An Introduction to Community Dance Practice

An Introduction to Community Dance Practice

Edited by
DIANE AMANS

palgrave
macmillan

First published 2008 by
PALGRAVE MACMILLAN

Palgrave Macmillan in the UK is an imprint of Macmillan Publishers Limited, registered in England, company number 785998, of Houndmills, Basingstoke, Hampshire RG21 6XS.

Palgrave Macmillan in the US is a division of St. Martin's Press LLC, 175 Fifth Avenue, New York, NY 10010.

Palgrave Macmillan is the global academic imprint of the above companies and has companies and representatives throughout the world.

Palgrave® and Macmillan® are registered trademarks in the United States, the United Kingdom, Europe and other countries.

ISBN-13: 978-0-230-55168-8   hardback
ISBN-10: 0-230-55168-8   hardback
ISBN-13: 978-0-230-55169-5   paperback
ISBN-10: 0-230-55169-6   paperback

This book is printed on paper suitable for recycling and made from fully managed and sustained forest sources. Logging, pulping and manufacturing processes are expected to conform to the environmental regulations of the country of origin.

A catalogue record for this book is available from the British Library.

A catalog record for this book is available from the Library of Congress.

10   9   8   7   6   5   4   3
17   16   15   14   13   12   11

Printed and bound in Great Britain by
CPI Antony Rowe , Chippenham and Eastbourne

Contents

This book is dedicated to the memory of Anke McMillan

Foreword

Community has long been identified as one of the founding themes of sociology, and at the same time it is famously difficult to agree exactly what it means. Back in 1955, sociologist George Hillery identified 94 definitions of 'community' in the literature and could establish no overall congruence of meaning except that they all dealt with people[1]. Not very helpful you might think, if you're trying to give an academic gloss to your latest strategy paper. And yet the word is all around us – often, it's true, just giving a cosy but vacuous gloss to a product or service, but also as a word we don't seem to be able to do without. Raymond Williams referred to it[2] as 'this warmly persuasive word', and I have argued for keeping the term 'community dance' for the reason that it is a thread through our history as a profession and its very generality unites all the different strands of practice. They're all about people, and they're all about caring about people.

Of course the experience of community has two sides: looking out and looking in. Community unites us but it also divides us, and a family, tribe, religion or nation is an experience of belonging for some and of exclusion for others. At different times in our lives (and maybe even in our day, in this fast-moving world) we need the experience of community more, or less. It's a truism that when we're in adversity we 'run for shelter' in a community – whether it's the family, our friends or our nationhood – and then when things are calm we can exult in our individuality and itch to be free of the warm but constraining embrace of the group. Human society is orientated around the oppositions evoked by community: in Western European culture the story of Romeo and Juliet is probably the most obvious example of our deep awareness of the Janus face of group membership, while the theme of inclusion/exclusion is also at the heart of folk tales the world over.

And yet, and yet. Genetically and culturally we are social beings and our whole history predisposes us to need and to care for others, even to the point of self-sacrifice for the group. We need others and they need us, but modern society conceals this in many ways, and the exhilarating freedom of urban life seems to offer a heady mix of self-determination and a succession of different experiences of community, which give us the feeling of belonging but without the commitment. Arguably this only works when you're feeling strong and independent, but in any case it only works if you can afford it, and many people are lonely and fearful in the city. Anyone looking at the totality of American film-making must be struck by the pre-eminence of fear as a theme: fear of nature, the dark, aliens, ghosts – 'the other' in a hundred guises. The problem is that if you make people afraid – or you make yourself afraid – sooner or later violence will follow. We need to counter fear with trust and care, and that's where dance has so much to offer.

Rudolf Laban wasn't the first person to argue that industrialisation was damaging communities, but he was probably the first dancer to use movement in groups as part of a conscious programme to counter what he saw as destructive individualism. Peter Brinson wasn't the first person to recognise the potential of dance in this respect, but he was the first to call it community dance in the context of a programme of institutionalisation which would make it a profession with its own values, philosophy, training and praxis. Today, around thirty years on from Peter's support for seminal practitioners like Fergus Early, and his founding of the training course at Laban, we can genuinely speak of the community dance profession. Still growing and developing, certainly, but a body of professional practice that is increasingly admired and emulated by dancers and policymakers worldwide.

This book is therefore timely and important. It offers a range of perspectives from some of the most experienced and thoughtful practitioners we have, and it includes practical guidance as well as insightful thinking about values and processes. Diane Amans has set out to provide an eminently useful book, and at the same time one that will stimulate debate and further thought. I have long argued that we need a rigorous debate and a common language in which to conduct it if we want to make our practice both transparent and shareable. This book makes a hugely helpful contribution, and the chapters by Diane, Sue Akroyd and Keyna Paul offer clear analysis, grounded in practice, that will be greatly helpful to students and others learning about this type of dance provision. Other writers – other voices – combine reflection and analysis, asking very important questions about process and, for example, the nature and role of performance in community dance and issues around power and learning. Helen Poynor, Heidi Wilson and Louise Katerega all look at participatory work and ask searching questions about its nature and structure, while Sara Houston tackles the always difficult question of just how we define and articulate the distinctiveness of community dance, at the same giving a valuable historical overview of thinking on this issue. Case studies describing work by Diane, Cecilia Macfarlane with Crossover Intergenerational Dance Company, Jabadao and Alan Martin all give interesting first-hand insight into processes and outcomes.

There are also contributions by four pre-eminent practitioners and leaders in the field. Rosemary Lee, Penny Greenland, Ken Bartlett and Adam Benjamin all offer personal perspectives which distil an enormous amount of experience and thought. These are provocative, moving and inspirational, as is their work, always.

Community dance is primarily a social activity, uniting creativity and physicality in a way that offers the experience of *communitas*, of solidarity and significance, in an immediate and grounded way. It's in that experience of belonging and being valued that human beings flourish, that we open up to learning and develop the ability to trust and be trusted. And it's on this that our survival depends, because unless we match our concern and care for individuals with a corresponding care for the natural world and for the injustices daily visited upon the poor and other minority groups we won't be living up to the values that inspire and sustain our practice.

Rosemary Lee, in her reflective and moving contribution, touches on these vital issues and asks if we 'in our small, local, unspoken way' can change the world. I think community dancers already have changed the world, and they'll continue to do so by changing individual people's experience of the world and of others, creating those magic moments in a workshop or performance that don't necessarily show us perfect community, but do give us the feeling of *what it would be like*. We all know there's so much more to do – I think this book will help inspire and equip us to do it.

Christopher Thomson
Director, Learning and Access, The Place

Notes

1. Hillery, G. A. (1955) Definitions of community: areas of agreement. *Rural Sociology*, **20**(2).
2. Williams, R. (1983) *Keywords: a Vocabulary of Culture and Society*. Fontana, London.

Preface

This book is intended for readers who are interested in the purpose and defining values of community dance together with the practicalities of delivering participatory dance projects. Although the profession is over thirty years old, and community dance work forms part of many dance artists' portfolios, we have surprisingly few reference texts for students and others who are preparing for employment in community dance. Following discussions with a group of senior practitioners, I decided to write a textbook which would focus on some of the key issues and debates, together with a set of resources for existing and emerging practitioners. It includes the kind of information and discussions that I would have found useful in my journey as a dance artist working with people in community settings.

Anyone who has ever tried to explain the rather bewildering world of community dance to students, staff from a different sector (such as health and social care) or someone who has never heard the term before will appreciate just how complex an undertaking this is. There is enough material for an encyclopaedia, never mind a textbook! The very diversity of practice is exciting, but it can seem confusing to someone who is trying to understand what community dance actually *is*. We need to be able to draw on the accumulated experience of practitioners in order to develop a theoretical framework for our profession. We already have a substantial collection of articles commissioned by the Foundation for Community Dance and published in their quarterly journal. I intend to add to this theory base and also refer the reader to other excellent sources of information.

The book contains a number of 'voices' – contributing authors are established artists, practitioners and academics who have all made significant contributions to dance. As these are a range of individuals with very different writing styles I hope this will appeal to the book's diverse readership. Some people enjoy analytical, issues-based discussion; others prefer shorter chapters with experiential accounts, case studies, interviews and examples of community projects. My own chapters have focussed on a selection of core themes and practical guidance. I have also included a Resources section containing 'toolkit' materials such as session plans, risk assessment forms, music list, contact details of useful organisations and examples of policies. Exercises throughout the book will suit learners who want to gain understanding and engage with key issues yet do not want to read lengthy texts.

As the value of participatory arts is now widely recognised, other sectors have become interested in working in partnership with dancers. We need to be able to explain what we do and how we might connect with other people's agendas. With the growth of community dance and the increasing diversity of settings in which dance artists are working, issues and challenges emerge. The more we engage in discussion and debate the better equipped we are to evaluate our work and develop a shared ownership of our extraordinary profession.

Diane Amans

Acknowledgements

Thanks to the many people who have shared their dances, ideas, thoughts and time. In over thirty years of community dance work I have met dancers and other colleagues who have delighted me with their creative energy. I can't mention you all by name but I am grateful for your generosity and friendship.

Thanks to participants and performers in Freedom in Dance projects, community dance students in the UK and Germany and Marple Movers. Thanks to the Foundation for Community Dance and JABADAO National Centre for Movement, Learning and Health.

Thanks to the contributors who have written chapters and the many organisations who have allowed me to include their material in the Resources section of this book; thanks to Arts Council England for funding research and development.

Thanks to Deb Barnard, Brian Beardwood, Sylvia Christie, Susan Smith and Chris Thomson, who have given valuable comments and support during the actual writing; thanks to Kate Haines and Palgrave Macmillan for advice with publishing the book and Petra Kuppers for comments on the early draft.

Contributors

Sue Akroyd is Head of Professional Development at the Foundation for Community Dance. On completion of her initial dance training, she began her professional life as a community dance artist with Ludus Dance, based in the North West of England, before becoming a full-time dance lecturer at Liverpool John Moores University. Her current role at the Foundation for Community Dance – in particular her work on Making a Move: an initiative to develop a professional framework for community dance – continues to stimulate her longstanding interest in the development and progression of community dance practice. Sue's ongoing professional enquiry centres on finding clarity of purpose within what we do and how we do it. She believes that by challenging ourselves to 'dig deep' and reflect purposefully on the whys and wherefores of ourselves and our work, we can open up new and exciting possibilities for our continued growth and nourishment as professionals.

Ken Bartlett is currently the Creative Director of the Foundation for Community Dance. He was previously Head of Arts and Cultural Services in Walsall in the West Midlands. Before that he worked in education as a teacher, Schools Advisor and as a member of the local authority schools inspectorate service. Ken has taught and lectured in Europe, North and South America and Australia.

Adam Benjamin Award winning choreographer and a teacher with an international reputation, Adam was joint founder and Artistic Director of CandoCo Dance Company (1990–98) and of Tshwaragano Dance Company (South Africa). He is the author of *Making an Entrance. Theory and Practice for Disabled and Non-disabled Dancers* (Routledge Taylor). He has made work for, amongst others, Remix Dance Project, Scottish Dance Theatre, Vertigo Dance Company, CandoCo Dance Company, StopGap, Adam Benjamin and Dancers, The Besht Tellers and A&BC Theatre Company. Adam was made a Rayne Fellow for Choreography in 2006 and now teaches on the Faculty of Theatre and Performance at Plymouth University. He performs with Rick Nodine and Jordi Cortes in the improvisational ensemble *5 Men Dancing*.

Penny Greenland MBE has over 30 years experience in a wide range of community contexts. In 1985 she set up JABADAO to bring about a sea change in the way education, health and community organisations work with the body and movement. Her passion lies not in the visual aspects of dance, but in the way it focuses the *feeling* of life itself. She has carried out research with partners in the early years sector on the impact of early movement on 'readiness for learning and readiness for life'. Penny delivers training for policy makers, advisors and staff in schools, nurseries, health care and community settings throughout the UK.

Dr Sara Houston lectures in dance studies at the University of Surrey. Her research into community dance has taken her into ballrooms, church halls, sheltered housing, ballet studios, offices and prison. Sara trained at the Laban Centre and was awarded a PhD from Roehampton. She is Vice-Chair of the Board of Directors and Trustees of the Foundation for Community Dance and sits on the Executive Committee of the Society for Dance Research.

Louise Katerega is a performer, choreographer, educator and mentor to people of all ages and varying levels of dance experience. She is especially acknowledged for her development work in the field of dance and disability, and in 2006 she worked with a disabled and non-disabled cast to create 'A State of Becoming'. This piece reached the semi-finals of the dance equivalent of the Booker or Turner Prize – the Place Prize. Louise has worked as an advisor for Birmingham Royal Ballet and is a trustee of the Foundation for Community Dance.

Rosemary Lee is a choreographer, director, film maker and performer. She also teaches and writes. Her creative output is diverse: large-scale site-specific work with mixed age community casts of up to 250; solos for herself and other performers; commissioned works for companies; films for broadcast TV, and most recently interactive installations. She is an *artsadmin* artist and an artist research associate at ResCen.

Cecilia Macfarlane trained as a teacher at the Royal Academy of Dance and as a dancer at the London School of Contemporary Dance. She is an Oxford-based independent dance artist with a national reputation for her work in the community. She is the founding director of Oxford Youth Dance, DugOut Adult Community Dance and Crossover Intergenerational Dance Company and co-founding director of Oxford Youth Dance Company. She is a Senior Lecturer in Arts in the Community at Coventry University. Her work is based on her passionate belief that dance is for everyone; she celebrates the uniqueness and individuality of each dancer. As a performer Cecilia is continually curious about expression, how movement can communicate so powerfully to others without the need for words. Her work is very influenced by her studies with Joan Skinner, Helen Poynor and most recently Deborah Hay.

Alan Martin is a creative dancer, musician, disability speaker and comedy actor. His life changed dramatically 13 years ago, when he got his first communication aid. He then gained relevant training and wide experience, which led to setting up his own business. Alan's clients include educational establishments and statutory and voluntary organisations. The aim of his work is to change attitudes to disability in life and the performing arts, and promote equality, independence and life choices through provision of the necessary support and equipment.

Keyna Paul is director of *lincolnshire dance* and responsible for steadily creating a culture within the county where dance and dancers are encouraged to thrive. She has played a key role in the development of dance for over 15 years working both at the grassroots level and as a member of national working parties and committees. She was a member of the Executive Committee of the Foundation for Community Dance, for six years serving as both vice-chair and chair. During 2004–2006 she undertook a part-time secondment to be Project Manager for the initial Dance Links programme as part of the PESSCL (PE, School Sport Club Links) strategy.

Helen Poynor is an internationally recognised movement teacher, director and performer. She runs the *Walk of Life* centre for non-stylised and environmental movement on the World Heritage coast in Devon/Dorset. Her approach has evolved out of 30 years of professional practice on four continents. She specialises in movement in natural environments, site-specific and autobiographical performance and cross art-form collaborations. Helen is co-author with Libby Worth of *Anna Halprin* (Routledge 2004) and co-edited *Dancers and Communities*, a collection of writings about community dance in Australia (Ausdance NSW 1997). Helen's training with Anna Halprin at the San Francisco Dancers' Workshop and Suprapto Suryodarmo from Java has served as the foundation for the development of her work. She is recognised by Suprapto as a teacher of non-stylised movement practice. Helen is a mentor for a number of established and emerging dancers and performers. She taught for five years on the Theatre and Performance BA at the University of Plymouth and is a Senior Registered Dance Movement Therapist.

Christopher Thomson read French and Linguistics at Edinburgh University before leaving to study Speech and Drama at the Guildhall School of Music and Drama in London. He performed with the Lindsay Kemp Company and with a number of small-scale dance companies, before becoming a founding member of Ludus Dance Company, and was Artistic Director of the company from 1983–86. From 1986–1991 he directed the Community Dance Diploma course at Laban. Chris is a former Chair of the Foundation for Community Dance, Vice-Chair of Dance UK and member of the Arts Council's Advisory

Committee on dance education. He is currently a member of the DCMS Dance Forum, helping advise government on the development of dance policy. Since 1991 he has been Director of Learning and Access at The Place, running a wide range of dance provision, from regular classes for children, young people and adults, to a variety of project work in schools and the community. Chris has spoken and taught about community dance in a number of countries, including Denmark, Switzerland, France, Finland, Italy and Japan.

Heidi Wilson is a Dance Development Practitioner with Powys Dance and a Dance Lecturer at the University of Wales Institute Cardiff. Previous work in the field of community dance includes two years as West Suffolk Dancer in Residence under the umbrella of Suffolk Dance National Dance Agency ((1993–95) and two years as the initial arts worker on the Gateshead Elderly Arts Project (1991–93). Heidi has a Masters in Dance Studies from the University of Surrey (2000) and a BA (Hons) in Theatre from Dartington College of Arts (1990). Heidi tutors and assesses on the Laban Guild's Dance Leaders in the Community: Stage 1 course and is a National Trainer for PE in School Sport (Sports Council Wales).

Part I
Definitions and Contexts

Introduction

As you read through the book you will notice that several contributors deal with the question 'What is community dance?' The first two chapters provide a historical perspective and include definitions and descriptions of qualities which characterise the work. The issue of whether anyone can call themselves a community dance practitioner is debated in Chapter 1 and continues to be a theme later in the book. (For example, Chapter 11 contains case studies which contribute to the debate by illustrating the very different backgrounds of four practitioners.) The questions raised in Part 1 are intended to provide a framework for discussion. Sometimes there are no easy answers; or there may be several answers, all of which are valid.

If you are new to community dance you may want to start with Chapter 3 to get a feel for the activities and people involved. You could then go back to look at definitions and historical contexts. If you are a dance artist who is looking for practical guidance in delivering projects you may decide to start with Part 5, together with the Resources section, and return to look at issue-based discussion when you have more time for reflection.

At the end of each chapter there are some points for discussion with tutors, students and colleagues. You may prefer to discuss different questions which are more relevant to your situation. One area which does deserve consideration is the use of language. Although the early chapters deal with some definitions I suggest you think about other terminology and notice the ways different contributors write about their work. The word 'professional', for example, is sometimes seen as controversial when it is used as a comparison with community dance. Other terms which are often used interchangeably are 'performers', 'participants' and 'dancers'. Dance is a performance art, so participants in a dance session are performing – they are dancers. Others see participants as performers only when they are involved in some kind of event where there is an audience made up of people who are not involved in the weekly sessions.

I think the meaning is clear in each individual chapter, but I have drawn attention to terminology as there are differences in the ways in which we community dance professionals use particular words. I hope you will share my interest in exploring these differences so that we can continue to develop a shared understanding of our practice.

Further Reading

Kuppers, P. and Robertson, G. (2007) *The Community Performance Reader*. Routledge, London.

Tufnell, M., Greenland, P., Crichton, S., Dymoke, K. and Coaten, R. (2000) *What Dancers Do That Other Health Workers Don't*. JABADAO, Leeds.

1 Community Dance – What's That?

Diane Amans

This is the first of two chapters which look at what we mean by the term 'community dance'. It includes definitions by a range of practitioners and other thinkers who have written about community dance over the years. In this chapter I also introduce some questions relating to key themes which will be addressed throughout the book.

- *What is the purpose of community dance? What are its qualities and core values?*
- *Who is delivering community dance and what should we call them?*

These questions are explored further in subsequent chapters – particularly Chapter 2, where Sara Houston looks more closely at definitions and Chapter 11, where I look at the role of the community dance practitioner.

- Community dance? What's that?
- Well it's, you know, working with different groups – doing dance projects.
- What sort of dance? Ballroom dancing? Street dance?
- Might be – it depends on the group and why we're doing it… Sometimes it's not a particular dance style – it might be helping a group make a dance piece about something they want to say

Defining community dance has always been something of a challenge. Since the mid-1980s there has been critical debate about the purpose, practice and defining values of community dance. As there is considerable diversity of practice in the profession there are inevitably differences in philosophy and approach amongst people who are involved in the work: as participants, artists, employers and agencies commissioning projects.

Definitions of Community Dance

The **Foundation for Community Dance** (FCD), which is the lead body for the profession, offers the following definition (FCD, 2006):

> Community dance is a strand of participatory dance practice defined by particular values, intentions, qualities and methodologies.
>
> Community dance includes a broad range of practices and styles and is not dance style specific.

On their web site the FCD says (FCD 2006):

> Community dance is about artists working with people. It's about people enjoying dancing, expressing themselves creatively, learning new things, and connecting to other cultures and to each other

In 2006 a survey of community dance workers produced these responses to the question 'What is community dance?' (Amans, 2006):

> Community dance is working with people using movement. Community dance can include set dance steps and free movement, it inspires and motivates. Community dance gets people moving who may not normally dance.
>
> Dance which mainly takes place with non-professional practitioners (though often facilitated by professional artists/teachers)
>
> Any dance activity, led by professional dance practitioners, which involves participants from an identified community and which is publicly funded, is community dance.
>
> Creating opportunities for anyone, regardless of gender, race, religion, physical or mental health, and ability, preconceptions (their own or others) or anything else, to be able to participate in a group dance experience that is positive for them
>
> Community dance is about dance not being elitist... it can be about creating pieces of work that break the stereotypes of what dance is and what dancers are, it can be about performing dance in non traditional places. It can be anything that we, the community, want it to be.

The people who produced these definitions reflect a cross-section of the profession and include lecturers and artistic directors as well as dance artists delivering projects. They were asked to attempt a definition for someone who has never come across community dance. Compare their responses with these comments written twenty years earlier, when there was already discussion about the nature and purpose of community dance.

What *is* Community Dance? What is its Purpose?

In 1984 Sarah Rubidge outlined the following aims and objectives of the 'community dance movement' (Rubidge, 1984):

- To de-mystify dance as an art form
- To provide opportunities for as large a part of the population as possible to engage in dance activity of some sort or another, irrespective of their age, class, or cultural background
- To reinstate dance as an integral part of the life-style of our society

Chris Thomson's article, given at the 1988 Dance and the Child international conference at Roehampton Institute, made an important contribution to our understanding of what community dance actually is (Thomson, 1988):

> the community dance movement in the UK sees itself as offering dance to everyone in a given community, on the premise that dance is the birthright and the potential of all human beings, and that this fundamentally human activity is in our rational and logocentric culture undervalued and marginalised – the experience of dance is often simply unavailable. The community dance movement... has been seen by many as having the potential to redress the balance in favour of dance, to start bringing dance back into the mainstream of our culture

In 1996 the Department of Dance Studies at Surrey University hosted a conference *Current Issues in Community Dance*. The speakers raised questions that continue to be debated.

> Twenty years on and though we have some broad agreements in community dance there are apparently almost as many philosophies as individuals involved in the work. We have not yet agreed a public account of the aesthetics and philosophy of community dance (Peppiatt, 1997)

> community dance has its own values, principles, methods – and it is more than education. It is also about converting the population, establishing dance colonies across the country and creating a dance empire (Siddall, 1997)

> The definition of Community Dance is an ongoing debate because of the apparent diversity of practice in the field: how is it possible to define something that by its very essence is individual to different geographical areas, funding structures, populations and aspirations of practitioners? (Jasper, 1997)

Community Dance Qualities (What it is About?)

In order to clarify the purpose of community dance the FCD published a description of qualities which characterise the work – see the box below.

Community dance is about:

- dance that engages directly with people as they define themselves, valuing and respecting who they are, their differences and what they bring individually and collectively to that engagement
- providing experiences that contribute positively to self-worth, self-confidence and a sense of wellbeing
- connecting people to experiences that are achievable – yet testing, over which they have a sense of ownership, control and belonging
- providing a framework for learning and making effective use of art form skills
- providing sustained support that allows people to grow, develop, gain a sense of achievement and make a contribution within their wider communities
- engaging people creatively in solving problems, seeking solutions and finding a form of dance that expresses their concerns, cultures and aspirations and thinking critically about their experience
- providing opportunities for people to develop more positive and active relationships with their wider communities

FCD (2001)

Who Delivers Community Dance – and What Should We Call Them?

- Are they artists, dance teachers or therapists?
- It depends on what the individual wants to be called. Definitely not therapists – though practitioners often say there is a therapeutic value in their work.
- Artists then? What's artistic about doing a session with special needs children or old people?

There are a number of terms to describe people who work in community dance. Originally the term *dance animateur* was used to identify dance practitioners who were working in community contexts. They were usually in full- or part-time posts supported by public arts funding. Thomson (1988) pointed out that some community dance workers preferred not to be called 'animateurs' – a term which the community arts movement had been using in the 1960s:

> interestingly it was not long before the word was seen as patronising in its assumption that communities needed 'animating' and it was dropped in favour of 'community arts worker'

Other job titles at the time included 'dance co-ordinator', 'dance development officer', and 'dancer in residence'. Since then workers in the field have adopted a range of job titles including community dance practitioner, community dance artist, dance teacher, dance artist, dance worker, community dance leader and community dance worker. 'Community dance artist' and 'community dance practitioner' seem to be the two most commonly used terms (Amans, 2006).

> Practitioners identify themselves as community dance workers whether they are freelancers or in full time posts. Some want to be known as artists, rather than community dance practitioners, possessing additional skills which enable them to work in the community. This could be interpreted as a claim for a more fitting title than 'worker', 'practitioner' or 'development officer' etc. to

Figure 1.1 Freedom in Dance *What you lookin' at?* Commissioned by Dance Initiative Greater Manchester for Big Dance 2006 'What you lookin' at? (*Brian Slater*)

reflect the status and/or character of their work. Many freelance artists with a portfolio career within various arts sectors, also use the term. It is a particularly metropolitan centred phenomenon where community dance practitioners work in a large population of dance artists. (Jasper, 1997)

Kevin Finnan (2003), from Motionhouse dance company, illustrates Jasper's point:

We are very clear that we are not therapists, care workers or missionaries. We are artists. We acknowledge that our own experience of our work has taught us that it can be therapeutic, liberating, empowering and affirmative.

Can Anyone Call Themselves a Community Dance Practitioner?

There are full- and part-time workers who have been appointed to work as community dance practitioners with dance agencies and independent dance companies, but, as Jasper points out, many freelance workers also call themselves community dance workers if this is part of their portfolio of work. They are just as likely to refer to themselves as artists, choreographers, teachers or performers. It will depend on the context and which particular 'hat' they are wearing at the time.

There are also other community workers, for example carers, day centre activity coordinators, leisure centre staff, youth workers and early years teachers who use dance in their work and who are members of the Foundation for Community Dance. They occasionally call themselves community dance practitioners – even if they have had no dance training apart from a two-day in-service course. Naturally this has led to confusion amongst **service providers** outside the dance world as there are no nationally recognised standards and it is up to each individual employer to ensure that the dance practitioner has the necessary skills and training to carry out the work[1].

It is not just service providers outside the dance world who are confused by the ambiguity surrounding who and what community dance workers actually are. Penny Greenland, director of JABADAO – National Centre for Movement, Learning and Health and a dancer of many years experience, is frustrated with the lack of structure and clear identity for dancers (Greenland, 2005):

I, for one, as a dancer wanting to work with other people's agendas, am sick of the lack of clarity that my 'profession' continues to have, because it gets in the way of developing new collaborations, new ways of working and new partnerships.

Figure 1.2 Freedom in Dance Intergenerational Project (*Linda Boyles*)

It is as if we are all 'General Practitioners' (and GPs with no shared under-standing at that). How can the public, or the government for that matter, know what we truly offer, or what they can expect from us, unless we tell them?

Prior to this article Greenland had already begun to articulate what dancers actually do and differentiate the many contributions dance makes to other people's agendas. Together with four other dancers she produced a book – 'What dancers do that other health workers don't' (Greenland, 2000) – setting out to define the territory for work in **dance and health**. Five years on Greenland questions whether the profession has made much progress and admits to a sense of urgency (Greenland, 2005):

The climate around us has changed, government is asking us straight forwardly what we can contribute, and I'm unconvinced that we are well placed to reply.

Greenland's concerns relate to the community dance profession's lack of detailed descriptions of core skills and competencies. Individual dance agencies are very clear in their own job descriptions, but there is no unified structure across the profession. This lack of rigour does contrast with other professionals' practice. Teachers, physiotherapists, architects and social workers, for example, all have their own clearly defined practices with a unified structure across the country. Whether they work in rural Suffolk or inner city Liverpool they will have nation-ally recognised qualifications and a forum for shared professional debate.

Community dance, on the other hand, incorporates many different strands of practice delivered by practitioners with a wide a variety of qualifications.

Conclusion/Summary

The definitions included in this chapter characterise a profession which creates accessible opportunities for people of diverse backgrounds and abilities to join in dance activities. There may not be a single overall identity, but the community dance world of the 21st century continues to reflect the **process-oriented** values of community dance since its inception in the 1970s:

- a focus on participants
- collaborative relationships
- inclusive practice
- opportunities for positive experiences
- celebration of diversity

The extent to which individual practitioners are working in a way which reflects the above values is determined by their experience, training and personality together with the aims of the organisation or project in which they are working. There is no externally determined set of criteria against which community dance activities are judged. Whilst narrow, prescriptive inspection systems would be in no one's interest, the community dance profession would benefit from a system of **quality assurance** which supports, celebrates and disseminates good practice.

Discussion Points

- What are some of the difficulties involved in defining community dance? (Chapter 2 also addresses this question)
- What term do *you* think best describes people who work in community dance – artist/teacher/community dance practitioner/or one of the other titles mentioned in this chapter?

Note

1. In Chapter 12 Sue Akroyd discusses developments in recognised standards and benchmarks for community dance practice.

2 Dance in the Community

Sara Houston

Sara Houston is a dance academic who has made a significant contribution to research and debates about dance. Here she discusses some of the tensions in defining community dance and summarises theories by key contributors such as Chris Thomson, Peter Brinson, Linda Jasper and Penny Greenland. This chapter explores the values associated with the concept of 'community' and the challenges of trying to find a generic term which satisfies people involved in what we call 'community dance'.

What is 'community dance'? It is a question that I often get asked and it is easy to churn out a pat answer: 'it's participatory dance activity that's done by amateurs and often led by professionals'. Yet such a statement does not do justice to the area of work in question. It is an introductory answer that raises many more questions and leaves out much that could be included in a definition. Community dance in the UK has been a success story where structures have been embedded into institutions to support the delivery of dance to a broad section of the population, and yet still community dance commentators debate the umbrella term used to describe the work. What is it about the term, or about the dance happening, that makes it such an area of contention?

The debate ensued when it was feared that by using a separate term for community dance, the community dance movement risked being marginalised as a second rate appendage to Professional Dance. Sue Hoyle gave an interview in *Animated* in 1994 when she was Dance Director of the Arts Council of Great Britain. Even though the movement influenced much contemporary dance and education, Hoyle maintained that it was unhelpful to segregate it. In her view, because of this influence, dance ought to be seen as an integrated 'culture' (Hoyle quoted in Ings, 1994, p. 2). More than a decade on, the fear of marginalisation is alleviated by the current interest and cross-participation by the dance profession in projects and workshops for and by members of the public. The high profile of the Foundation for Community Dance as a policy-forming body contributing to national debates on dance has also encouraged cross-participation. It has given a certain legitimacy to the separate term 'community dance'.

The debate continued, however, with issues that are still current. In discussing the tensions in the definition of community dance, Linda Jasper remarked that, 'there are problems with retaining a separate title for what can be seen to be an activity that crosses many sectors' (Jasper, 1995, p. 189). In the cited article, she debated whether community dance 'should be distinguished as separate from other dance practice, or be included within all Dance fields' (Jasper, 1995, p. 181). It can be seen as an educational practice, a life-empowering formula, an artistic outlet, an enjoyable pastime, or even several of these definitions at the same time. As well as crossing these sectors, community dance also traverses many styles of dance, a variety of venues and spaces and a large demographic. A weekly North Indian Kathak class for adults in a church hall can be labelled 'community dance', just as much as a three month project in a theatre for aspiring young ballet dancers. A one-off workshop in Street Dance on a strip of waste ground for anyone inquisitive enough is still characterised in a similar fashion to an intensive year-long course in contact improvisation for visually impaired adults. Some, such as Frank McConnell (2006), have also argued that traditional folk dance can also be regarded as community dance.

In an attempt to order such a variety of dance, Chris Thomson's categorisations (1994) have been useful. Thomson expounded the view that there were three types of community dance practice: 'alternative', 'ameliorative' and 'radical'. He describes the 'alternative' as emphasising a holistic approach incorporating the execution of the physical with therapy for the mind. In this way, the practice also links to other complementary and therapeutic services. He sees alternative community dance as seeking 'to create meaningful ritual and "boundaryless" experience' (Thomson, 1994, p. 25). It is not clear exactly what this entails and even whether a 'boundaryless' experience can happily sit alongside ritual that has strict patterns and boundaries. Nevertheless, whether the experience for participants is 'boundaryless' or not, Thomson argues that practitioners working in an alternative fashion subscribe to a holistic, therapeutic philosophy. The 'radical', in contrast, emphasises empowerment for participants to overcome discrimination or oppression. It is based around ideas on community action, with the activity often associated with social welfare provision. The 'ameliorative', promotes the participant's sense of well-being and offers a wide range of dance activity. It is often associated with recreation and leisure and as a result is, as Thomson says, 'well-integrated into [the] economic and institutional order' (*ibid*). According to him, in contrast, radical community dance helps participants challenge this institutional order where it has failed them in some way.

In a conference paper published in 1995, Linda Jasper argued that the majority of community dance groups could be considered ameliorative. She suggested that this is because of a belief amongst practitioners in 'dance for all', which is grounded in the tradition of dance as education. Jasper also pointed to another classification of community dance that involves 'community building', which is clearly distinguished by Jasper from mainstream community dance. She argues that (Jasper, 1995, p. 187):

> these are distinctive working principles that seem directly to address the concept of dance as a medium for community development, and in particular the individual within the community. These working practices could not be particularly mistaken for dance in other contexts.

Her discussion is drawn from the views of Penny Greenland, director of JABADAO. JABADAO classes itself as a national development agency for specialist movement work and could be seen to be radical under Thomson's terminology. Among its activities, it unusually offers education and training in movement specifically to health, social and community development workers. Although JABADAO holds the belief that movement 'includes, enables, embraces' (JABADAO, 1995, p. 1) people of all physical, emotional and intellectual abilities, the main thrust of the belief is that it builds more effective communities (Jasper, 1995). Communities can grow through movement, which is a powerful communication tool that everyone possesses in however small a quantity.

Greenland herself acknowledges that her views are not mainstream, but it is principles like these that occupy the rhetoric attached to arts projects coordinating with British and European government schemes, such as the urban regeneration programme. In connecting to social policy, François Matarasso (1998) suggests that the arts can become 'a force for development in a complex world'. Arguably, one of the reasons that community dance has developed a relatively high profile is that there has been a burgeoning of work with the socially excluded – for example, young people at risk, offenders, marginalised older people – which has been funded by channels made available through a government agenda that has made social inclusion a priority. The radical has become mainstream, as Thomson noted in 2006, and in doing so, community dance has established itself as an institution.

A term that becomes institutionalised does not solve any of the debates, but it does provide a standard label that can be used to describe the area of dance. The terminology becomes useful then when it is necessary to give pointers, rather than an in-depth explanation. Thomson (2006, p. 6) writes:

> Clearly, in specific contexts we can talk about youth dance, or dance with young people at risk, or dance with older people, so we have – or can create – practice-specific terms that aren't as vague as 'community dance'. However in some situations I find I need the overarching term, not least when I am talking about the phenomenon in other countries, or to anyone who doesn't have a clue about what community dance is.

He goes on to acknowledge that the term would still need explaining, but so would any other label, which is also noted by Alysoun Tomkins (2006, p. 33):

> As I write this article I can observe people dancing and participating in dance activity in a studio at Laban [one of the UK contemporary dance conservatoires], but they are not partaking in community dance. Titles such as 'Participatory Dance' and 'People Dancing' are non-specific.

Replacing 'community dance' with 'participatory dance' or 'people dancing' merely replaces one set of complications with another.

Why was – and is – the word 'community' used instead of, for example, 'participatory'? The concept of 'community' is a slippery idea that fails to sit comfortably, or quietly around any complex praxis. Perpetually challenging previous definitions of the notion, 'community' has been used as a principle upholding a particular way of acting or living by divergent commentators.

One theorist, Benedict Anderson, in his 1983 analysis of nationalism, pronounced that, 'all communities larger than primordial villages of face-to-face contact (and perhaps even these) are imagined' (Anderson, 1991, p. 6). He argued that because members of a nation do not have a face-to-face, communicative relationship with all other members, even though they consider themselves as belonging to the same community through a 'deep and horizontal comradeship' (Anderson, 1991, p. 7), the nation is an imagined community. His work is significant in that it highlights, to the people involved, the importance of inventing a community.

The sanctioning of the label 'Community Dance' as an entity in itself precipitates something imagined. As with a national identity (singular) that includes many different cultural affiliations, the community dance movement (singular) also, as noted above, contains a great variety of projects with different aims, for a wide cross-section of people. Anderson's concept is working here in the sense that with so many different types of project, the classification 'community' as a cohesive term seems too limited. There is no one community that binds diverse dance projects together.

Dance as an activity links the groups, but the difference in the movement forms, aesthetics and specific aims could seem to give the umbrella term 'dance' an opacity that sits uneasily with the defining adjective of community. One collective characterisation of community dance is the fact that projects are designed for the amateur, rather than for the professional dancer. Yet why title it *community* dance? Why should the term mean 'for those who do not do this for a living'? Is this what is meant by a community? Do all amateurs – whatever their aims and intentions – form a unified group to the exclusion of professional dancers? In fact, as noted above, the dance profession plays an important role in the sector. So with the above discussion borne in mind, it is possible to see why the label 'community dance' cannot be thought of as a singular defining entity unless it is taken as imagined.

But there is another way of looking at the word 'community', which has to do with values, rather than material descriptions. It is more than one hundred years since the German sociologist Ferdinand Tönnies (1963[1887]) published his ideas on 'community' and 'society'. According to him, 19th century industrialis-ation forced the decline of the community. One hundred years later, it was again a common theme among academics, politicians and other social commentators. Post-modern philosophers like Frederick Jameson (1991) and Communitarians such as the philosopher Charles Taylor (1992), have decried the fast-paced, super-ficiality of modern life. Communities are being devoured by an encroaching alien-ation, spawned by versions of the modern, consumer society (Featherstone, 1995). Politicians worldwide on both the left and right have preached for the return of a sense of community, either through a nostalgic vision of shared tradi-tions, or through an emphasis on civic responsibility. Some religious organisations have also called for the reintegration of a value system into the core of Western secular life to reignite feelings of community.

Theorists and advocacy groups have had diverse attitudes as to why a sense of community has been lost, what should be done about it and what it exactly means in the first place. There are also views (Nancy, 1993; Cavarero, 1997) that not only support the notion of community as being relevant to present-day society, but also hold that a sense of community can still be found in many situations and will always be there. It is not a question of it being 'lost' as much as being created or people being ready to experience it. These views hold that active participants are the keys to establishing a sense of community.

Following this thread, Peter Brinson argued that community arts created com-munication between people through collective creativity (Brinson, 1991, p. 130). Tomkins reminds us that the origin of the word 'community' comes from the Latin to give among each other (Tomkins, 2006, p. 31). The idea behind the term 'community dance' is not to signify geographical allegiances (although it might), but to alert us to its guiding principles nurtured within an activity that brings people together to work in reciprocity. Not all projects will engender long-term, harmonious relationships or deep social bonding, but fundamentally dance is a practice that requires cooperation and communication, a sharing of physicality and mental agility that may precipitate creative energy and communal feeling in the moment of the dance.

The word 'community' might not translate in the same way in other languages (Ames, 2006), but the notion behind the dancing transcends semantics. Those projects that uphold the ideal that dance is about a communion amongst partici-pants are buying into the notion espoused by the community dance movement. Even though some groups may not outwardly engage with the idea, the values maintained by community dance practitioners within their work signify an attachment to the notion behind the term in question. As long as there is identification with the ideals for which community dance stands, then arguably the term 'community dance' is a valid one.

Discussion Points

- Do you think there are any problems in seeing community dance as something distinct from other dance practice?
- Sara Houston mentions 'the ideals for which community dance stand' – what do you think she means by this?

3 Community Voices
Diane Amans

Taking part in dance activity can be a powerful and life enhancing experience. In this chapter people tell their very different stories about what dance means to them. In addition to participants from a range of community dance projects there are the voices of artists and other community workers involved in projects.

Dancing Nation – Young Performers

In 2000 the Foundation for Community Dance commissioned a film to show examples of some of the dance activities taking place in community settings. Simon and Amayra were two of the young people featured in the *Dancing Nation* film.

Simon

Simon is a member of a break dance group in Warrington. He was 15 at the time of this interview and had been dancing with 'Street Beat' for 18 months.

> What would I be like if I didn't dance? I'd probably be a bad boy. I'd probably be on the streets doing things, getting into trouble, stuff like that. Dance changes me –it takes the aggression off the street, diverts it into dancing, onto the dance floor. Inside me is a fire – when I'm dancing it's let out. It's another side of me if you know what I mean. (FCD, 2001, p. 16)

Amayra

Amayra is a young woman who has been dancing since she was ten years old. She combines street and African dance and performs with a group called DC (Dance Creators)

We've become known around the area as the young black kids performing – people want to know what we're getting up to. We express old 'African' and new 'street' – something our younger and older audiences relate to. We perform to parents and grandparents, generations who didn't get to dance, to celebrate the way that they would wish to. Our generation has now got that chance.

I love to perform, I like what the audience can give me... if I do something right I know by their reaction. If they're feeling it, I'm definitely feeling it. Movement is motion, emotion – if we're feeling it, it comes across stronger when we're performing. (FCD, 2001, p. 40)

Impact on Adult Performers
The experience of dancing in front of an audience is both exhilarating and terrifying for some community performers.

Sylvia
Sylvia is a woman in her seventies who had been dancing with a local community group for six months when she took part in a performance project with Freedom in Dance. Here she describes how she felt in the early stages of the project.

The second weekend, doubts didn't just creep in, they burst, screaming, into my brain. You can't do it, they yelled. You're too old, too fat, too stupid, too inhibited. You'll let them all down. I was seriously worried about my own brain – my memory was letting me down left right and centre. I bought some gingko biloba, but you can't expect miracles. Surely I should be able to remember a sequence of actions? I can remember poems, quotations, shopping lists, names of plants – why did I find myself dithering about wondering what the hell to do next? It felt like senility was waiting in the wings to grab me. I hated the idea of going on and letting the group down; I also hated the idea of giving up and giving in to old age and lack of confidence.

Six weeks later Sylvia performed at the Lowry in Manchester, as part of a community dance showcase.

An extraordinary thing happens on a real stage, in a real performance. A huge euphoria grips you; you find yourself grinning insanely in the direction of the audience – look at me! Look at me! – and you find, for the first time that day, that you know what to do, when and where to do it, and look like you're having the time of your life.

Which you are, actually. I wouldn't have missed it for the world[1].

Chrissie

Chrissie is an active retired woman who had been dancing with Amici Dance Theatre for 20 years when she took part in the *Dancing Nation* film.

> Performing to an audience is quite heady, 'champagne like'. And that feeling –
> that heady feeling – comes from the audience. If you're enjoying the produc-
> tion and you know the audience is enjoying it, you feel as if your feet are just
> an inch above the stage... it's like an aircraft taking off – you lift into the air –
> take off. But the excitement of dancing doesn't only take place on the stage in
> front of an audience, it takes place in our ordinary sessions, every Wednes-
> day, when we perform or improvise – the music speaks to your soul and you
> express it through your dance. And that feeling of take-off or uplift is there just
> as strongly (FCD, 2001, p. 24)[2]

Edward

Edward lives in sheltered accommodation in Tameside, Greater Manchester and attended a weekly dance session which took place in the residents' lounge. Initially he had some reservations about joining the group, but he soon began to appreciate the freedom to enjoy spontaneous, playful movement:

> It's like a senior playschool but you don't feel a fool because we're all doing
> the same[3]

Jeremy

Jeremy is another dancer who appreciates the chance to play. He began dancing when he was in his mid-thirties and became involved in community dance pro-jects through his children.

> Dance... allows us to play. We can shed all the rules and inhibitions of ordinary
> life and, with the right tuition, discover less cluttered and more straightfor-
> ward ways of being ourselves without words and without the usual rules of
> personal space... We dance because it is fun and, through the laughter and
> playfulness, we rediscover the child in each of us. (Spafford, 2005)

Artists' Perspectives

In this section several dance artists give an insight into their work with community groups.

Luca

Luca Sylvestrini, artistic director of Protein Dance, has written about his experiences of choreographing work for groups in different community settings. Luca believes that 'commitment' and 'artistic ambition' are just as important in participatory dance projects as they are in work with professional dance companies.

> I am aware of and respect the differences of these two worlds and I am not trying to change them. In fact I try and challenge those differences by often asking non-professionals to have a professional attitude and professionals to borrow the enthusiasm and spontaneity that non-professionals have.
>
> educational and community choreographic projects ... have gone hand in hand with the creation of the company's repertory. Although separate, these two areas of activity have been feeding each other and share aims and values. (Sylvestrini, 2006)

There are other dance artists who express a similar commitment to high artistic standards regardless of which group of performers are involved. (See Chapter 8 for Rosemary Lee's approach to working with groups in a range of different contexts.)

Hannah and Craig

Hannah Paice and Craig Horton are choreographers from Resonance Dance and, until the 2006 Urban Moves Festival in Manchester, they had mainly worked with children and young people. They accepted a commission to choreograph a dance piece for an intergenerational group and they found that it also offered valuable learning opportunities.

They were initially concerned about health and safety as they had never worked with older people. They learned to adapt their approach to take account of the different energy levels and learning styles of their diverse performers.

> we learned to teach small chunks of material and let the older performers, in particular, digest it for a week before we looked carefully at it... We allowed for mistakes and missed counts as some of the cast were more musical than others and we used a variety of cues for movement which worked extremely well[4].

Hannah and Craig involved the dancers in creating the choreography and enjoyed the unique contribution made by each of their performers:

> We feel after seeing so much professional dance, it was exciting, interesting and refreshing to see untrained dancers move in a more natural, personal way and performing with the same confidence.

Impact on Support Worker

Jean

Jean is a special needs teacher who acted as support worker on a dance project involving adults with learning disabilities. She was surprised at the amount of time the dance artist allowed for responses and said it was the first time she had seen a real person-centred approach.

> It's not simply about getting through the exercise/activity but about offering it and observing/working with/assessing the response, if any. This enables the practitioner/facilitator to give a measured and individual response to the participant. It also allows you to assess, over a period of time, some notion of development and sense of enjoyment. I'm thinking of Ricky and the feather blowing exercise and how giving him his own time to do things enabled both his own and the group's enjoyment at his response.[5]

Case Studies

So far the 'community voices' have revealed different ways in which dance has impacted on a range of individuals. The following case studies give a more detailed account of some community dance projects and include:

- Crossover Intergenerational Dance Company
- Creative Dance with Older People
- Integrated Dance
- JABADAO Early Years Project

Case Study 1: Intergenerational Dance

Cecilia Macfarlane

Cecilia Macfarlane is an independent dance artist who also works as an Associate Senior Lecturer in Arts in the Community at Coventry University. She directs and performs with Crossover Intergenerational Dance Company which she founded in 2003. Here she describes her work and includes quotes by members of the audience who watched performances of Dragon's Tale.

Crossover Intergenerational Dance Company is the result of a natural evolution in a dance journey. Since coming to Oxford in 1986 as an independent dance artist, my work in the community has evolved very organically. I started two creative contemporary dance classes for children and this led to the creation of Oxford Youth Dance, which offers children and young people of all ages the opportunity to create and perform their own work under the direction of professional dance artists.

In 1992 DugOut Adult Community Dance Company was formed, offering parents and other adults the opportunity to discover and celebrate the dancer in them. This led naturally to projects in which parents and their children could dance together. In 1997–98 I created and directed 'That's What Parents Were Created For', two projects for fathers and their sons and mothers and their daughters, performed at Pegasus Theatre and at the Richard Attenborough Centre in Leicester. Over the last seven years, I have developed intergenerational dance in many different settings.

Crossover has allowed me to work with a small group of dancers of widely different ages for a significant and regular amount of time. Currently there are nine dancers (four female, five male), aged between 7 and 66.

I wanted to look at the stereotyping that goes with specific ages and particularly research the movement that can accompany these conventions. I wanted to explore the diverse ways in which we think, feel and move at different ages and the similarities that we share and to challenge the familiar stereotypes that surround my art form.

> I saw Crossover alongside two other dance performances. I haven't seen live dance before... and of the other two performances I would say they were kind of what I expected – athletic young people doing interesting energetic things with their bodies. Whilst I enjoyed those performances I wasn't especially moved and wouldn't rush back to see dance of that type. With Crossover however, the interest/energy was still there, but not just of the youthful athletic type – the nature of the troupe meant that the expression seemed far more expansive – due to the fact that your troupe contains people of a variety of ages and different abilities. It made the other performances seem limited – as if they were musical instruments with fewer notes available, whereas Crossover expresses a more diverse range of humanity and human experience. I found that very beautiful, real and inspiring. There must be so much more you can do with such a lovely set of notes like that!

Crossover aims to offer dance performances and workshops by and for intergenerational audiences aged 0–100 that are physically demanding, artistically challenging, socially inclusive and fun. We promote the idea that people of all generations can find a common language through dance. This common language is not only accessed by the people involved in the making of work but by the audiences that come to see that work:

> I don't find dance easy to get close to – shape and movement doesn't necessarily work for me – but with Crossover's performance I really didn't want it to end; it spoke to me and had such resonance. It spoke to me of working

together, of finding areas that are of common interest and making things collectively and how there is so much strength and joy in this; this is important and vital to us as human beings.

Dragon's Tale

Dragon's Tale is the third of three substantial pieces that the company has made and is touring at the moment. It explores the history and heritage of fairgrounds: from the afternoon merry-go-rounds enjoyed by toddlers and grandparents to the edgy techno beat of the late night twisters and dodgems, the piece looks at how the different generations can occupy the same public space alongside each other and find their own way of playing. It was performed first at Warwick Arts Centre to an audience of a thousand 7- and 8-year-olds and their teachers and then was next performed at Oxford Playhouse. This event included not only the nine company dancers but also 200 dancers aged from 2 to 86 to celebrate how different generations can come closer through dance. These two hundred dancers truly embodied the notion of community as they represented the history of my work in Oxford, spanning generations and families, some of whom have been dancing with me for the last 21 years.

The next stage of *Dragon's Tale* will be a tour to rural Oxfordshire to include local communities and give them an opportunity to dance in this piece.

> I found the whole evening truly inspiring... Your wonderful piece showed how neither age nor disability is a barrier to creating and performing an interesting and thought provoking and well balanced piece. I say balanced because

Figure 3.1 Crossover Intergenerational Dance Company *Dragon's Tale* (*Naomi Morris*)

everyone was able to show their true talents and for those talents to be used sensitively without patronising.

I realised quite early on in my career that, as an artist in the community, I don't work in a vacuum, it isn't just about giving, it's also about receiving and with Crossover it is a perfect balance. It's an opportunity to create and be creative in an environment that is totally committed to the task of dance exploration and therefore continually feeds my practice as a dancer.

Case Study 2: Creative Dance with Older People
Diane Amans

This pilot project took place in Stockport over a period of six weeks. Participants met twice a week for a two hour session which included afternoon tea. The aims of the project were to explore themes of interest to participants using movement, music and words. Additional aims were to promote mobility, confidence and creative expression.

I had funding to do a pilot project with older people and a perfect venue in our local theatre. It was an exciting opportunity to work with other artists and offer something different to the senior adults in my community, but initially I found it really difficult to recruit participants. I went to speak to residents in some of the local care homes, but they were not very enthusiastic:

You don't know what it's like at our age – you get too tired to do things
What do you mean, creative movement?

I was sure I could devise activities that they would enjoy if only I could persuade them to join me. In the end I stopped mentioning dance and invited people to join me for free afternoon tea with home made cakes. That seemed to work – I soon had a group who liked the idea of an afternoon outing with a free taxi ride.

After the refreshments we sat in a circle and introduced ourselves. I was joined by a writer and two other dancers who acted as support workers. There were 10 participants, aged from 69 to 86 years; some people lived in residential homes and others lived independently in the community. They were all mobile but several used walking aids and were not able to walk very far.

I explained that we would like them to join us in a creative project and they agreed to take part – with the understanding that they did not need to return next week if they did not enjoy it. After some gentle breathing exercises and name games I led seated warm-up activities and then some standing exercises using the chair for support. They soon seemed more relaxed and enjoyed a tango dance with their hands.

I introduced creative work by mirroring in pairs and by the end of the session they were all keen to come back. It soon became clear that they were very interested in learning how they could increase their mobility and were eager to talk about how the dance sessions were benefiting them.

> *Doris*: This dance work – it's given me the confidence to go upstairs without using the lift. I've surprised the staff.

> *Edie*: I felt 'down' when I came but it's made me feel better.

> *Hilda*: I'm starting to use my hands again – writing and tying my shoelaces. I haven't done that since my stroke. It's these exercises and the movement. Coming here and seeing the others dancing – it motivates you.

The participants attributed their sense of wellbeing to the warm up exercises but I observed that it was the creative dance which seemed to really motivate people. Taking part in stimulating and unusual activities increased the range of movement and encouraged interaction between members of the group. We used different props such as light floaty scarves, balloons, fans and masks. We also experimented with body shapes and balanced on each other with chairs for additional support.

In one session I wanted to help participants experience a greater range of movement and feel strength in their bodies. I had noticed that many of their dances were rather tentative and I wondered how they would respond to different qualities of movement. In the warm-up they enjoyed stamping and pushing and we developed this into a seated contact improvisation. Participants sat in a circle facing outwards and the dance artists moved from one to another, making hand contact with members of the group who pushed us away. Even a gentle push acted

Figure 3.2 Freedom in Dance Tameside Elders Project (*Matthew Priestley*)

as an impulse for a dynamic lively response from a dancer. Participants smiled and leaned forward in their chairs, anticipating the next contact. They really seemed to come alive in this session and we could feel a greater energy in the group.

One particularly successful feature of this project was the collaboration with a writer. Sylvia made notes and created poems based on observations and comments she overheard. One afternoon we used natural objects as a starting point for discussion and movement. Participants were invited to choose something and describe it with their hands. Jessie focussed on a blue shell – her hands following its spirals and curves. She became totally absorbed in her dance whilst Doris and George moved their hands along the twisted convoluted shapes formed by the willow twigs they held.

At first Mary was reluctant to join in this activity. When we invited her to look at the willow twigs she shrank back in disgust, saying they looked like worms. 'No thank you' she said when offered a piece of driftwood. Later Kath, one of the dance artists, brought the driftwood back and encouraged Mary to touch it. They talked about where the wood might have come from – what kind of tree, what kind of weather it had experienced.

Mary said 'I would never have thought of this – never have looked at a piece of wood. I would have thrown it away'. As she left that day Mary raised her arm in a farewell salute and said 'Thank you... I will look... I will look'. Mary often found communication difficult, but Sylvia incorporated her words into a poem and Mary was delighted.

Looking
I would never have thought
An old, dead piece of wood
Had something to give me.

I would never have thought of this
This touching... feeling...
I would never have felt its velvet skin
Never have touched its rough heart.

I would have thrown it away, unvalued
But now I have imagined
the tree it came from,
the wind that swayed it,
the sky it reached for.

Now I will look at other things –
Unvalued
I will look, I will look
I will turn my hand to something new

The optimism expressed in this poem captured the atmosphere of this group.

Although the project lasted only six weeks it definitely had an impact on the confidence of participants. It also had a powerful impact on the artists involved. Each week there was something to surprise and delight us. A 'special moment' we will all remember is when Jessie told the group she'd been into town to have her ears pierced. 'It's the first time since my stroke that I've felt able to go out and cross the road on my own. Doing this dance – it's made my legs stronger. I've always wanted my ears pierced and look – I've had it done!'.

Case Study 3: Inclusive Dance Workshops
Alan Martin

Alan Martin, a former student at LIPA (Liverpool Institute of Performing Arts) is a dance practitioner who leads workshops for disabled and non-disabled people. He uses an electronic voice communication aid and adapts activities for participants in a wide range of settings. Here he describes what dance means for him.

Until I was about 32, the only thing I did, that you could loosely call 'dance' was after several pints in the pub during karaoke sessions. I really enjoyed this, but mainly because of the company and the alcohol. I thought that the idea of *me* dancing was completely crazy until I attended a short dance course run by

Figure 3.3 Alan Martin (*Frank Newman*)

CandoCo in Liverpool (just for a laugh!) and they showed me a little of what creative dance was all about, and that absolutely anybody who has a pulse can join in dancing.

I'd thought that a person like me, with seriously restricted control over my movements, and a wheelchair user, would never be able to do what I now do, which is to earn my living from giving inclusive creative dance workshops and performances to all sorts and ages of people, all around the country.

In the 12 years since I first 'saw the light', I have joined many community dance organisations, attended as many workshops as possible to build my skills and knowledge, learned workshop leadership skills at LIPA in Liverpool, worked to share my enthusiasm voluntarily for several years, and now I have my own thriving business. My work is much in demand, and I'm delighted at my success.

Dance, to me, is a great means of communicating feelings and emotion. This is significant in my case, as I have no natural speech and use an electronic speech aid to communicate and lead my workshops. I believe that I'm the only dance workshop leader (in this country at least) who uses an electronic speech aid and also an electric wheelchair.

Dance is so much more than just an art, or an exercise. It's a means of self expression and a statement about myself. It says, 'Here I am, look at me, value my physical difference, and appreciate what I am doing'.

It says that I'm confident in my body, and have lots to teach you about valuing people who are 'different'. I'm proud of myself, but not in a conceited way. I just want to show everyone the joy and benefits of creative dance, and teach people how to make dance fully inclusive.

Inclusion, to me, means planning sessions so that all the activities can be adapted to fit any ability, not, as is still often the case, making sessions for non-disabled dancers and tagging on accessible bits to fit the rather embarrassing presence of a disabled dancer. Sadly, inaccessible studios and performance spaces and discrimination are still the norm in dance – even in community dance settings. A few years ago, on approaching a local dance group, I was told that I wouldn't be able to keep up and do the right steps, and basically to 'forget it, and get lost'. It's very satisfying to now be entering my school groups in dance festivals, and showing the 'mainstream' dance world just what people with disabilities can accomplish.

Here is an account of a two-day project with children in a special school in Haslingden, East Lancashire. As with most of my work in schools, many unexpected challenges cropped up and had to be worked around. Getting up at 5 a.m. to travel there was a difficult start for me and finding the school was not easy. The room we had to work in (although mostly an uninterrupted space) was small, and looked even smaller when five pupils arrived in wheelchairs, one on a bed, one in a frame and eight walking. They were accompanied by several members of staff.

We began with introductions; pupils quickly accepted that I communicated with an electronic speech aid, and a couple of my class also did. It was not an issue.

Who needs to tell me anything about themselves? Is everyone OK with being touched? Let's warm up our imaginations first. Let's see who can do what with this Liverpool Football Club scarf! *Was that the fire alarm?* Everyone went outside for an hour, while this was sorted out. Quick rethink about warm-ups.

Back inside, after the break (everyone took the interruption in their stride).

Let's start warming up our bodies now! We began warming up, first everyone copying my moves, soon progressing to the pupils leading, with their own moves. We could have carried on with this all day. Barriers fell; confidence grew; communication with movement developed and leaders were emerging. Everyone was happy and excited as there was a performance next day to think about. Not much space to do moving around the room exercises, so find a friend to work with, and stay in the same place! Learn to focus on your friend's movements and pretend you are looking in a mirror. Change the leader when I shout 'change'.

Stop now. Show us all what you've been doing, one pair at a time.

This gave most of the group a short rest, whilst they watched the others.

Soon it was lunchtime and I enjoyed a smashing school dinner. We were just starting the afternoon session when the press arrived wanting to get pictures of our performance. Children were taken outdoors and pictured in artificial poses – again and again. Back inside and warm up again. See how many hands you can shake in one minute!

Let's get on with choosing a theme for our dance. (Thank goodness they chose 'under the sea' – a subject I had ample props and music for.)

What's under the sea? Frogs? Well, possibly! Mermaids, sea horses, whales, jellyfish, crabs, dolphins. We all chose a creature to make a dance about. What a lot of different ways those beasts get around! Let's show the rest of the group how you each move. Soon we had many moving creatures. What else? Seaweed. Flowers? Well, perhaps. Water, pebbles, gravel, sand. What sounds do those make? A performance was coming together. How can we show the water, waves etc? As luck would have it, I had a long piece of sparkly blue fabric in the van.

There were too many bodies to develop this dance in the space we had (tomorrow we would perform in the big school hall). For the time being, a small group chose to work in a side room with one of my assistants. They created sea sounds by moving in the Soundbeam[1] – this is an excellent device which can produce sounds of all sorts from even the tiniest movements. One of my better investments! The end of the school day came too soon, and the children went home full of ideas about how animals under the sea move and sound, and how the waves perform.

Next morning (another 5 a.m. get up!) we started promptly. No fire alarm, but, even more interesting, a team of inspectors arrived who 'had to see what we up to'. They almost joined in the dancing – if I'd had longer, I could really have done something with them! The morning flew, with costume fittings, trying out the music (my own composition), practices and so on. Then another photographer arrived – different newspaper. Who can be photographed? Who cannot? I suppose publicity is great, but it takes up too much 'dancing time'.

After the dining hall had been cleared of tables and chairs we had half an hour to set up. No time for a rehearsal – but then again, the audience don't know what it's supposed to look like. Go and have 5 minutes break, then we're on!

The whole school assembled, some showing interest in the 'funny bloke in the wheelchair, with the voice box'. We were ready, so I gave a quick introduction and backed into the audience space, from where I was able to conduct the dance without the rest of the audience realising what I was doing.

The magic of live performance happened, and it went better than perfectly. Pupils who had little movement during practice found hidden reserves and amazed everyone. Nobody knew that the frog was not meant to stay in front when the dolphin was dancing.

Case Study 4: Developmental Movement Play
Penny Greenland

JABADAO is a national agency which set out to create a 'sea-change' in the way education, health and social care settings work with the body and movement. They created an approach called 'Developmental Movement Play' (DMP) and, since 1998, they have been involved in a long term action research project across England. Here Penny Greenland describes how JABADAO practitioners have used 'everyday dancing' to challenge the prevailing culture in early years settings.

Dancers who are happy to work with playful, ordinary movement seem like ideal people to draw attention to the way our culture has sidelined a fully physical response to our lives. JABADAO practitioners – 'everyday dancers' – are adults who bring to ordinary life an ease and comfort with being physical. They aim to highlight what happens if we ignore this side of human nature and they offer simple ways to develop a more full-bodied response to learning, health and wellbeing.

In 2002 fourteen settings (Sure Start Projects, a private nursery, a special school and outreach projects) joined us for three years of evidence-gathering about the value of a new way of supporting children's movement play. Two members of staff from each setting started by attending DMP training, then took it back to their centres and developed new ways of supporting movement play in their own individual ways.

At the start, these early years practitioners were nervous about spontaneous movement. Even though they were from a world that is thoroughly used to supporting play (role play, block play, small world play, heuristic play...), this movement play was uncomfortable. Our job was partly to act as role models for a

Figure 3.4 JABADAO Developmental Movement Play (*Mike Barrett*)

different way of being in the body and partly to present theory (pandering to our cultural norms) that would give them permission to 'be daft'.

After the course we met quarterly to share stories, top up on theory, swap the games their children have invented and... to move and play together. Over the period of three years all the practitioners radically changed the way they worked with movement with their children – and most felt very differently about moving themselves. Where once they took to chairs at the drop of a hat, now they rolled, romped and lay on the floor for preference. Quite simply, they made a completely different relationship to movement themselves and saw children's movement differently as well.

> You ask something of a child and you expect to hear an answer. I see answers now.... They move beautifully and if we did not give them opportunities to express themselves through movement then we would not see that answer through their bodies. (Kate Johnson, Parklands Children's Centre)

Back at their settings:

- All moved/removed tables so children could be on the floor more (a developmentally more useful place), rather than at chairs and tables

- All valued 'early' movement more (rolling, crawling, belly crawling and lying on backs and tummies)
- All created new movement areas in their settings – places that children could move when and how they wanted, bearing safety in mind
- All made a passionate commitment to the importance of movement as an underpinning for all learning

The children's self-confidence is really blossoming.... We have noticed that children are more considerate with their friends and they understand how each other is feeling. (Amanda Willis, Goosehill Private Nursery)

In their evidence about children's movement they noted that:

- Their children's strongest movement preference was for spin-tip-roll-fall activities
- Their children's second preference was for push-pull-stretch-hang-buffet about play
- They all agreed that very few children were distractingly over-excited by their involvement in movement play
- They all agreed that most children risk assess all the time as they play, and that it is important for adults to provide the most movement play for those who don't – so they can learn through practice and support.

After three years we rounded up and analysed the evidence gathered across all the settings and presented it to the whole early years sector. At the conference, the workshops were mostly led by early years practitioners, passing on – to other practitioners in similar settings – the ways they had developed of supporting movement play.

We are now in Cycle 2 and continuing perhaps to prove the blindingly obvious. But in this culture things about movement always seem strangely hidden, even if they jump up and down in front of us.

Conclusion

This chapter included a diverse range of 'community voices' – people of different ages and backgrounds who have shared some very positive experiences. Their stories illustrate the wide-ranging impacts of being involved in community dance activities, from the point of view of participants, facilitators and dance artists. Although projects take place in many different contexts, participant reactions reveal a remarkable unanimity in the beneficial results experienced.

Discussion Points

- Consider the comments by participants in the above dance projects and look at the Foundation for Community Dance's community dance qualities outlined in Chapter 1. To what extent do you think the projects described in this chapter have these qualities?
- In Case Study 1 Cecilia Macfarlane mentions stereotypes associated with different age groups and stereotypes surrounding dance as an art form. What are these stereotypes and how can dance artists challenge them?
- In the project described in Case Study 2 there were initial difficulties in recruiting people to join a dance group for senior adults. Why might older people be reluctant to take part in such a project? What can dance artists do to encourage participation?
- Case Study 3 gives us the flavour of an inclusive workshop run by Alan Martin. He plans sessions 'so that all the activities can be adapted to fit any ability'. Think of three dance activities with which you are familiar (they might be warm up exercises, a set dance or a creative dance task). How would you adapt the activities to suit the needs of *either* a 10-year-old child who uses a wheelchair (manual) and has a moderate learning disability and autism *or* an adult who has done little exercise for 30 years and cannot see?
- Why do you think staff in early years settings practitioners might be nervous of spontaneous movement? What does Penny Greenland mean when she refers to 'everyday dancers?'.

Notes

1. Soundbeam is an electronic device which converts body movement into sound and images.
2. Community dance project evaluation (unpublished), Freedom in Dance (2004).
3. Tameside Healthy Communities Collaborative, project evaluation (unpublished), Freedom in Dance (April 2003)
4. Evaluation report on 'Big Dance' Intergenerational Project (unpublished), Freedom in Dance (2006)
5. Salford project evaluation (unpublished), Freedom in Dance (March 2003)

Part 2
Issues and Challenges

Introduction

The introductory chapters looked at the defining values of community dance and drew attention to some of the many issues and challenges experienced by those of us who have chosen to work in this profession. This next section includes critical reflection in the areas of diversity, inclusive practice, power relationships and duty of care. To begin with Ken Bartlett invites us to 'love difference' and his chapter outlines the differences that he believes we need to value and support. He is also particularly keen that dance artists are able to understand what people have in common when they are involved in dance – as participants, observers and makers of dance. 'Finding common humanity' is how Ken describes it. Whilst Chapter 4 is a fairly brief look at diversity it does include a number of key themes which are referred to in other chapters: if you are interested in how community dance values are nurtured in our emerging practitioners, you will find Sue Akroyd's perspective very interesting (see Chapter 12). The question of diverse aesthetics comes up time and time again, particularly in Part 3, which deals with community performance.

Another challenge for dance artists working on participatory projects relates to 'inclusive practice'. In Chapter 1 I argue that 'inclusive practice' is one of the process-oriented values that characterise community dance. It means encouraging people to engage in dance and being flexible enough to accommodate their different ranges of needs. So, should community dance projects be open to all comers? Do we need general practitioners who can make dances with any diverse group of people? Actually, I think we probably do. If you're not sure about whether community dance projects should be open to anyone and everyone, ask yourself what would be a reason for excluding people? Sometimes it is appropriate to have a closed group because of the context of the work (an after-school club or a project in the criminal justice system for example), or because the funding specifies work with a particular section of the community. Whatever the context of your work you need to have thought through, beforehand, who the participants will be and what you need to do to engage them in a positive dance experience.

Louise Katerega's chapter deals with inclusive practice and some challenges presented by power relationships in an integrated project. Louise worked as executive assistant to Tom St Louis, who is a disabled dance artist. She describes her role as staying in background whilst supporting Tom, who acted as artistic director and choreographer. I find it fascinating to read about how Tom managed the support staff in this project. He is clear about defining roles, and his ground rules for support staff highlight awareness of the need for these staff to experience the workshops as dancers (rather than carers) so that they have a better awareness of how they might best support disabled dancers. In the Resources section you will find guidelines which Generation Arts give to support workers and other venue staff. These guidelines are intended to make sure that both participants and carers have a positive and safe experience.

In Chapter 6, Penny Greenland argues for community dance practitioners to have an understanding of duty of care measures so they can create 'shared standards'. This is about having a responsibility to take 'reasonable care' to protect people from risk of harm. Few would argue with this, but when it comes to defining 'reasonable care' there are some contentious areas. One of these is the practice of filling in health questionnaires – part of the duty of care procedures in many dance agencies. What do you do if participants refuse to complete them? How do you keep people safe if you have no information about their health background? On the other hand, individuals have a right to privacy and may have good reason to be suspicious of yet another form-filling exercise.

Figure P2.1 Freedom in Dance Intergenerational Project (*Matthew Priestley*)

There are no easy solutions. I do find health questionnaires useful – I have included an example of one of mine in the Resources section . However, they are only one small part of 'reasonable care' and there are times when it is neither appropriate nor practical to use them – when working with people who do not read, for example, or vulnerable people who do not have an understanding of their own health status. Also, in one-off 'drop in' sessions it may make sense to just make sure the activities are low impact and that people are reminded to take a rest when they need to. As dance artists working on community projects we need to be flexible and imaginative in order to exercise our duty of care to others and to ourselves.

As you read through Penny's chapter I encourage you to try and answer her quiz questions and discuss them with other people. Make a note of any areas where you are unsure or feel you don't have the knowledge or experience to answer the question.

Further Reading

Arts Council England (2004) *Action for Access*. Arts Council England, London.

Arts Council England (2005) *Keeping Arts Safe: Guidance for Artists and Arts Organisations on Safeguarding Children, Young People and Vulnerable Adults*. Arts Council England, London.

Greenland, P. (2000) *Hopping Home Backwards: Body Intelligence and Movement Play*. JABADAO, Leeds.

Jasper, L. and Siddall, J. (1999) *Managing Dance: Current Issues and Future Strategies*. Northcote House, Horndon.

Juhan, D. (2003) *Job's Body: A Handbook for Body Work*. Station Hill, Barrytown.

Thompson, N. (2003) *Promoting Equality – Challenging Discrimination and Oppression*. Palgrave Macmillan, Basingstoke.

4 Love Difference: Why is Diversity Important in Community Dance?

Ken Bartlett

Ken Bartlett is the Creative Director of the Foundation for Community Dance. In this chapter he discusses the importance of recognising and valuing our differences whilst also seeing what we have in common. As community practitioners we have significant opportunities for contributing to an inclusive culture in dance – this chapter sets out some of the reasons to 'love difference'.

Community dance practice over the past thirty years has built up a tradition of being excited by the possibilities offered by different people and different dance traditions. Community dance artists have sought to extend access to and participation in dance to the widest range of people in their communities and have also chosen specific identifiable groups within those communities with whom to work. They have taken on the challenges set out by successive governments to demonstrate the value of the arts, and dance in particular, in the fields of health, education, disability, social exclusion, youth, aging and criminal justice. And there is now a growing body of evidence to demonstrate that being involved in community dance activities does contribute positively to people's lives, individually and collectively.

The United Kingdom is one of the most ethnically and culturally diverse nations in the modern world. Immigration has been part of how our nation has developed for centuries and has happened for a range of reasons – escaping oppression and fear, and seeking better economic opportunities being key features.

Community dance as a body of practice has, as it has developed, sought to make links with people not usually closely engaged with mainstream arts practice – young people, older people, disabled people, culturally diverse people and people with low incomes. In addition, community dance artists have actively sought to engage with services and agencies where they think dance has a positive contribution to make – the health service, the criminal justice system and education.

Community dance artists demonstrate a range of purposes in their work – teaching the skills of specific dances, developing people as artists, introducing people to specific dance genres, promoting creativity, promoting self-worth and self-confidence and promoting social inclusion and social cohesion.

However, underpinning these different purposes, a set of values has developed which distinguish community dance from those dance experiences based on more straightforward curricula. These include a belief that everybody can dance with intention and purpose; that we build on what people bring to the engagement – personality, individual body signature, previous experience, personal expectations and aspirations, family and cultural background; and the importance of the individual within and as part of the group, of personal and social development alongside artistic development, of the arts process from creative experiment to effective performance, and the necessity of including everyone, whatever their difference. We build on what people *can* do, rather than what they can't achieve.

There is also a multitude of dancing communities across the UK that are based on historical associations with places and cultures and on particular styles of dance that appear in different contexts and at different times – some of which are based on sophisticated and developed rule systems, while others emerge apparently spontaneously from within wider popular culture, seemingly without rules or regulation. With each of these dancing communities there are diverse audiences who seek out the dance and dancers with whom they identify and in which they see themselves appear.

If we accept that everybody can dance and that we can apply the underpinning principles and values of effective community dance to any dance style or any culturally inspired dance tradition, we also have to accept that there are diverse aesthetics at work in dance that are not based on the Western European tradition of how the dance looks but on how it feels.

Working within the frame of 'world dance' – to borrow a term from popular music – challenges us to think of different ways of transmitting or teaching dances based on approaches which recognise that, culturally, dances have different origins, meanings and modes of transmission. 'Western dance forms share a commitment to the role of the gifted who have a special talent, while many non-western forms still have an inclusive function in community life where it is assumed that everyone will participate' (Greenwood, 2007). We also need to recognise that individual participants have different ways of learning and may not respond positively to a pedagogy that is dominated by sorting the gifted and the talented from the rest. In the narrow framework of the professionalised aesthetic, set out in ballet and Western contemporary dance, the majority fail. So we have to find ways of teaching and transmitting an engagement with dance that allows 'everyone to reveal their individual signature' (Macfarlane, 2007) and where 'everyone has their turn "centre stage"' (*ibid*).

So what are the differences that are important to support and value in community dance?

- Differences between individuals
- Differences based around cultural identity and what is important in our worlds
- Differences of aesthetics in different dance situations
- Different reasons for participating in dance
- Different learning needs amongst individuals and groups
- Different methodologies and pedagogies to ensure that people have the most positive experience in their dancing
- Different bodies that can produce different dancing opportunities and solutions
- Different contexts in which dance takes place and has meaning
- Different audiences that widen the opportunity for dance to be valued in wider society.

Whilst I believe it is important to recognise and value all these differences, and that it is important for community dance artists to embrace them into the core of their practice, I think we should understand why we need to. For me, it is in the sharing of our differences in our dancing, that we see and recognise what we have in common, for if, when we engage in community dance, we can enter dialogue about our differences, we can promote greater understanding for the individual within the group and for the group as part of its wider community.

I also believe that we need a more compelling and inclusive narrative for dance in this country, one that allows us not only to see the differences and use them, but also to see what is common when people dance, make dances and watch dances. This inclusive narrative would be characterised by people striving for excellence, doing the best they can – paying attention to the quality of their dancing, having a say in what the dance is about and how it is made, having a voice about who the audience is and the context in how the dance is seen and experienced. Also, they would reflect seriously and critically about how successful or otherwise the dance was in achieving their vision and aims. If we look for the 'Common Wealth' of dance and the people taking part then dancing truly achieves its potential in making a difference to people's lives and those of our communities.

In embracing the different, as Janet Archer, Chief Executive and Artistic Director of Dance City in Newcastle, says in another article from the Spring 2007 edition of *Animated*: 'I really hope that everyone can keep seeing those sharp silvery beauteous moments that come out of embracing each other's individuality with warmth and openness. I profoundly believe that we can move towards a more secure and humane society if we do' (Archer, 2007).

Discussion Points

- Do you agree with Ken Bartlett that 'there are diverse aesthetics at work in dance'?
- Can you think of any practical ways to value and celebrate diversity within a community dance workshop? (The Resources section has suggestions for inclusive activities and ideas for celebrations and special occasions)

5 Whose Voice is it Anyway?

Louise Katerega

Louise Katerega is a choreographer who has worked in a range of community settings and has considerable experience of working on integrated projects. In this chapter she describes 'Station Master' – a performance project with Dance Dangerous, which is a Northampton-based community company run by disabled people. Louise gives an honest account of how she dealt with an interesting dilemma and she raises some thought-provoking issues about power relationships in community dance practice.

First Stop

It's my favourite kind of phone call.

At the end of line is the familiar voice of a trusted friend and colleague representing the collective voice of a community dance organisation whose aims and practices, I believe, represent all that's best about British community dance. I have the advantage of long trusting relationships with the owners of both that individual and

Figure 5.1 Louise Katerega and Tom St Louis (*John Hogg*)

that collective voice and, what's more here, they are offering to pay me to do my favourite thing – choreograph – in my favourite field – integrated dance.

The caller is Miriam Keye, a former mentee of mine, now a friend and colleague, like me, living and working freelance in the East Midlands.

She is calling in her capacity as part-time administrator for 'Dance Dangerous', which is a community project governed exclusively by disabled adults providing integrated workshops and performance opportunities in Northampton. The company had decided to make a performance piece based on 'Starlight Express'. They were looking for a choreographer to help them create a piece in time for the forthcoming STOP Disability festival.

All Aboard?

Miriam puts their cards on the table: 'The company has been considering all the artists they have worked with in the past year to choose one to make a piece on them. You and Tom St Louis got equal votes, so we feel we really have to offer it to you as you have the experience of running a project start to finish. Tom could maybe come and assist'.

Tom St Louis is a disabled dance artist – a wheelchair user like the majority of Dance Dangerous – with a couple more years' experience in integrated dance than me. It's also been a more consistent part of his practice. Though he was a builder for more than twenty years before he became disabled, unlike me, he has a formal qualification (HND) in dance. Tom's my senior in years (24 to be precise), life experience and integrated dance generally, having worked nationally and internationally as performer/demonstrator/teacher with acknowledged master in the field Adam Benjamin, co-founder of CandoCo. He has also worked as an actor with acclaimed Graeae Theatre. A few weeks prior to this conversation I saw him produce his first 20 minute professional choreographic work on 'Cultural Shift', East London Dance's breakthrough programme to encourage the country's first disabled choreographers where all of this experience patently shone through.

How come I just got offered his job? And more importantly what are the consequences all round if I take it?

I believe the answer to the first question lies in the fact that it is difficult enough for a disabled person to train in the practical side of dance in the UK let alone the organisational aspect. Yet self-management is a key aspect of working freelance and, crucially, inspiring an employer's confidence.

Add to this that, in Tom's individual case, his paralysis causes some difficulty writing and emailing – skills often needed when setting up a project or taking notes in rehearsal. The difficulties go deeper than this, however. Despite completing his HND successfully he has always battled against a limited early education and always had difficulty speaking and writing in standard English – it being his third language after the French dialect of his native Dominica and Caribbean 'patois'.

In other words, Tom may not simply come across as being the administrative type in terms of the very middle-class conventions which pervade British arts practice. I, though my degree is in Film & Literature, have always been comfortable with speaking and writing, find it easy to convert to 'artspeak' and thus may seem more conventional in my communications with an employer. Of the two of us I must seem like the quickest and easiest person to employ. Making dance happen is an arduous road for all of us involved in doing so. If there's a quicker simpler path, of course, we want to take it. And I fully include myself in that!

Having known Tom for a decade, however, and watched him successfully run an integrated project in Soweto, South Africa, I am convinced of Tom's innate intelligence, organisational skills and abilities. What if it's the case that, linguistically, he sometimes simply needs a translator?

In terms of the second question about the consequences of my taking the work: well, a piece gets done, I get paid, and Tom need never know the conversation took place, or I could ask him to assist me. Dance Dangerous get what they ask for. But would I be giving Dance Dangerous what they *stand* for? Their very existence is a model of empowerment for disabled people in decision making about art. Wouldn't my taking the job over Tom undermine that completely?

If the only issue is that Tom might need support with managing a whole choreographic project, what if I was *his* assistant instead?

I look at the consequences again: Dance Dangerous gets an experienced dance artist with in-depth personal experience of wheelchair use and mechanics; an emerging choreographer gets a national opportunity to expose his work, and the STOP Festival gets work by an artist it exists for – a disabled artist. Dance Dangerous continues to build its national reputation for innovative practice – and I still get all I *really* need, which is pay for the time I put in and not to let down a group of a group of people whose enterprise I so believe in. By standing aside, it seems I might in fact do everyone more good.

'What's your total budget?' I ask Miriam. 'Can we go back to square one and reconfigure the project so Tom and I combine his artistic skills and my mentoring ones to still guarantee you the quality work and positive creation process you're asking for?' And Miriam, sharing Dance Dangerous values as she does, trusting my judgement based on our past relationship, generously does so.

Here's how it all panned out.

Ready for the Off

During project planning in April/May Dance Dangerous was between administrators – Miriam had finished her contract and Linzi Lee, the new administrator, was about to start, so my organisational skills were doubly useful. Tom and I met and drew up a document for Dance Dangerous – not unlike a mentoring agreement for us, but which also communicated to Dance Dangerous our roles and responsibilities in relation to each other.

Conducting Ourselves 1: Getting Tom in the Driver's Seat

Tom's role as choreographer was to:

- research 'Starlight Express', which Dance Dangerous had asked be the starting point for the work
- complete the choreography
- decide on lighting for the work

Tom achieved all of this with no difficulty other than the unfortunate fact that 'Starlight' was not touring as a production at the time. However, he was able to work from programme information and the musical score.

He comments: 'The whole idea for the commission was an interesting challenge. I saw an obvious link between roller skates and wheelchairs. I had the idea of keeping the wheels of the chairs close together the way they are on a train. Disabled dancers could create the idea of a train the way able-bodied [sic] couldn't. I had ideas about trains, platforms and barriers... I used the actual 'Starlight' music to inspire me. Though in the studio I found more contemporary music went with what we'd made'.

Signs and Signals

Tom stated his personal aim for the project as 'recognition', defined in detail in the wish list below:

- to be credited on a poster as a record
- have good quality DVD/video to keep for further self-promotion
- receive some positive comments by dancers and audience
- to see a written article about myself as a disabled choreographer – for example in a newspaper

Linzi, even though this was one of her first administrative jobs, proved to be both meticulous and brilliant in all aspects of it – especially marketing. Tom had local media coverage including TV and, at the end of the project, he left with excellent quality photographic and DVD evidence of his work. Participant and audience feedback on the work was universally positive.

Conducting Ourselves 2: Keeping Louise in the Back Seat

My role was that of 'Executive Assistant', a role defined by Australian dance artist Philip Channels (now Education Development Manager for StopGAP) who supported Tom in a similar way during 'Cultural Shift'. 'Executive' refers to having an excellent dance skills/literacy base and 'assistant' refers to playing second fiddle artistically plus compensation for Tom's loss of manual dexterity.

I was to be:

- literally Tom's 'right hand' writing notes in rehearsal, typing emails and if necessary fetching and carrying equipment in rehearsals. All written work, artistic or administrative, was to be written as dictated by Tom.
- a sounding board for the choreographic and leadership process
- facilitator of Tom's lighting design in technical rehearsal so that Tom could concentrate on the group. (In the event this proved to be doubly necessary as the light box was not wheelchair accessible.)

The practical timetable of my input was:

- 5 meetings – 1 preparation, 3 during rehearsal, 1 to contribute to the evaluation of the project
- plus up to five phone calls about the piece
- and no more than 2 quick calls per week re practical things

In the event, Tom asked for, and in my view needed, no help at all choreographically or with leadership of the piece. He prepared meticulously for each session in ways that surprised even me, always on the ball with CDs and track numbers and, though it was a physical struggle to do so, always providing basic notes for whoever was videoing or operating the music. Rehearsals always ran smoothly and he held an easy authority over participants and attendant care staff. Tom puts this down to laying down clear ground rules in his first session. We agreed that I wouldn't be present at this session, which may also have helped clarify the leadership.

Conducting Others – We Hope You Enjoyed Your Journey

Maintaining effective relations with support staff in integrated projects is vital in freeing a choreographer to deal only with artistic and not personal participant needs. Tom's ground rules, which were aimed at creating an appropriately professional and continuous working atmosphere, were as follows:

- no support staff in the final performance unless they were performing as dancers themselves
- support staff encouraged to join in introductory workshops (as dancers not carers) to boost their own confidence and widen their understanding of physical interaction with disabled people
- after the initial session each disabled participant to be responsible for his/her care needs on the dance floor. For example if the belt to keep you in your

chair becomes undone it is your responsibility to alert your support worker to fix it, not for the support worker to enter the dance floor and fix it while you are working

Tom had to reinforce this latter point at first:

In the beginning any slight thing wrong and the carers were in there... they soon got the message, however, not to come onto the dance floor unless asked and to go as soon as their job was done. The dancer's job is to look out for themselves and each other – like they will have to on stage in performance.... I avoid spending much one-to-one time with individuals. This helps them become more self-reliant and when they leave the workshop they can take that discipline back into their own environment. I got the impression the disabled participants were only too glad to be away from their carers.

Pulling the Communication Cord

Crucially, we laid down the ground rules of communication between Tom, Dance Dangerous and myself over the project from the beginning:

All correspondence to be copied to Linzi, Tom and Louise. Tom is central leader and decision maker on the project, so although information may pass by/be copied to me, it must come to Tom first or at the same time and any actions on it eventually be decided upon by Tom.

This was where we felt there was most danger in power relations swaying in my favour rather than Tom's, simply because I might be seen as more senior and/or simply have inherited the role as first point of contact for the project. Tom did feel that there was a slight tendency to turn to me as first port of call. We stood firm, however, sticking to our plan to keep me out of the picture much of the time.

I wasn't present for the final casting of the piece, which, according to Tom, was a turning point when he began to be acknowledged as leader. He said 'The penny finally dropped with them when I wouldn't have any arguments and I wanted the three able-bodied [sic] dancers who were there to all be in the piece'. In other words, Tom's authority as project leader stemmed from the moment he asserted his artistic authority, which was the message we were hoping to get across.

Indeed, the most interesting, tense and revealing moments of the whole process revolved around the inclusion of the non-disabled dancers. Another crunch point came when one of them spoke to Tom privately about feeling uncomfortable with a duet he'd included because it was not with a disabled partner. Discussion arose as to whether Tom was obeying the 'rules' of an 'integrated' piece.

Tom came to me with this dilemma wanting to stand his ground as, choreographically, he felt the piece needed this dynamic duet to lift and balance the energy of what was a generally slow piece. I backed Tom in his thinking and encouraged him to stand his ground asserting that it was his right, as the artist Dance Dangerous had brought in, to be just that – an artist trying to create the best art he could for the benefit of the company.

This incident does raise eternal questions for me, however, about where the lines between art and politics are drawn in the field of integrated dance. Who draws them, when and why? Perhaps the only answer *Station Master*[1] offers is that each project is different, each partner must work out beforehand where he/she draws own their lines, and lay them down in relation to the project's agreed priorities and negotiate throughout.

The duet was included and there were no objections. Tom explained that his choice was for the artistic good of the piece and 'because it belongs to Dance Dangerous, which includes – not excludes – non-disabled dancers'. Tom's own personal take on the dancers he works with is that: 'as a choreographer it's important to me that I become known as not working with just disabled people. A choreographer works with anyone'.

Looking Back Down the Line...

So did Tom's presence as a disabled role model make a difference to Dance Dangerous as an integrated group? Evaluation questionnaires describe participants as feeling 'more confident, more comfortable and more at ease' with a disabled choreographer at the helm. As a fellow choreographer, I definitely felt that Tom used the many wheelchairs with far more innovation and efficiency that I would have done.

Looking back, *Station Master* stands for me as one of my proudest achievements in community dance – not so much for what I did as for what I stopped myself from doing; not so much because of what happened when I was there, but because of what occurred because I strategically absented myself. Writing this – which is last thing on Tom's recognition wish list – I realise the weight of our responsibility and the wonderful *possibilities* we have as community dance artists to influence whose voices get heard through our practice. And not just by the dances we make, but with whom and how we choose to make them. And from the moment the phone rings, not just the moment we step into the studio.

If I had said yes at the end of the line that day, whose voice would have been heard in *Station Master*? Mine. Fine – but I *had* to ask the question: does the world need one more non-disabled choreographer working on another disability dance piece? Answer: not really.

Because I said no – a creative 'no' but 'no' nonetheless – I see three communities benefiting from an exchange of voices, none of them mine. First of all I got out of the way, so that Dance Dangerous could communicate directly with one of their own – who understood their choreographic needs far better than I ever could; secondly, I got out of the way so that the public and dance community could hear

Tom's choreographic voice; lastly it seems this has now helped a community miles from all of us to celebrate and benefit from the return of a prodigal son.

The experience of 'Station Master' has led to a wonderful next step in Tom's career and to his voice reaching a community even closer to his heart and life experience – his own. Having now called the shots and watched me up close running a community dance project, in summer 2007 Tom will be creating work in his home village, Colihaut, in his native Dominica:

> The project gave me the confidence to set up a 1 month site-specific project for Fete La Saint Pierre, the yearly festival of the village's patron saint. I'll create a dance/drama piece for 18 non-disabled people aged 10–50 years, about friends and family, harvest and Saint Peter. I will probably go back to some of our old *Station Master* paperwork to help me with the organisational side. I might have given it a go without having done that project, but as things are I *know* I can deliver.

So, clearly, no careers were harmed in my refusal of this project. And of course you are now hearing all the many community voices raised in this project through mine here. Which keeps me wondering... next time the phone rings... is there anything any of us could *not* do for the future of community dance?

Discussion Points

- What do you understand by the term 'inclusive practice'?
- Should community dance projects be open to everyone?
- When you have discussed these two questions have a look in the Resources section, where Caroline Bowditch gives her perspective on the same questions. Caroline is a performer and choreographer who has created exciting pieces which promote disability equality.

Note
1. *Station Master* was the title of the dance piece that Tom St Louis choreographed for Dance Dangerous.

6 Reasonable Care

Penny Greenland

In this chapter Penny Greenland challenges us to think about how we keep people safe in community dance work. The light-hearted quiz questions do not come with a handy set of 'correct answers' – this is deliberate. I suggest you imagine yourself in these different situations, explore your options and discuss them with other people. This will help you to really engage with the issues and identify what you need to do to equip yourself to 'take reasonable care' of the people you dance with.

I realise that many readers will want more than open ended discussion and, immediately after this chapter, there is a quiz which does give some concrete answers. Also, you may decide to go on training courses in Duty of Care and Safeguarding (Protection of Children, Young People and Vulnerable Adults). The Resources section will signpost you to information about these courses together with sample risk assessment forms and health and safety questionnaires.

Here's a quiz for you.

1. You are running a high-energy street dance workshop in a lively youth club and the work is going well. You ask the group not to chew gum as they work as it is potentially dangerous. Two lads laugh at you and refuse. Do you:
    (a) Stop the session. You can only continue if no-one chews gum.
    (b) Let them continue, because it's their club after all, and they need to take responsibility for themselves.
    (c) Try to get them to stop, but when they go on refusing back off because you don't want to spoil things for the whole group.
2. You arrive at a residential home for frail older people to run the first session with a group of residents. Unfortunately, there has been a death today and the assistant manager, who was going to join you in the group, can no longer attend. Because everything is in turmoil she asks you to carry on, on your own – 'It will be a nice distraction on a grim day'. Do you:
    (a) Willingly agree, glad to help out in such sad circumstances.

    (b) Politely refuse, saying you don't know the group well enough and you don't feel it would be safe to go ahead with movement activities on your own.

    (c) Compromise and suggest you could spend time chatting with a group instead, using the time to get to know residents a little better.

3. At the start of a community class an older woman, attending for the first time, comes to you and says, 'I have a pain in this part of my back (indicating lower left). What do you think it is? And can you advise me which bits of the class I should miss out?'. Do you:

    (a) Welcome her to the class and say that exercise will probably do her good, but advise she takes it easy if something really hurts.

    (b) Tell her not to join in until she has sought advice from a health practitioner.

    (c) Tell her you cannot give specific advice, but your class will emphasise the need for everyone to take care of themselves throughout, so carry on anyway[1].

How did you do? I haven't supplied the bit which usually follows this sort of quiz; and certainly no thumbnail sketch that tells you just what sort of community dance worker you really are. You know the sort of thing: 'Score 1–20. Watch out! You are so keen to please everyone you avoid taking important decisions and the people in your sessions might be at risk as a result'. Or, 'Score 30–50. Wow! No-one is going to get hurt in *your* sessions. You have every insurance policy going and you'd rather sit and do nothing than risk anyone twisting an ankle'.

Figure 6.1 Freedom in Dance Intergenerational Project (*Linda Boyles*)

Truth is, in the real world there are no easy answers. In fact, each answer raises another myriad questions. Taking care of people is a complicated business with many value judgements hidden within. Inevitably, when a society creates shared measures to try to ensure uniformly 'good enough' practice, many individual sensibilities are likely to be trampled underfoot. '**Duty of care**' – all the questions above refer to some aspect of this relatively new catchall phrase – is just such a beast. It is an attempt to round up, and structure, the responsibilities we owe others as we work. At the turn of the millennium you would have been hard pushed to find the phrase in common usage. Now it pops up constantly, in a rather vague sort of way, clearly indicating some moral and professional imperative, but never quite defining it. It goes hand in hand with some other unsettling catchall phrases like 'health and safety', 'risk assessment', 'employer's responsibility', 'professional indemnity' and 'civil liability' – frightening sorts of phrase that clearly have precise definitions and procedures somewhere, if only you knew where to find them; things that feel as if they might threaten the very thing that you, as a community dancer, were put on this earth to do: dance with people.

Back to the quiz.

4. Circle the definitions that most closely fit your own position:
    (a) Community dancers automatically take good care of the people they work with. They don't need special training to tell them how to do it.
    (b) Arts work is different; freedom from bureaucracy is essential or the work itself is altered.
    (c) I wish I really understood what is expected of me.
    (d) If we risk assess everything we do we'd never move for fear of being sued.
    (e) Community dancers have to join the real world if they want to be taken seriously.
    (f) My work is about nurturing open, trusting relationships. Why would I want to buy into legislation that is about watching my back?
    (g) There's too much paperwork in this world; nothing changes because of it.
    (h) These are the kinds of measures that are written by people sitting in offices, not people working on the ground.
    (i) I just wish someone would give me some clear guidelines for all these measures and I'd happily just stick to them.

'Duty of care' has no precise legal definition, but there is a clear common law responsibility (built up through case law) to 'take reasonable care' of the people you work with. This duty is established whenever a practitioner holds themselves out as ready to give professional advice (they may have ten years experience or ten weeks). Suggesting ways to move is the 'advice' we community dancers give.

What is 'reasonable' has to be defined by implication, rather than definition. Unfortunately, clarity about 'reasonableness' tends to develop when things go wrong, rather than when they go right. 'Negligence' is defined as a 'breach of the duty of care which results in damage' or 'a failure to exercise the degree of care... in protecting others from a foreseeable and unreasonable risk of harm'.

In a nutshell then, you have a professional responsibility to take '*reasonable* care' to protect others from '*unreasonable* risk of harm'. When push comes to shove, there is a heavy emphasis on reasonableness here. It all comes down to what you – or more pertinently, an aggrieved person in a court of law – deems to be 'reasonable'. And that's a tricky one. I don't expect there is a community dance practitioner alive who doesn't feel they take reasonable care. But I know, because I've asked, that different practitioners take very different views of what is, and isn't, reasonable in any given situation.

5. What do you think is reasonable here? Answer yes or no to each question:
    (a) Participants are fine to wear socks as they work even though the floor is varnished wood and slippery.
    (b) A participant aged 101 must be asked to sit down after dancing four dances on the trot, because you have a duty to make sure she is safe.
    (c) A member of your group, returning after having an operation, should be able to make their own decision about how soon to start exercising again.
    (d) A member of the group with a recent diagnosis of cancer is delighted to be part of your exercise group because it makes her feel so much better. However, you cannot let her join in unless she brings written medical approval for exercise.
    (e) You run a group for a mixed group of children in a busy community centre. The changing facilities are in a public space, out of your sight, with many people having ready access. You have done a Child Protection course and know that this is an issue. As there are few alternatives is this acceptable?
    (f) The sessions you are running are high energy and involve much lifting by the men; you recommend high protein drinks to help build their strength because you have heard, from colleagues, that they are very effective. Is it reasonable for you to give this advice?

There are some very strong preconceptions within our profession – things that have become embedded in practice which are very difficult to challenge. The sock thing is one of them: for some practitioners it is completely acceptable to work in slippery socks on a slippery floor – it is just what we dancers do. For others it is unthinkable. And dancers are often used to getting changed in very public places; surely being open about the body is just part of the dance experience?

Here is another tricky issue.

6. Returning for the third day of a five-day holiday project, several young women in your group say they are very stiff and found it difficult to get out of bed this morning. As the morning wears on one is quite weepy and say she doesn't

think she can continue – she is just too uncomfortable. She says she will ring her dad who will come and fetch her. When her dad arrives and expresses concern, do you:

(a) Tell him stories of when you trained and say that stiffness is just part and parcel of developing strength and flexibility. She's tired; she'll be better in the morning.

(b) Tell him that this is a course for intermediate level dancers and suggest she looks for something a bit closer to her ability level next time.

(c) Tell her to go home and have a hot bath.

(d) Spend the evening reviewing the material you have given the group this week and revise it for the remaining days, taking things more gently.

As you wrestle with this one, think about this legal definition. 'Actual bodily harm' is defined as 'any harm which interferes with the health *or comfort* of the victim'. Victim? Surely not the language of a dance class? Well, is it acceptable to send someone away feeling very stiff because 'no pain, no gain'? Or is any amount of pain unacceptable?

Reasons to Consider Duty of Care

Most of us with long careers leading dance work will have had one or two incidents in which, if someone had wanted to, they could probably have sued us for negligence. Not because we were particularly careless, or because the injuries were particularly devastating, but simply because, if someone is really of a mind, it isn't difficult to contrive a situation that puts a dancer firmly on the back foot. But people don't go around trying to sue community dancers. It's good, creative work, attracting good and creative people. Paranoia is not a good basis for artistic practice.

Well, let's get really grim for a moment. Have you been stopped in the street recently and asked if you have had an accident – *any accident* – that you might claim for? Let's suppose you were someone with a mind to make a few bob. (And I know some very nice people who, when pushed, have made a spurious claim – 'I'm hurting no one but the insurance company and they can withstand it' – ending up with £3,000 or £4,000.) If you decided to have a go, and had to choose between the various knocks and bangs you have sustained over the last three years (that's how long you've got to back-track, by the way), who would you choose as a potential source of these surprise funds? The big local council or corporation, with lawyers and plenty of experience of this sort of claim? Or the community dancer, armed with all the goodwill and good intentions in the world, but with little by way of legal backing? Hmm...

So is this the reason to develop a duty of care policy? Well, it's *a* reason, but not a good enough reason. Duty of care is not primarily about fear and blame; it is about all-round good practice. Duty of care is about bringing together all the disparate policies and procedures that we are increasingly asked to provide – by insurance companies and funders, local authorities and individual bookers, each in turn covering their own backs. The real value of putting duty of care at the centre of our practice is that we can make sense of all these demands in ways that are appropriate to our practice, rather than someone else's. As we do this, we also protect ourselves against the (remote) possibility of mischievous claims against us. If our procedures are as good as they should be – *because we want them to be* – we don't even have to think about the fear and blame culture again.

There is another reason to adopt this duty of care focus. It is the way we can justify public trust in our work. My own interest in duty of care was kick-started by a health worker in GP referral scheme who was eager to include dance within the range of activities promoted by his GP Practice. He asked a group of very experienced dancers a simple question: 'What qualifications do you have?' Bewildered by the burblings he received in reply – 'a degree'/'years of experience'/'I was a professional dancer' – he tried another tack. 'How can you prove that your practice is safe? I have to be able to justify anything we offer on the same terms as any drugs we might prescribe'. More burbling: 'I've never had any problems'. 'The work just isn't dangerous', 'I'm a trained teacher!'. He drew breath. 'Aerobics teachers take a test and gain a certificate that proves they know how to keep people safe. It means I can hire them. What do you have?' Irate burbling, puffed up chests, high dudgeon. I have no doubt that the dancers' practice was of the highest quality; I don't doubt that their different experience and training equipped them to take very good care of the people they worked with. But they had no way of *proving* it.

More quiz:

7. You need a new car. Do you:
    (a) Look in the Yellow Pages and ring the garage with the name you like best.
    (b) Look for a dealer with membership of a professional body which offers some protection if something does go wrong.
    (c) Ask for a full log book and records but don't trouble if it isn't available – 'I'm selling it for my brother who's away in the army'.
    (d) Ask if you can have an AA safety check before buying, but happily agree with the seller not to bother because it would take extra time.
    (f) Say nothing when you find an irreparable fault just one month after purchase. After all, it was your fault for not knowing more about cars in the first place.
    (g) Count yourself very lucky when the car dealer turns out to know rather a lot about insurance as well (he's just sorted out his own), and take his advice about which company to use.

When you look for advice or services from other professionals, there are probably certain things you hope to be able to take for granted. Oddly, they are often things that community dancers don't feel they have to provide – membership of a professional body with clear codes of practice and explicit statements regarding training or competencies; open record-keeping systems; clarity about what the trader is *not* competent to offer, as well as what they are competent to provide, a commitment to shared standards across their profession. These aren't frightening things that erode our individuality; they liberate us from those middle-of-the-night anxieties about what it is we *should* have done in order to comply with whatever legal requirements we *ought* to know about, but don't... quite.

Good Procedures

No one asks us for a Duty of Care policy, but I suggest that this is the (missing) central policy which binds all the others together. From this simple principle – putting people's best interests at the heart of what you do – you can make fresh sense of your diversity and equal opportunities policies, health and safety procedures, those dratted risk assessments, safe-guarding, data protection and use of personal information systems. They cease to be dust-gathering, meaningless, time-consuming annoyances that you do because someone says you have to, and become, instead, small kindnesses, careful considerations, part of the gift.

A duty of care policy has two components: things that minimise the chance of anything going wrong and things that help the situation if something does go wrong. Hurray – we can talk openly about the possibility of things going wrong instead of ignoring the possibility. We don't have to brace against the unthinkable, head in the sand, but can acknowledge that things *do* go wrong from time to time and plan accordingly. What a relief.

8. Your builder completes your new conservatory but creates a crack all down what was the exterior wall. He says it was an unforeseen accident, but he hopes it won't cause you any trouble in future. Do you:
   (a) Apologise for your wall being so awkward and ask him to help you wall-paper over the unsightly crack.
   (b) Ask him to use his professional insurance to compensate you fully, so that you can have any necessary and expensive repair work carried out.
   (c) Agree that with any creative endeavour there is always some risk involved, so it's as much your responsibility for wanting a conservatory just there.
   (d) Ask him why he didn't tell you about any possible risks, as they arose, giving you a clear choice at all stages of the process.

Keeping people's best interests at heart is not difficult or unfamiliar. It's what we want for ourselves, and what we owe others. It need not limit our creativity or compromise the relationship we have with the people with whom we work, as long as we don't let it. The grudging lip service that I often hear given to risk assessment, the writing of a new policy, or worst of all, record keeping, feels far more damaging than a refreshed, unified approach to looking after people because it is the right thing to do.

Record keeping is an essential part of duty of care. Of course it is our awareness and adaptability within the practice itself that actually keeps people safe from harm, but it is the records that *clarify and communicate* how we carry out our duty of care, and highlight the tricky bits where things threaten to, or actually do, go wrong. Records don't have to be long; but they do need to be fair and insightful. The skill of writing brief, helpful records is one that I feel should nestle, with equal importance, alongside the practical dance skills we hold dear. It is simply part of professional practice.

All of this is time-consuming of course, although not as much as many fear. Larger organisations often feel that they are already stretched to bursting simply maintaining their existence without more attention to background work; individual practitioners quake at the thought of having to write policies, or produce reports, all on their own. I sympathise, but where matters of protection from harm are concerned I can't see that anyone can be exempt.

9. Your grandmother – who lives in a residential home and struggles with osteoporosis – tells you that a community dancer is visiting to run exercise sessions. When you ask the Manager for some more detail you discover that this is the dancer's first job after doing a six-week introductory course on dance exercise for older people. He is hoping to build up more work, but is just getting going. In view of this:
    (a) You don't feel it is fair to expect him to have leaflets about his work, or information about policies. After all, he is just starting out.
    (b) You are too embarrassed to ask if he has any experience of working with people who have osteoporosis, as he seems rather nervous. He is clearly very well meaning and wants to do his best. After all, it's great that he's coming in at all.
    (c) You feel protective of your grandmother and ask the dancer how he will be working with her in this very mixed ability group. After all he is here to support your grandmother, and the others, not the other way round.
    (d) You casually ask the dancer who he got his CRB check through, and whether he has the POVA addition (protection of vulnerable adults), but when he doesn't seem to know about it you back off, not wanting to upset him.

As our profession grows up there is much to be shared between us about how to develop duty of care standards that are simple, streamlined and helpful to all concerned. As new practitioners train to lead dance work, duty of care measures should be seen as part and parcel of the necessary skills – every bit as person-centred and loving as the movement work. Keeping people's best interests at heart is not difficult or unfamiliar. It's what we want for our selves and what we owe others. Creating shared standards for such measures within our profession will not limit our creativity or compromise the unique nature of our artistic endeavour. It will enable others to see clearly on what basis we ensure that those who work with us are protected from harm.

10. You come to the end of a day working with a mixed-age, mixed-ability group of people new to dance. It has been a huge success, but there was an injury along the way. What do you want for yourself at 2 a.m. the next morning?

   (a) When the fall happened you suggested the injured party sat out for the rest of the day and had a brief chat with their mum when she arrived to pick them up, saying you thought there was no real problem but you advised no more dancing just to be on the safe side. Now you are lying awake wondering if the ankle is all right and if there will be any come-back.

   (b) You are lying awake having endless conversations in your head between you and your manager: what forms should you fill out tomorrow? Whose insurance would cover this accident if it does turn out to be a problem? Do you have that insurance? Who will speak to the mum if she rings?

   (c) Having written a brief accident report (that you have signed, dated, filed confidentially and passed to the woman who organised the event), and spoken on the phone to the injured party after they got back from A&E where you advised them to check it out, you are sound asleep.

Sweet dreams ...

Exercise 1: A duty of care quiz (with answers this time)

1. To whom do you have a duty of care?
2. What is a 'vulnerable adult'?
3. If you are working with children, young people or vulnerable adults are you considered their carer?
4. What is 'risk assessment'?
5. Do you need to have your own public liability insurance?
6. What a CRB Disclosure Check?
7. Are there any recommended staffing ratios for dance workshops?

See p. 200 for the answers.

Exercise 2

Penny Greenland refers to record keeping as 'an essential part of duty of care'. Imagine you've been asked to run a ten week dance project with a mixed age community group.

- What information do you need to gather before and during the project?
- Devise a simple system for recording this information (either in a notebook or a pro-forma to use in a loose leaf file)
- Where would you store your records and how long should you keep them?

Discussion Point

- In the introduction to Part 2 I raised the issue of health questionnaires. Can you think of situations when it would not be appropriate to ask people to fill in such a form? What other ways are there of finding out what you need to know to keep people safe?

Note

1. As community dance practitioners we are not qualified to give advice about specific injuries/medical conditions. If a participant needs such advice they should be referred to a health practitioner.

Part 3
Community Dance Performance

Introduction

This section looks at the connection between the process of making dance and the experience of sharing what is made (the product) with an audience. Heidi Wilson sets the chapters in context by discussing reasons why dance is presented to an audience and ways of viewing the work. This is an interesting area: what are we looking at when we watch community dance performance? Which lenses are we looking through? Does a dance excite us because of the demonstration of technical skills or because of the presence of its dancers?

Chapter 7 looks at audience responses and the impact on the community performers – something that was briefly mentioned in Chapter 3. If you are interested in looking more closely at the relationship between community performers and their audience I recommend *The Community Performance Reader*, edited by Petra Kuppers and Gwen Robertson, which goes into this subject in much more depth.

A recurring theme in this book is the way we use the words 'professional' and 'community'. In the following chapters Heidi Wilson, Rosemary Lee and Adam Benjamin all refer to these terms in different ways. Rosemary states, from the outset, that she finds such labels unhelpful. Heidi draws attention to the fact that some members of the audience compare community performance with 'professional' work. Adam poses the question 'What...distinguishes "community" from professional dance?'. You might like to discuss this with colleagues and tutors – what are the implications for us as a profession if our community work is seen as something to be compared with professional work?

In Chapters 8, 9 and 10 I asked each of the artists to give us a flavour of how they work with groups to make dance pieces and how the work is presented/performed for an audience. As an artist working with community groups I am particularly interested to learn how other people manage to recreate, for an audience, those special moments which occur in workshops. Rosemary Lee calls these 'the moments we aspire to' and points out that these happen far more often during

Figure P3.1 Freedom in Dance *Landscape Rhythms* (*Joel Fildes*)

sessions than in a performance at the end of a project. As you read through these and other chapters make notes on leadership styles and think about how *you* facilitate dance experiences for other people.

Further Reading

Bannerman, C., Sofaer, J. and Watt, J. (eds.) (2006) *The Creative Process in Contemporary Performing Arts*. Middlesex University Press, London.
Kuppers, P. (2007) *Community Performance: An Introduction*. Routledge, London.

7 Community Dance in Performance

Heidi Wilson

Heidi Wilson is an experienced practitioner who has carried out research into the impact of community dance performance on audience, performers, artists and project partners. Here she presents a theoretical framework for community dance in performance and a summary of research findings during her work with Powys Dance (a community dance organisation in mid-Wales). This chapter contributes to discussions about 'community' and 'professional' dance and includes a consideration of the following:

- *Why hold community dance performance events?*
- *Viewing and evaluating community dance*
- *A community dance aesthetic*
- *The process/product debate*

Community Dance and the Wider Dance Ecology

Community dance is often characterised as being participatory in the sense that community dancers are actively engaged in the process of creating, defining and presenting their own dances. This is distinct from engagement in dance product as an audience member where influence over the event is generally restricted to whether to attend or not, where to sit, whether to remain for the duration of the performance and how hard to clap and cheer to voice your approval or otherwise. There is not usually ready access to the performers and choreographer during the making process or post performance. These two distinct practices have historically been labelled 'community' and 'professional' dance, respectively, creating an unhelpful and erroneous assumption amongst some that 'community' equates with 'amateur' and therefore of a lower standard and that 'professional' always implies excellence and excludes a participatory element. Clinton and Glen (1993) offer the following clarification of community arts: 'The activity is distinct from traditionally funded "high art" in that the activity is more than likely to have a purpose beyond its aesthetic value'. The Arts Council of Wales defines Community Arts as, 'arts professionals creating opportunities in communities for people to develop skills, and to explore and communicate ideas through active participation' (Arts Council of Wales, 1996). Current debate on what to call community dance has crystallised some of these concerns (see *Animated*, Summer 2006).

Recent approaches are more sensitive to this historical divide and attempt to present a coherent and united dance ecology. Whilst still acknowledging a difference in intention and practice between participatory and performance work, a review carried out in 2005 by the National Assembly for Wales acknowledges the professionalism inherent in both by identifying that there are 'career avenues for professional dancers' in both 'a community or performing sphere' (National Assembly for Wales, 2005).

This division is the result not only of different practices but also an inevitability of historical funding structures. The Draft Art Forms Strategy of the Arts Council of Wales states: 'the previous funding patterns have always made a distinction between dance which is considered to be community dance and that which has been considered to be professional dance. With time the dance sector itself has come to the conclusion that it is in fact more organic than that... practitioners working in the field have to have skills that span the whole spectrum of delivery' (Arts Council of Wales, 2007).

The Process/Product Debate

The difference in intention between community and professional dance practice has been explored through identifying the emphasis which each places on the process or product of dance making. Akroyd states (FCD, 1996):

> People-centred community dance practice is characterised by an emphasis on process as opposed to product and by the conscious 'tailoring' of content and method to suit the specific context and needs of a group.

This belief resonates through community dance practice and is often employed as one of its distinguishing features. It is explored in some detail in a framework devised by Peppiatt who uses professional dance performance as a benchmark from which to distinguish community dance practice (Peppiatt, 1996, p. 3):

> The territory of community dance activity is everywhere except professional dance performance. The driving force[s] in the world of professional dance performance are essentially different from those in community dance.... Professional dance performance has important links with community dance activities but is essentially focused on professional performance itself (training, creation, performance and touring).

He emphasises the point by claiming that the territory of professional dance is, 'everything FOR performance', whilst community dance is, 'everything AND performance'. He further claims that the process is the main product of community dance, whether or not that process is demonstrated through a conventional product or performance.

Thomson explores this idea further but tries to avoid an either/or, professional/community split (Thomson, 1996, p. 3). He proposes the use of a curved continuum with 'process/intention' at one end of the continuum and 'product/form' at the other end. The continuum is curved to acknowledge and emphasise that all works contain both process and product (of some kind). Professional performance would tend to be at the 'product/form' end of the continuum with community dance at the other, although not always necessarily so. Akroyd cites an example where a youth group request to work in a very technical way toward a specified performance thus placing themselves at the 'product/form' end (*ibid*).

Matarasso (1994, p. 9) recommends a broadening of the notion of product:

> what needs rethinking is the concept of product. Of course it may be a finished poem, the performance of a new piece of music, or a show in the local town hall, but it can mean much subtler things. A single gesture, a hand shape, a verbal image, a chord sequence, a rhythm held, a facial expression – there is

Figure 7.1 Powys Dance (*Ian Dixon*)

no end to the things that can constitute real, tangible artistic product. Because these things are often small, they may pass unnoticed by the casual observer of a workshop. Because they can be hard to explain to someone outside the group, or someone with little or no experience of the work, there is a temptation to stress the process. But the product – the thing that each of us is trying to work towards – is what gives purpose to the learning process and its importance must not be underestimated.

Rosemary Lee picks up this point when she reflects on her experience as a choreographer who works across the community and professional dance sectors. She is often involved in projects with non-professional dancers and describes what it is she looks for in a dancer which may not be realised in a formal performance but as part of the working process (Lee, 2004, p. 2):

> It is the transformative potential of dance that I find so intoxicating and I rarely tire of seeing it if I get the scent of its possibility. My most memorable and moving moments as a viewer have been watching participants in workshops. It is the beauty of seeing something unfold before you, happening for the first and only time before your eyes.

Marks (1998) believes that Thomson's continuum implies an artistic process thus 'maintaining its identification with art rather than therapy, sport or recreation'. Being identified as artists is important for many community dance practitioners – particularly those working in contexts where other agendas have a high priority. Whilst working on an arts and health project Storey and Brown felt that what they 'perceived as an inward looking, therapy-oriented approach might militate against the potential of artistic processes that can create something that can be shared with others' (White, 2005).

In summary, performance is an established component of much community dance practice but it is commonly associated with an extension of the working process on which greater value is placed. The suggested divide between the worlds of community and professional dance finds a focus in the process/product debate.

Performance as Part of Community Dance Programmes

The development of performance skills is mentioned specifically in Powys Dance's Statement of Values and as an aim of Powys Dance's Artistic Policy (Powys Dance, 1999). Performance events by community dancers constitute a regular feature of Powys Dance's programme. These range in scale from informal sharings as a component of sessions through to festival events in formal theatre settings with full technical support and a paying audience. Three dance festivals held in 2000 formed the focus of this research. The events were similar in that they all occurred in theatre settings. Groups were drawn from Powys Dance's network of community classes representing a range of ages and abilities. They also included performances by an all male group and a special school.

The majority of community dance organisations include a performance element in their programmes. Peppiatt and Venner (1993) identified that 77% of community dance practitioners surveyed saw the encouragement of dance performance as part of their role. A review of the other community dance organisations in Wales revealed that all hold performance events every year (Wilson, 2000). In keeping with Powys Dance these range from informal events to formal showcases. Organisations also link with high-profile national performance events when opportunities arise.

Why Hold Community Dance Performance Events?

The different stakeholders involved will inevitably have different responses to the above question. Existing research on community dance in performance proposes common aims of celebration, sharing of skills acquired (which can be broadly categorised as educational and artistic aims) and profile raising (associated with accountability to partners and funding bodies). Scholey (1998) identified the following aims of community dance performance following discussion with community dance practitioners:

- to function as an extension of the process (which is the community dance experience);
- to make dance and develop knowledge of dance vocabulary;

Figure 7.2 Powys Dance (*Ian Dixon*)

- to provide participants with an artistic experience;
- to provide participants with an opportunity to celebrate and demonstrate their achievements;
- to provide an opportunity to raise the profile of community dance to funding bodies and community stakeholders;
- to provide participants with a form of exercise in a safe environment.

Amans (1997) suggests similar reasons for presenting community dance through performance:

- to show what has been created (an end product);
- to demonstrate newly learned skills;
- to show work in progress (*i.e. a stage in the process*);
- as a celebration;
- to satisfy funding bodies.

The Community Dance Performer

Concerning the effect of performance on the community performer, Trueman (1998) looks specifically at the relationship between self-esteem and dance performance employing a model based on Maslow's theories of motivation (Maslow, 1970). She concludes (Trueman, 1998, p. 21):

> from the data available, it seems that the link between performance and self-esteem is indeed very strong. This link is dependent upon the public nature of the performance, the exposure of self during performance, to some extent the esteem from others post-performance, the community built by the cast, and the creative investment in the performance.

This is borne out by anecdotal evidence from community dance performers. A young man participating in *Third Symphony – Men at War* (part of ACE Dance Included) made the following statement: 'it was a real high. It was a good feeling performing in front of people. It made me feel pleased everyone enjoyed it' (Arts Council England, 2006).

Jeremy Spafford, a community dance performer with Dug Out[1], talks about the link between the process of making dance and the value of sharing a product with an audience (Spafford 2005):

> The creativity is crucial. We are not simply exercising or learning steps – though we do that – we are also researching ways of expressing how we feel about ourselves and the world and then refining our movements with care and attention. Despite the laughter and playfulness, it is wonderful to watch the seriousness with which members of the group will approach a dance task or performance. It feels as if it really matters.

Whilst performance can build an intimate community of dancers this community extends beyond the performers to encompass the audience. Some community dance performance projects are specifically designed to achieve this. Leap of Faith dance and performance group for people aged fifty and over in East London managed to create a completely new audience in Stratford Circus (Risbridger, 2005):

> People who've lived in the area for years were surprised to discover that this venue and cultural centre existed, and delighted to experience an event specifically for them. The sense of community was overwhelming, with people spotting friends they recognised from the borough but hadn't seen for years.

This example of community development through the vehicle of a community dance performance helps illustrate Matarasso's model of evaluation developed to explore the social impacts of participation in the arts. His research considers the areas of: personal development; social cohesion; community empowerment and self-determination; local image and identity; imagination and vision; health and well-being. He concludes that (Matarasso, 1997):

- Participation in arts activities brings social benefits;
- The benefits are integral to the act of participation;
- The social impacts are complex but understandable;
- Social impacts can be assessed and planned for.

Performance events make visible some of these impacts and provide evidence of activity. In 2006 Arts Council England explored models of good practice in dance within a range of social exclusion settings and their report refers to performance as 'a very tangible and shared achievement (which) appears to have a great capacity to boost the confidence and self-esteem of those taking part. When asked what they had felt most proud of, many participants talked about performing in front of an audience and the reaction of an audience' (*ibid*, p. 21).

Education of a Community Dance Audience

It may be that witnessing performance serves to educate a community dance audience (Jasper, 1996). In some instances the presentation of community dance work takes direct account of its audience. In seeking to create meaningful and accessible multimedia performances which would appeal to older generations Niki McCretton (2006) used projections and voice to 'refer to what is happening on stage, which enables the more abstract passages of dance and imagery to exist in a semi-explained way, allowing the audience to feel comfortable with what is unfolding at all times'. This strategy serves to support an audience in coming to understand a new or challenging aesthetic, or simply to feel supported in finding meaning in the more abstract and non-literal aspects of dance.

Viewing Community Dance

Dance, like all the arts, can be practised in many ways and with varying degrees of distinction. It has art's basic function of articulating the values that people use to create meaning in their lives. That, simply put, is the defining characteristic of what, in Western culture, is called art: it expresses and communicates values (Matarasso, 2005).

The refinement of the movement language which is used to express and communicate these values is perhaps the key difference between a community and a professional dancer. Aesthetic concerns codified within the execution of a technique often present a benchmark by which professional dance work is judged. This critical stance is clearly inappropriate for much community dance and has fuelled discussions concerning a community dance aesthetic. If there is one what should be its defining features? Matarasso decries the levels of physical virtuosity demanded by some dance techniques employed in the professional arena: 'in some forms, dance has become tyrannical in its pursuit of certain ideals of physical beauty'. He also identifies a parallel development in dance practice: 'people with all kinds of physiques and of all ages can be marvellous dancers' (*ibid*).

What else makes a good dancer if virtuosic technique and a uniform body type are not appropriate? Val, a 67 year old dancer with Dug Out articulates the performance experience for her. 'When dancing I live totally in the present. I am not anticipating tomorrow or regretting today – I am totally in the now' (see Spafford, 2005). Val's perception of her performance state reflects a quality that choreographer Rosemary Lee seeks in her performers (Spafford, 2005):

> What am I waiting to see? A glimmer of embodiment. A sense that the dancer is overtaken with the activity they are engaged with in such a way that every cell in their body seems involved. They are in synch, they are whole, they are present.

(See Chapter 8 where Rosemary discusses her practice in more detail).

A community dance performer lacking the cover of perfectly executed technique behind which to hide is more likely to appear as him or herself in performance. Their body becomes the medium and the subject of the dance:

> As a form that is inseparable from the physical presence of a person, and whose language is rooted in the communicability of experience through movement, it is essentially humanist. It claims, by its very presence, respect for the physical integrity of the person, and their autonomy of action. It values the individual, by focusing attention on them directly; and it values cooperation between individuals (*ibid*).

When viewing and evaluating community dance performances Thomson suggests that the audience is applying an 'inclusive framework' which extends beyond that of a professional performer/audience relationship. Many community dance audiences are made of people who are connected to the performers in some way.

A framework for appreciation of community dance will include precisely those things usually omitted from the dispassionate critical view. Our knowledge of who is dancing, and why, and where they have come from, and what it means to them, enriches rather than invalidates our appreciation of their dancing (Thomson, 1996, p. 8).

Wolff (1993) identifies such knowledge as the 'extra aesthetic' elements of a work. She believes that the artistic value is not undermined by examining a work in its social and historical context, quite the contrary, 'the origin and reception of works is thus made more comprehensible by reference to social divisions and their economic bases'. Willis (1996) calls for a 'grounded aesthetic' which takes account of the context of consumption (and production) whereby quality is not judged solely upon 'the cerebral, abstract or sublimated quality of beauty' inherent in a form but on its actual reception by consumers.

Findings

The following section considers the findings of two aspects of fieldwork undertaken, namely audience questionnaires and interviews with performers.

The Audience

The fieldwork revealed that over 94% of respondents attended because a relative or friend was performing. This suggests that the community dance audience is viewing the work within an 'inclusive framework' (Thomson, in FCD, 1996), taking 'extra aesthetic' considerations into account when attending a community dance event.

When asked to evaluate the performance they had seen using a ranking scale, 72.4% considered it 'excellent', 26% 'good' and 1.4% 'fair'. No one judged the performances as 'poor' or 'very poor'. To try to establish what criteria these judgements may have been based on, respondents were asked a single open-ended question concerning what they valued about the evening's performance. Their responses fell into roughly six categories as follows: artistic considerations; seeing the enjoyment of the performers; the diversity of people performing; perceived effort demonstrated and achievement and experience gained (broadly educational aims); community considerations; and entertainment value.

Artistic Considerations

A high number of responses were given which were concerned with the artistic achievements of the performers. Their responses included reference to dance technique, where 'range of dance movements', 'lifting' and the use of 'body movements to express emotions and feelings' were mentioned. One respondent referred to the 'brilliant choreography' and the topics covered by the different dances. Other comments concerned the appreciation of performance skills, such as: 'wonderful individual performances – an inspiration to us all'. Production qualities were mentioned as well, 'large choice of music, costume and lighting'.

There is an indication that some audience members may have been making comparisons with professional performances. One respondent felt it was 'an excellent amateur effort' obviously judging it within a range of other amateur performances, whilst another valued the 'professionalism and dedication of all the performers', presumably feeling that their achievements bore comparison with those of professional performers in a positive way. Yet another referred to the 'sophistication of the performance'. Value judgements such as 'high standard' and 'excellent' were also used. The research revealed that 63.7% of respondents attend dance performances other than Powys Dance Festivals and of these more than half see both professional and community work, indicating that they have a critical framework against which to assess community dance.

Seeing the Enjoyment of the Performers

This aspect of performance was valued by the majority of respondents with such comments as, 'the enthusiasm and enjoyment on the faces of all the performers' and 'seeing everybody enjoy a wonderful evening'.

The Diversity of People Performing

Several respondents valued the opportunity to see people of different ages and abilities performing together. One respondent felt strongly about the accessibility of dance as 'something people of all ages and ability can enjoy'. One event included an all-male group prompting a positive response from audience members who enjoyed seeing 'boys dancing in large numbers'. The findings suggest that the opportunity to see performers who challenge the dancing stereotype is certainly valued highly in a community setting.

Perceived Effort Demonstrated and Achievement and Experience Gained

These can be characterised as broadly educational aims centred around the performer. Responses within this category included such things as: 'achieving and producing good work'; 'commitment from young people'; 'hard work and effort'; 'enthusiasm and dedication'; 'opportunity for young people to perform'.

Community Considerations

Responses which fell under this category have similarities with those above, although they embrace the wider community. 'Involvement', 'taking part' and 'working together' were highly valued, as were 'great atmosphere' and 'team spirit'. One respondent said it was 'good for the children taking part and for the community'.

Entertainment Value

A number of responses expressed enjoyment and entertainment: 'sheer delight'; 'the fun of it'; 'entertainment value'. They also enjoyed being part of an audience valuing, 'the general appreciation of the audience' and 'the complete participation of the audience'. These comments are associated with having a good night out, a potential aspect of community dance performance which is rarely, if ever, mentioned!

These findings reveal that the respondents value the Powys Dance Festivals for a range of reasons including artistic, educative and social.

Performer Questionnaires and Group Interview

This aspect of the fieldwork focused on a group of twelve 9–11-year-old boys who worked on a ten-week performance project with Powys Dance. Through analysing the boys' responses in relation to Trueman's findings on the relationship between performance and self-esteem there is a strong correlation between her conclusions and the boys' experience (Trueman, 1998). Trueman identifies five features linking community performance to self-esteem. I shall take each of them in turn.

The Public Nature of the Performance

All the boys claimed they enjoyed the experience of performing, even one child who did not enjoy the overall project. For one respondent it was his favourite part of the whole project. Reasons as to why they enjoyed the performance varied. Many felt it was fun and interesting and they enjoyed being on the stage. Public recognition of their achievement was also important, 'showing people our dance' and 'because you can dance in front of people' were reasons given by two of the boys. The pressure to produce an end product for the performance was important to one boy, 'it was a chance to put everything we had learnt together'. Most of the boys expressed anxiety at the prospect of performing, all except three of them said they felt 'nervous' or 'scared' prior to the performance, these feelings seemed to originate from concerns over 'messing up' or 'going wrong'. When asked how they felt after the performance many of them said they felt 'relieved' and 'glad' but also 'proud', 'happy' and 'pleased I had done it'. They all felt more confident having done the performance. One boy commented, 'I feel we could do it again now we know what it is like'.

When asked if they felt it was important to do a performance as part of the project only one boy said 'no'. Most of them saw the performance as a vital element, reasons for this seemed to centre around the public nature of a performance – a desire to share work produced and to be seen to be accountable. Their responses included: 'what would be the point otherwise?'; 'otherwise your work and time would go to waste'; 'to check we had learnt something and see if you could do it under pressure'. One boy viewed the performance as a gift: 'it was a surprise for my nanny and other people'. All the boys had someone special in the audience who had come to support them – either family, friends or their head teacher. This was very important to them although it made them more nervous, comments included, 'all those people there!' and 'my mum was videoing us'.

Exposure of Self During Performance

This aspect is clearly linked to the public nature of performance and was an enjoyable and important element for many of the boys. One boy very honestly said, 'it's like showing off to lots of people'. Another boy said, 'people got to see me and remember me' – the performance experience made him feel singled out and important. Other dancers commented on feeling 'famous' and appreciating the chance to demonstrate their skills – 'I enjoyed doing my cartwheel'.

Esteem From Others Post-Performance

Many comments showed that the boys valued the audience applause and the very positive feedback they received from friends and family. Another important factor was their own reflection on their work. On watching a video of their performance they all thought it looked good – better than they had expected it to, especially, 'the dancing bit and the driving the cars'.

Community Built by the Cast

They felt that the teamwork needed to create their dance piece was important to their experience of the project. Two of the boys commented on how much they had enjoyed working with a partner. All the boys except one said that they enjoyed working in a group. Their comments included: 'in a group you can share each other's ideas'; 'I like working with my friends'; 'there were more people so we could do more things'; 'because if you get it wrong it's not just your fault'. They also found the responsibilities of being part of a group quite challenging. When asked if they found anything difficult four of them said keeping quiet was difficult and also keeping still at the sides of the stage. There were also concerns about the execution of their dance in performance, such as, 'the timing', 'holding up the pyramid', and 'remembering the dance and lifting the tyres'. They felt it was 'cool' being out of school together on the day of the performance without their teachers. They enjoyed meeting some of the other performers (especially the girls!), and seeing the other pieces which were performed.

Creative Investment in the Performance

Many of the boys' ideas were incorporated into the piece. This was very important to them – they felt pleased and proud that their ideas were used. Following the performance they also discussed ways in which they would like to develop their piece if they had the opportunity to perform it again, their comments included: 'add more to it'; 'work on the doubles'; 'more good music'; 'get more experience'. All except one would like to be involved in another performance project.

Conclusion

Performance is a valued element of community dance practice and appreciation of a performance event is enhanced by knowledge of the context against which achievement can be judged in a realistic and grounded manner. This does not diminish the expectation of high-quality performance but embraces it within a relative and inclusive framework where the performance is recognised as simply a moment within a longer developmental process.

Discussion Points

- Summarise Heidi Wilson's discourse on the key distinguishing features of 'community' dance and 'professional' dance. Can you identify any problems in seeing them as two separate aspects of dance practice?
- What do you understand by the term 'a community dance aesthetic'?

Note

1. Dug Out is an adult community dance group based in Oxford and led by Cecilia Macfarlane.

8 Aiming for Stewardship Not Ownership

Rosemary Lee

Rosemary Lee is a choreographer, director, film maker and performer. Her creative output is diverse, and includes creating dance with mixed age community groups. In this chapter she reflects on her work as a choreographer in a range of varied contexts. Rosemary reveals why she does the work she does and explores our responsibilities as leaders: 'It's about the larger picture – what underlies what we are fundamentally doing – beneath the specifics'.

Over the last twenty years as a choreographer I have chosen to work in diverse, challenging settings, be they a familiar theatre, the largest red brick building in Europe or a waterfowl sanctuary; working with casts as small as 1 and as large as 237. I have made live works, dance films for broadcast and, more recently, interactive installations. There are many reasons for developing my work in this way and for the perhaps startling range of performance situations I have chosen. They have enabled me above all to reach new audiences and to explore quite different relationships with them in each context, and have also allowed me the privilege of working with a wide range of performers of all ages and of varied experience.

Early on in my career, I sought to try to ignore certain divisions: 'professional'; 'non-professional'; 'community'. Some might name a work with a cast of 13 dancers of all ages as a 'community' piece. Such labels, at least as regards my own work, seem to get in the way, making people look at the performance with different eyes. For me, each piece is firmly the next in my body of work; I aim to bring no less rigour to the so called 'community' piece as to working with a professional dance company. I aim for the same artistic standards and production values, and I also try not to be swayed into perceiving the work with a different, perhaps less critical, lens. I want all my work, regardless of its cast or context, to be considered critically as art. If it falls short of that, the responsibility is with me as a maker. This desire to try to avoid labels is sometimes problematic, but for the most part it keeps me asking questions of my own practice and its role in society, and helps me feel less trapped within sets of hidden rules and agendas.

My motivation and respect for working with this wide range of performers are threefold. Firstly I believe fundamentally in the positive power of groups of people coming together for a common creative purpose and the extraordinary effect that has on both individual and group. Secondly, I love to watch people dancing – whether they are trained or untrained. Their movement often speaks to me and inspires me more deeply than their words can. Thirdly, I want my works to reflect and communicate our common humanity, and sometimes I can do that more successfully by having a cast that is of all ages and of varied experience.

> I am watching an adult, a theatre director I think, in his shoes and summer linens on a hot summer day at the Festival Hall. He is partnering a nine-year-old boy who is a fantastic, natural, lithe mover and tiny. They are improvising together; the boy has his small hand stuck firmly to the adult's hand. The man looks flushed and a little dishevelled, his glasses are steaming up, but he is enthralled and exhilarated as he tries to follow the boy, who leaps and ducks, spirals and whirls. Their palms hold firm in this time of unspoken connection and energy. They come from such different worlds, different ages, different races, different economic backgrounds... but this dance transcends all that and brings them together into an intimate *pas de deux*. The dance is unfolding before them[1].

When I see a disparate group of people, brought together for a project, have their trepidation and anxiety melt away within an hour of dancing together, when I see an adult performer, whose daily life does not include children, begin to dance and engage with their nine-year-old partner with care and interest, when I see a child, who has rarely been in a setting of equal status with an adult, begin to value their own contribution with new-found pride – then I feel privileged to have been a facilitator and to have witnessed those moments. I feel a sense of stewardship, not ownership, as I try to create fertile settings where change and transformation can take place. Dance has a subtle but intense, powerful force. It can be a true equaliser in a society where hierarchy, divisiveness and rifts between individuals and groups seem ever greater. Is it fear and suspicion that make us perversely feel more secure if we widen these gulfs and more afraid if we build bridges to discover and trust common ground?

> The children view each other suspiciously across the grim dirty gym. I think to myself 'this is going to be tough' – and it is. The children are from different schools, a wire fence apart but with such suspicion and dread of each other. I set my expectations a little lower. I think to myself – if I can even get these children to acknowledge each other on the way to school after this project, then

it's a step forward. By the end of the project they could joke and imitate each other, learning each other's names eventually and knowing their peers' movements inside out[2].

He is late always and in a dream. He, like his classmates, loves the part of the day when they lie down and close their eyes, and I come round and gently test to see if they are relaxed, lifting a limb and seeing if it drops down easily. They lie so still and try so hard to be relaxed, excited when they feel my hand on their arm or hear me near them. This is their favourite part every day, which puzzles me initially since they are such live wires and so unstoppable. Each time we do this, they begin to release more, allowing the ground to cushion them. Some of them have to be woken – he often. I later find out that he, at nine years old, has to get himself and his sibling to school as his mother is so ill, being addicted to drugs, that he often cannot wake her up. This sweet, sleeping, gifted lad has seen more of the horrors of life than I have. Why should I wake him and remind him of reality[3]?

Looking up the definition of the word 'community' I was reminded of its root being the same as that of the words 'communication' and 'common'. This reminder made me realize that it was in this family of words that I could find a way of linking various strands of my work with my reasons for being an artist. My work in all settings is about seeking to find common ground where we can meet without the differences that divide us predetermining the relationships made. This meeting place may be between the individual participants themselves or between me (the choreographer) and them, but equally important for me as a

Figure 8.1 Rosemary Lee: PASSAGE 2000. Commissioned by The Royal Festival Hall with support from Rescen and DanceEast (*Photo © Pau Ros*)

maker is the meeting place between the work created and the individual audience member. The whole process from start to finish is about finding and making connections. Whenever I try to write about my work I find myself coming back to E. M. Forster's famous quote from *Howard's End* – 'only connect'. In all the work I make as an artist my aim is to connect with others, however subtly, and share with them something of what is precious to me, something that speaks non-verbally of our human condition. At my most idealistic I venture to say there is universality to this connection that dance alone can illuminate.

The philosopher R. G. Collingwood called dance the 'mother of language' – preverbal, and our first means of expression (Collingwood, 1938). It is through our bodies that we encounter and experience the world and through our bodies that we communicate our responses to it. Our senses connect us to each other and to the world, they guide us through our lives, discovering as we go. We empathise easily with the loss of a sense or a limb, or the struggle to breathe, perhaps more easily than we can empathise with an emotional or belief struggle. We have this in common – we all have bodies and senses, fundamentally individual and shaped by our different life paths, but also fundamentally the same. What binds us is our ability to sense, to be aware.

Further affirmation came when speaking to the late poet Michael Donaghy, who told me that in his mind, dance was the mother of the art forms and that all words could be traced back to a physical action. Hearing this validated my trust that dance was not a frivolity, not a poor relation to text-based art forms – far from it: it has an ongoing fundamental place in our history and is at the heart of language development. There are times when we need to get beneath words, beneath the labels, that can only ever be one step removed from the experience sensed, to a more profound, unspoken method of expressing ourselves and communicating.

What excites me when I watch a child scamper across a school hall, or a senior dancer stand alone, or a highly experienced professional fling herself through the air? It's simplicity, humility and a sense that you are seeing the person without other complications. Dance can be both profoundly exposing and revealing: it comes close to reflecting truly what it is to be alive and reminds the dancer and the watcher of that life force. In these moments I feel I see a transparency in a performer – it is as if you get a clear glimpse of humanity. (Sometimes I see this more easily in untrained performers who have not been masked by the fine finish or style of a technical training – though as the training is changing this is less the case.) My wish is to make their glimpsed humanity visible and palpable to the audience. In witnessing this they may discover a moment of connection, a moment of intimacy on that common ground. Perhaps we sense something within ourselves – which we cannot put into words – made manifest in a performer in front of us. Or is it a sense of seeing the performer's own uniqueness, potential and grace, or maybe that we feel more deeply alive and present together? It is probably all these things. There are times when it seems as if I am seeing their inner light, their potential perhaps, their 'themness', their spirit. However we explain it, it fills me with hope. In a world of cruelty and injustice, a world where market forces seem to have invaded every part of our lives, seeing this inner light reminds me of the things I cherish in being human, being alive.

> They are standing together side by side; the workshop audience is semi-cir-cled around them. They have their eyes closed, listening and waiting. Neither knows who will make a cupping support with their hand offering it into the charged space between them. Neither knows who will glide their head out into the space searching for the hand to rest their head in. I watch this simple task, they are exposed, revealing to us their unsighted experience of waiting and sensing. The image once found of the head cupped in the other's hand concludes this patient waiting. It is times like this when I feel sane, when I feel a different sense of being alive[4].

In a performer, whether they are highly trained or a non-dancer, old or young, I am looking for that transparency, that simplicity. When a dancer is so at one with their dancing, so unselfconscious, so engaged that the dance fills every single cell in their body, when they and the task they are engaged in become inseparable – then they become compelling and beautiful. These are the moments we aspire to, where you cannot tell the 'dancer from the dance' in Yeats' words. When I have experienced this state I sense completeness and surrender; it is simultaneously humbling and empowering. I believe that this state can promote a profound sense of healing and wellbeing, not easily found. These are transformative moments – it is actually tangible when this embodiment happens; the dancer experiences the affect of the dance and the viewer sees it. Such moments are rare, but I believe we are all capable of experiencing them.

> I am preparing children for some filming where they will be distant on a hill standing silhouetted against the sky. I want them to feel huge and powerful in order to expand their presence. I talk to them of weather gods, imagining that they can alone command the weather bringing in thunder from the north and sunshine from the south just by the vast monumental gestures they improvise with. I see one transformed from the quiet and reserved boy to a beautiful statuesque figure, dignified and powerful as he spreads his arms to the skies with utter confidence. I am stunned by his presence. Afterwards I ask him qui-etly if he felt that and he nods to me with a changed face, and in that moment he and I know and share. Nothing more needs to be said.[5]

In the early 1980s community art was, it seemed to me, constructed either as grand spectacle or speaking on a smaller scale of the stories of the participants in their particular situations. Seeing such work inspired me to make dance works that involved huge casts, but without spectacular effects; work that, despite being on an epic scale, could create subtler levels of engagement for the audience and perhaps deeper levels of communication. However, I sometimes felt fraudulent that I came with ideas and an imagined sense of the work I wanted to create, say, in response to the site in a compositional way rather than devising from scratch with a group. My task then and now is to find ways to allow the dancers to take owner-ship of their dancing within those authorial ideas and structures that I have in my head.

> I had in mind that the dancers would swirl fast, arms held to the sky and then leap high and fall onto the ground and repeat this in a frenzy of energy and abandon. I see them all with anoraks over their floor length robes, hoods up shivering and awaiting the rain as the thunderstorm approaches. I feel it is impossible to ask them to do this and guilty for having them out in this weather and to have even entertained the idea of their dancing in this way on this hard ground. They see my concern and with more gusto and enthusiasm than I can muster as their facilitator they start to swirl and leap over and over, arms up to the rain. They are powerful and filled with the energy and spirit of this idea made physical as the rain pours down on them. I am humbled and the technicians gaze with wonder as these performers of all ages defy my doubts and exceed my expectations.[6]

Governed by practicalities and funding, my earlier work was often made in a short time frame, but recently I have been fortunate enough to be able to work for longer on projects. The dance is able to grow more from the performers and my response to them.

What I try to do in all my work, whether the dancers are highly trained or not, is to find ways of enabling the dancers to inhabit the piece that I envisage without losing *their* identity and without their being disempowered in any way. I am always treading a line between responding to the participant and responding to my artistic imperatives. I find I have to be highly attentive to both concerns, as if the balance goes awry the piece will not be successful for me. I liken it to watching my long-term collaborator, designer Louise Belson, draping cloth around the body of the wearer and pinning and cutting to their body until the shape arrives. The costumes she makes have her distinctive authorial response to the work I am making, while being made for and with its individual wearer, rather than being an anonymous, finished garment to be handed to them. In my work, the dancer's movement comes from their response to images and tasks that I have given them. These are highly specific images and tasks that I judge will bring, in the dancers' responses, the very particular embodied quality or energy I envision or may have glimpsed as potential.

> I imagine a character that has tremendous inner drive and passion, a kind of heated intensity that is uncomfortable to be near. We work on embodying the very essence of each of the four fundamental elements that our bodies

Figure 8.2 Rosemary Lee: PASSAGE 2000. Commissioned by The Royal Festival Hall with support from Rescen and DanceEast (*Photo © Pau Ros*)

know deeply and instinctively, being made of all of them. We come last to fire. I trust that maybe tasting the distinctive quality of fire possessing the whole body might give a flavour of this imagined energy. One of the movements we finally use in the film comes from imagining the quality and energy of fire darting up the core of the body[7].

Imagine the steps of a wader with long jointed spindly legs and the spines of a porcupine raised on your back[8].

She is the billowed sail of a galleon; full of air pressing her forward and you are the anchor line rooting her to the spot[9].

A sculptor might say that, through being so closely attentive to the material they are working with, they are led to the sculpted shape. As a choreographer, I am trying to become intensely familiar with the dancers and their dynamic together so that the work created comes from them – is indeed theirs as well as mine. That is not to say I am only reactive to the present. It might be more accurate to say that I am reactive in order to be more successfully proactive. I liken my most recent work to portraiture; I am trying to support and thus allow the dancer to dance in a way that is most revealing of what I see as the essential quality or spirit of that individual. However, I am keenly aware that this is my personal response to them.

Lately I have been making fewer live performances, in part because I find I am better able to work with the idea of portraiture in a film medium. However, the thrill of seeing a piece find its life, shape and logic once an audience is present, the exhilaration of seeing dancers claim the work and make it their own, and the joy of feeling an audience connecting with the work cannot be equalled and I know I will return to it. But live work is not, I have realised, always the best way to give the participants an experience of growth and change or to reflect their individuality. Those exquisite transformative moments I have described happen more frequently within workshops and process-led projects than in final performances. The unforgiving environment of the stage can prove too harsh for their delicacy. In performance, other issues – nerves, memory – intervene to make the situation more about the outside rather than the inside. Therefore, in certain projects, the experience of the participant might be better served in discovery rather than in trying to hone a performance.

My most memorable and moving experiences as a viewer have been watching participants in workshops. This is why I continue to teach workshops so that I can witness those alchemic transformations taking place. It is the beauty of seeing something unfold before you, happening for the first time before your eyes, in the present moment right there, never to be repeated again. It feels a luxury and one I never tire of. Knowing the task that the dancers are engaged with alters your perception, allowing you to experience the dancers' discovery in an empathetic way that deepens your engagement and enjoyment. You discover with them at the same moment as they do.

> We are working on finding cushioned support from the air that surrounds us, coupled with a sense of length through the limbs and out into space along gossamer-thin, delicate lines. Suddenly the whole group seems to float above the floor, like gulls on thermals off a summer cliff top. The dancers surprised themselves as they hovered without a shimmer of doubt, the whole group shares the support as if uplifted by the common image. They are all on one leg, high up on tiptoe and they could stay there it seems forever, the air rising up under their ribs and arms to lift them[10].

Essentially what I am aiming for in any workshop is to bring the dancers 'home' in their bodies. I want them to feel completely at ease, centred, free of anticipation or judgment. It is then that they can then discover new qualities and feel an affirmation of their potential to go further. Everyone needs to be included, respected and treated exactly the same way, with the intention of freeing people from the comparisons or assumptions of their status that only get in the way of dancing, being irrelevant. They need to feel they belong and that they all share this common ground together. I have to find the right way to make people feel comfortable in themselves, with me, with the group, in the space and in the moment. I try to sense this very quickly and respond to my instinct of what might be the best way to achieve it. This could range from intense image-based improvisations to playful light tasks or to running riot. It depends on the group and what I sense their overall energy is, and where it needs to go to set it on its journey for the workshop.

> One of the children is blowing a bit of fluff across the floor; one of the seniors responds and on hands and knees blows it back. Pretty soon all 13 of us are down, our faces to the floor in a tight circle gently blowing the fluff from face to face giggling. This became a ritual and transformed into our nightly warm up of throwing an invisible treasure or secret to each other silently before going on stage together[11].

It's crucial for me to discover where I feel the flow of a workshop needs to go in order to release the potential of the dancers and of the event itself in the best way. It almost feels as if I am searching for the path that is already there. I do have a plan and sometimes follow it, but it's how I introduce things, what pace I go at, what I say, that are directly in response to the group in front of me. Do I need to keep going and push them to pass a threshold within a task in order for them to find the freedom I know they haven't discovered yet? Do I need to change things; do I need to encourage speed or stillness, listening or abandon? Do I need to take them unawares a little as surprise can sometimes bypass doubts and anxieties that are the enemy of finding one's own distinctive dancing voice?

> I am nervous; these are my colleagues in other art forms. I am supposed to be giving them a taste of my working practice. We end up crawling and prowling like lions, meeting each other side by side on all fours and trying with all our might to push the other over. I am surprised by this development and worry as I pursue it that I really have gone down the wrong path. But it brings us together physically without the embarrassment of tentative touching and the exposure of standing up, and it releases the powerful inner drive of each artist there within a very physical and direct non 'dancey' task. The spontaneous laughter that ensued also serves as a welcome release for all of us[12].

In order to encourage each participant to find and broaden their expressive and qualitative range, I rarely demonstrate but rely on my voice, carefully chosen words and visual images – again in response to what I observe in the group. What words and images will most effectively allow them to find the qualitative state I am after? Some words seem to give the body a clue almost before the brain gets in the way to interpret it. I want to catch the innate intelligence that is in us all, but which seems to get diverted or blocked by the more cerebral approach we have been taught to use. I am usually trying to encourage dancers to stop thought processes that might hinder the body finding its more instinctive response, taking the thought from the forehead and letting it settle further back in the skull. The quality of their engagement is as interesting to me as the resulting movements.

I am watching them but I am losing focus; I can't see; nothing seems clear. Rather it seems held and restricted, tame. I ask them to 'lift the lid off' their dancing for the last couple of minutes of their improvisation and suddenly there is clarity and energy and intention and I could watch them for hours and they could dance for hours[13].

What I am trying to do in any situation, whether it be teaching, performing, watching or creating a piece, is respond to the present, to be here and now. This is actually exactly what I want of the dancers too, so teacher, audience, maker and dancer ideally need to be in a similar state. This state of being present is one of openness and receptivity in both body and mind, open to the host of possibilities and hyper attentive and sensitive to the present. It is an acute awareness coupled with real ease that promotes a state where one can inhabit the present moment. This receptive place for me is one of infinite openness. This is easier said than done, as anticipating the future or judging the past can so easily fill the dancers' thoughts. To let go of these interferences and trust and surrender to the present gives us the possibility of having true presence and grace. It is this presence, this transformative potential that I find so continually inspiring. Watching participants in workshops when they fully inhabit the dance – or rather the dance fully inhabits them – affirms for me what it is to be alive. We return to that state of connectedness again.

As an artist one is a life-long student and observer, and I want to foster a life-long curiosity in each person I work with. I want to help them be proud of their imagination, own their dancing, broaden their horizons and thus sharpen their perception and awareness of themselves and of the world around them. If dancing helps us to find our feet on the earth then it can also help us to be more aware of the world we inhabit. Dancers who have worked with a respectful, inclusive, creative approach tend to be the most tolerant, open and non-judgemental people I know. They often question and explore givens that others take for granted; they think laterally. They know through dancing what it means to be truly cooperative and collaborative, knowing about listening, leading, following, allowing and making decisions; they know what it means to share. So if we can foster this outlook in all those we work with, couldn't we in our small, local, unspoken way change the world?

Discussion Points

- What is it about Rosemary Lee's working methods and leadership style that allows 'transformative moments' to happen?
- Compare Rosemary Lee's methods of leading dance workshops with Helen Poynor's approach (see Chapter 9).

Notes

1. This was a huge workshop for all ages in the Festival Hall ballroom, the Southbank, London. This took place before the performance of *Passage*, a work for 13 dancers of all ages (2002).
2. First workshops with two classes of 10 year olds from neighbouring schools in the heart of the East End. Part of *Apart from the Road* Whitechapel, an interactive installation built into the fabric of Whitechapel library featuring each child's dancing, poems and bookmaking (2004).
3. A workshop at a primary school in Dagenham held over the course of a year to create the original *Apart from the Road*, an interactive installation built into the fabric of Barking reference library featuring each child individually through their dances and poems (2001).
4. Rehearsal for *the suchness of Heni and Eddie*, an 'inside out' performance/lecture-demonstration that unpicked and exposed the layers of discovery within the creative process as an intimate duet simultaneously unfolded for the audience (toured 2006–07).
5. As 3 above.
6. Rehearsal for *Haughmond Dances*, a site-specific promenade performance with 237 performers of all ages at Haughmond Abbey outside Shrewsbury (1990).
7. Rehearsals for *greenman*, a film for broadcast made with Peter Anderson, featuring performer Simon Whitehead (1996).
8. Image for nine-year-old Tom Evans, who danced *boy*, a film for broadcast made with Peter Anderson (1995).
9. Image for Ricochet Dance Company when making *Treading the Night Plain* (1996).
10. Improvisation in workshop for dancers at Winterlab, Independentdance (2006).
11. Workshop/rehearsal for *Passage*. The cast of 13 dancers ranging from 8 to 70 plus years old are beginning to work together (2001).
12. Workshop for ResCen artists (2001). Centre for Research into Creation in the Performing Arts based at Middlesex University, http://www.rescen.net/.
13. Many workshops over the last few years, adults and young people.

9 Yes, But is it Dance?

The dances of daily life... non-stylised dance as a medium of expression

Helen Poynor

Helen Poynor is a movement teacher who has developed an innovative approach to non-stylised dance and site-specific performance in natural environments. Here she discusses her practice and includes a 'score' which illustrates her methods of facilitating movement. Helen also challenges the reader to think about issues such as:

- *the relationship between non-stylised dance and the aesthetics associated with 'real' dance*
- *how technical training in a particular style influences dancers throughout their careers*

The answer to the question in the chapter title depends on what dance is and on how it is perceived, understood and practised.

Does it, for example, involve pointed toes, bare feet, a lithe body, lightness and flow, a high centre of gravity, a sense of rhythm, sprung floors and mirrors?

Have you ever considered dancing in walking boots as you hang upside down between two rocks or halfway up a tree, or running along a ridge on the skyline, or with your wheelchair as your dancing partner?

I have been working with non-stylised dance for over thirty years as a performer, dance-maker, teacher and director specialising in work in the environment but also moving and creating performances in the studio. I work with adults who come from a variety of backgrounds, including trained dancers and others who have experienced 'alternative' approaches to dance or other movement/body-based disciplines, and members of the public who have little 'specialised' experience of dance and artists of all disciplines.

One of the of the biggest problems with opening up how we think about and practise dance is the baggage that we carry about what dance is. Unfortunately those of us who have trained technically in dance at some stage of our career carry more baggage than anyone else. Because we have worked hard and committed years to mastering a particular dance form or style/s we have more investment in what dance is or should be than others. Our training leaves its mark long after we have moved on to other things. It was ten years after I abandoned the ballet training of my youth that I finally kicked the habit of automatically pointing my toes when I danced. Studying a stylised form with a firmly established movement vocabulary and set of aesthetics instils a series of beliefs about what is and isn't part of the form, what is or isn't 'right' and by extension what is or isn't dance. These beliefs take root in our bodies, which are trained to manifest them, and become 'second nature'. Having invested so much of our identity, so much dedication, time and effort to become dancers, it can be very challenging to question these principles, some of which may not even be conscious.

The Myth of a 'Real' Dancer

Is there a way of being able to work more freely, more creatively, more inclusively and still benefit from the discipline, precision and sense of presence that we carry with us from our formal training? Can this serve us in our work with others in a way that does not disempower them, making them feel inadequate or confirming their suspicion that they are not a 'real' dancer?

How can the democratic approach to creativity which is at the core of community arts philosophy and practice be reconciled with the potential elitism of dance as an art form?

Whose Dance is it Anyway?

If we accept that any body is potentially a dancing body (and without this premise it is not possible to work in community dance), then we need also to accept that any movement has the potential to be a dance movement. Every body has experience of movement (although perhaps less in our sedentary society than previously) from floating in the amniotic fluid before birth, through the development stages of infancy and childhood games, to all the functional and expressive movements of daily life. By working with dancing bodies whose movement range does not comply with an accepted dance vocabulary, dance is created and expressed through an individual movement vocabulary which can be elicited and extended through skilful facilitation.

What makes a movement or series of movements dance? Is it a degree of 'extra-daily'[1] stylisation even if the style is highly personalised? Is it a quality of embodied presence in which the body is 'alive' and 'radiating', manifesting a kinaesthetic awareness of the whole body and of the body in space, opening a channel through which the self finds expression in the body? Does this expression have to be rhythmic or is it the embodiment of a heightened relationship with time as well as space?

What is Non-Stylised Dance?

How does non-stylised dance relate to stylised dance training? Is it possible to train in it? How can it be taught? What is its relationship to improvisation? To performance?

How can a trained dancer access ways of thinking about and working with dance which can break down some of the restrictive assumptions that have surrounded dance as an art form? Is it possible to discover ways of working that do not reflect the hierarchical structure of most technique classes with their formal lines and the trained body of the teacher (the 'real dancer') in front of the class as the model by which students judge themselves, a judgement which is reinforced by their critical assessment of their reflection in the mirror?

By contrast, the notion of creative dance is sometimes unfortunately associated with something worthy but undisciplined and unskilled, a form of self-expression in which 'anything goes'.

Non-stylised dance indicates dance in which the movements are not prescribed by a pre-existing technical vocabulary (even one that can be extended and developed) which has to be learnt like the rudiments of a language before one can express oneself fluently or even proficiently. It does not rely on steps that are put together in sequences in order to create dances. Nor does it entail a dance vocabulary based on an 'abstract' aesthetic like ballet or on the body type or physical abilities and preferences of the originator of the form.

The ideal in non-stylised dance is that over time each individual generates their own way (or style, if you like) of moving, which is continually evolving. As a result there is a smaller gap between the person and their movement, because it is not mediated through a pre-existing form. The link between the person moving and the movement expression is direct; their movement reveals rather than conceals who they are, making them more rather than less visible, allowing them to 'shine through'. There are memorable, radiant moments in workshops when a participant becomes fully present in their movement and they can be seen in all their individuality rather than as someone struggling with, or mastering, a particular style. Nevertheless it is also true that since a teacher of non-stylised work is working with a series of physical principles there is still a tendency for a basic style to emerge, precisely because these principles become embodied in the dancers (which is of course the intention) albeit (and this is a crucial difference) embodied in different ways. All stylised forms include a coherent system of physical and aesthetic principles, but these are generally encoded in a learned choreographic vocabulary, which is not the case in non-stylised work.

The physical principles I work with include: skeletal awareness; released joints; the integration of the upper and lower body through the spine, and the integration of the limbs and the torso (both of these support a sense of the interconnection of the whole body and the ability to allow movement to flow freely through the body); a three-dimensional awareness of the body and space; a mobile sense of grounding, a clear but permeable sense of the body's boundaries; and the ability to 'follow' a movement as it evolves and moves through space. These principles are explored through guided physical and creative tasks or scores such as moving between standing and lying, moving at different levels, and pair work including hands-on work in guiding and following. Different teachers of non-stylised practice incorporate different principles into their work. My approach has been significantly influenced by my early training with Anna Halprin at the San Francisco Dancers Workshop and with the Javanese movement artist Suprapto Suryodarmo, to both of whom I am deeply indebted.

Figure 9.1 Helen Poynor (*Annie Pfingst*)

Facilitating Non-Stylised Dance

I aim to set tasks with sufficient structure to enable participants to feel secure enough to explore in their own way without getting drawn into insidious self-criticism. Too little structure can be as anxiety-provoking as too much. I support this exploration by giving as much validation and encouragement as possible to the group and to individuals while they are moving. Feedback received while moving is more likely to be integrated kinaesthetically than feedback given later, which may be understood conceptually but less easily integrated physically. It is not appropriate to offer 'corrections' early in the process and perhaps is only ever relevant if there is information about the task or about the body which has not been fully understood.

The tasks need to be achievable, open to interpretation and easily engaged with at different levels so both more experienced members of the group and newcomers are stimulated by them. It is helpful to start from familiar movements (I often start with walking), especially if assumptions and movement habits are going to be challenged. I aim for a focussed but light, non-judgmental atmosphere where people don't need to feel they've failed if they misinterpret an instruction. A sense of humour is essential especially at your own expense – but not at that of others.

The atmosphere established in the group is crucial. I encourage participants to get to know one another's names, to work with different partners and cultivate an accepting, non-competitive attitude to one another. There is time for the dancers to share their experiences with each other or with the group. Receptive, non-judgmental listening is encouraged. I remind them how different their bodies are and emphasise that the work is about each person's individual experience rather than about looking or feeling the same. I encourage participants to avoid comparing themselves competitively or detrimentally with one another. I often start a workshop by asking each person what their hopes (or expectations) and fears are. Then at intervals, for example at the beginning of a new session or day, go round the circle and ask people to give a brief 'weather-check' on their current condition physically and if appropriate, on their feelings and state of mind. After moving I may ask people to notice any reverberations they are left with including sensations, images and feelings[2]. This can serve as a way to integrate the experience of moving and as a bridge to communicating it to others. Inviting participants to draw or write freely, directly out of their experience of moving, using shape, form, colour, language and imagery to reflect their movement without analysis or interpretation, is another way of validating their experience. It may capture a 'flavour' of the movement and provide the ground from which to be able to share it with others. I invite participants to be receptive to and non-judgmental of each other's drawing or writing without superimposing their own interpretation or experience. Oil pastels (infinitely preferable to wax crayons or felt-tips), large drawing pads or rolls of paper, and pens and paper are provided.

Dancing can be a private or a social experience. Some people like to move with their eyes closed and experience themselves moving in their own self-contained universe; for others, closing their eyes can provoke intense anxiety. Some people lose a sense of themselves and their bodies when moving in relation to another, while others find it difficult to sustain their own movement without some outside stimulus, for example a partner or music.

When running a session you need to be able to judge the mood in the room and make an appropriate decision to support it or encourage a change. For example, if at the beginning of the session people are lying quietly or stretching on the floor you may chose to start the session from there, perhaps putting on some gentle music and encouraging them to develop what they are doing into a creative exploration. On another occasion it may be appropriate to energise the group, waking them up through a structured warm-up or some lively music (the *Buena Vista Social Club* works wonders!) At times it may feel as if you are pushing against a general sense of inertia. This may mean that people are tired and it would be supportive to introduce something quiet and nurturing (perhaps some hands-on work in pairs), or it may be that there is some underlying issue in the group which needs airing through discussion. This of course requires a flexible attitude to leading. A clear plan is helpful, but you need to be able to adapt it to the circumstances. I find it is always a good idea to have a few extra ideas in reserve. If you don't have a sense of what to do next during a session, perhaps because things are going differently than expected, try not to panic and rush on regardless, but take a moment to breathe, to feel your own body and to see what comes. The moment of not knowing will rarely feel as long to the participants as it does to you! If you need longer give the group a tea-break and take ten minutes to relax or move yourself.

Your own level of self awareness will influence how you lead a group and what can take place within it. Be as honest with yourself as possible about your own responses (although clearly it is not always appropriate to acknowledge these in the group). Admitting that you are nervous may help others to admit their own nervousness and relax. Participants need to feel secure in your holding of the group, but it doesn't necessarily help them to gain self-confidence if they put you up on a pedestal as the 'expert'. (On this note: figure-hugging professional dance clothes can serve to set you apart and be intimidating for participants who may not comfortable with their body image.) It is important to be aware of your own preferences and blind spots. It is human nature that you will resonate more with some people than others. This, combined with your movement and aesthetic preferences, may mean that some participants' movement is harder for you to 'see', and therefore to appreciate and support, than that of others. Try to be open to what the participants have to teach you both about your own assumptions and about new possibilities. The image of setting out on a journey together with an attitude of interested curiosity is a healthy and creative one. It will also stand you in good stead when things don't turn out quite how you expected and it is easy to feel disappointed or critical of yourself or the group. Your function is to support something to grow, not to inhibit or control it. Like a gardener or a midwife, you need to nurture the emerging movement and creativity of the individuals and the group to facilitate their gaining confidence in themselves, allowing their physical potential and creative expression to blossom to its fullest. Who are you to say red flowers are better than multi-coloured ones?

One way of supporting participants to inhabit their bodies as fully as possible is to prepare your sessions by moving rather than sitting and thinking. The more at home you are in your body, the more it will support them to feel comfortable in theirs. Much, which may not be verbalised or even conscious, is communicated and received through our kinaesthetic sense. Especially in an environment where the body is the primary means of communication the participants, like children, will be particularly sensitised to receiving non-verbal cues. In this respect it is important that you recognise your own comfort zone. You will obviously be more at ease if you are working within it. At the same time there is much you can do to extend your comfort zone by broadening your experience. The more you experience your body in different ways, the more you expose yourself to different experiential working processes, including physical activities that are not stylised dance – for example 5 Rhythms, Halprin work, Feldenkrais, Release, Tai Chi – the richer your work will become, not only through acquiring new skills and ideas but by broadening your experiential knowledge of your body in movement.

The Body in Motion

In order to support a quality of embodiment in movement I endeavour to find ways that stimulate, or offer starting points for movement that are physical rather than conceptual. Translating ideas into movement can produce movements that are superficial or external and leave one feeling alienated rather than 'inside' the movement. One way to start is from the physical structure of the body. There are many simple ways of doing this, for example inviting people to feel their feet on the floor as they walk through space, imagining leaving a trail of footprints behind them. This is more effective in bare feet but only if people are comfortable taking their shoes off and the floor is clean, splinter-free and not too cold. Then work through the body from the feet up, gradually enlivening and releasing each area of the body as the dancers continue to travel through space, until the whole body is moving freely. A basic knowledge of anatomy is helpful, but there is no need to blind people with science. Helping people to experience the interconnections between different areas of their body through a sense of their skeleton and released joints can facilitate whole body awareness and the ability to allow movement to flow freely through the body. People often find it easier to move their arms, which are used expressively in daily life and are associated with dance, than their torso, and experience little sense of connection between the two areas. The centrality of the spine makes it the obvious starting point to increase awareness and movement in the torso. This has the added advantage that, as a result of the sedentary lives many people lead, their backs often benefit greatly from some attention. Simple exercises to release and feel the spine on the floor can be used. Extracts from Anna Halprin's (1979) *Movement Ritual* are useful but there are numerous other sources[3]. Working in pairs, supporting each other through attentive witnessing and gentle touch, enhances the experience and establishes a sense of mutual support between participants.

Working actively with the body's structure and continuing the theme of interconnection between the body parts, I encourage participants to explore the relationship between the foot, ankle, knee and hip joints as they move freely through space. (This can develop out of the simple walking described earlier.) We then focus on the interconnection between the legs and the pelvis and the relationship between the pelvis and the earth through the feet. Similarly, the relationship between the pelvis and the spine can be explored with the pelvis serving as the bridge between the upper and lower body. The experience of the spine connecting the pelvis, rib cage and head enlivens the whole torso.

The counterpart of this work with the legs is working with the upper segment of the body connecting hands, arms and shoulder girdle with the neck and head and eventually the upper back and rib cage. These explorations can be repeated many times in different ways until there is a sense of familiarity with and freedom in the whole body, and participants can feel how a movement in one part of the body subtly reverberates through the whole organism. The emphasis is on encouraging people to experience a three-dimensional sense of themselves in movement. Our visual sense (encouraged by dance studios with mirrors) tends to encourage an external, two-dimensional experience of our body. Combined with the western cultural tendency to have a relationship with the world which is primarily frontal this means that we often lose a three-dimensional sense of our body in space. One way of counteracting this is to bring awareness into the back and highlight the interconnection between the front and back of the torso, for example between the area between the shoulder blades and the chest, and between the belly and the back of the pelvis.

Non-stylised movement emphasises an experiential knowledge of the body, so it is fundamental to the practice to allow participants to have their own experience and not to be overly directive. Throughout these explorations it is important to support each person at their own level, encouraging those who are tentative and providing more of a challenge for those who are more experienced. While validating an individual's strengths they can also be invited to explore other possibilities; for example, more extroverted dancers can be encouraged to listen to their body's subtle responses and the introverted ones supported to claim more space. Validating each person's different qualities challenges any predominant assumptions in the group about the types of bodies and movements which are acceptable as dance.

Encouraging group members to work with as many different partners as possible broadens their experience as they learn from moving with people who are very different from themselves. Some bodies, for example, express yielding and flow, the qualities of water, while others have a strong sense of definition in space, the quality of rock. By witnessing one another and moving together participants can gain an appreciation of each other's qualities and begin to explore new possibilities. See the practical exploration at the end of the chapter.

Towards Performance

How is it possible to move from the process of non-stylised movement described above towards performance? Is it possible to craft a performance that does not rely on learnt sequences of steps?

The concept of 'scoring' is central to my work with performance, both working in the studio and site-specifically. The term 'score' is used by practitioners in a variety of ways, but my own approach is firmly embedded in the RSVP cycles devised by Anna Halprin and her husband Lawrence, an architect and environmental planner. The cycles were originally devised as a way of working collaboratively within the creative process which could be applied to any creative enterprise from choreography to city planning. The letters stand for Resources, Score, 'Valuaction' and Performance[4]. I use scoring as an alternative approach to choreography. There are many different ways of presenting scores: they can be understood as maps of processes, they may be visual incorporating language or they may be a set of simple instructions which are open to interpretation. The purpose of scores in this context is to communicate, to generate creativity and facilitate artistic expression rather than to control others. Scores may be closed (precise) or open, or anywhere along this continuum depending on the intention and the stage of the artistic process. The central feature of the RSVP cycles is that they facilitate a cyclical rather than a linear process. Scores can be used at every stage of the process of creating performance, from initial explorations to generate movement material and themes, to finalising the proposed shape of the performance.

It is preferable to have a significant period of time working with a group before embarking on the process of performance making. This allows time for the group to gain confidence in themselves and the trust necessary to explore new possibilities as well as refining their body awareness and movement skills. During this time resources are also generated for creating scores which could later lead to performance. These resources include movement material and themes, interactions, ideas and the strengths and weaknesses of the group and the individuals within it. One of the beauties of the RSVP cycle is that it encourages you to view potential obstacles as resources. For example, if there is a member of the group who does not fit in easily and perhaps has very different resources from the rest of the group this non-conformity can be incorporated positively into the performance score. For me the process of creating performance with a group does not start from a preconceived idea but from what I have witnessed as the group have been working together. In other words, the starting point comes from the group's responses to the initial scores that they have been given.

One of the biggest decisions that needs to be addressed is how collaboratively you want to work or how realistic it is to work in a specific situation, and what is your role as a facilitator or director. This needs to be clearly agreed with the group to avoid misunderstanding. Rather than scoring collectively I tend to feed scores back into the group that have been suggested to me by their previous work – for example images, characters or movement resources that have arisen. Participants can then recognise that the scores being offered have evolved out of their own resources, enabling them to claim a degree of ownership of the piece. The scores guide the evolution of the piece at each stage of its development. It is not a question of creating a score and then just rehearsing it (a more conventional linear process from idea to product), but of reflecting on what has been happening and building on that experience by moving on to explore new resources, create new scores or refine existing ones. Combining a positive evaluation of the process so far with action is the Valuaction phase of the RSVP cycles.

It can be both an exciting and a challenging process for a group to create a performance apparently out of thin air. Admitting that initially you do not know what the performance will be like can generate anxiety, but your confidence in the working process is all that the participants have to rely on. Tolerating the unknown is a necessary part of the creative process, one that any director/choreographer needs to be able to handle personally but also needs to be able to 'hold' their performers in, trusting that solutions will come out of the process and supporting the performers to find their own solutions.

It is possible that in the move towards performance preconceived ideas about what dance is may arise again, for you as well the group, the associated anxiety and pressure triggering a desire to return to recognisable territory. Mapping how a series of familiar scores could build towards performance is a productive way of allaying such fears, giving the group and yourself something to hold on to. These scores may indicate pathways through space, themes, movement activities and qualities, and other resources such as props or music. Different scores within the same performance may be more structured or more open to interpretation. Scores may indicate what an individual or group is doing, when and where they are doing it and the theme and intention or atmosphere of each section as well as the transitions between different phases. A roll of lining paper (cheap and available from any DIY store) and coloured felt tips can be used to map the evolving shape of a performance score. The score, which may develop through a series of variations before it is finalised, serves as a way of communicating decisions that have been made as well as highlighting aspects of the performance which need to be discussed or finalised. The challenge in the later stages is to keep the process alive rather going through endless repetitions which can become lifeless and lose all sense of embodied presence. If the physical and creative ground work has been done before embarking on the performance element of a project this will serve the group well.

Clearly the balance between structure and spontaneity in any performance score will be affected by many factors, including the group, the situation, and the intention and theme of the performance. It is worth noting that while some people are energised by the presence of an audience others may find it challenging to maintain an embodied sense of themselves when they know that they are being watched. The score is the safety net which supports the performers individually and as a group on their journey through the performance – a journey which is of course shared with their audience.

Practical Exploration

The following score is designed to help participants explore the different movement landscapes generated by the movement of various individuals.

1. Get into groups of three. Each group works in a specific area of the room. Have paper/notebooks and pens near you at the edge of the space.
2. One person from each group enters the movement space and begins to move; the intention is not to perform but to follow the movement impulses which arise, allowing them to develop.
3. The other two group members sit in a relaxed but attentive way, aware of their own bodies and breathing, and allow themselves to 'receive' kinaesthetically as well as visually the movement of 'their' mover. Try not to be distracted by the other groups.
4. When they are ready and have a feeling for the movement landscape that is emerging, one of the two witnesses enters the movement space supporting and responding to that landscape. It's not a question of imitating the movements of the first mover or of direct interaction with them but of finding a way of experiencing what it is like to move in this environment. The original mover continues to follow their movement, allowing it to develop even if this means that the movement qualities change.
5. In time the second witness enters, responding as above until the three movers from each group are moving in a shared movement environment that has been 'seeded' by the first mover.
6. When the agreed time is over (I use Tibetan chimes to indicate time) each group allows the movement to find its own completion, returning to stillness. Beware of the temptation to construct a 'tidy' ending. Remain in stillness long enough to recognise the sensations, feelings, atmosphere and images that linger.

7. Without talking take a few moments to write freely out of the experience of moving. The words do not need to be shaped in any formal way and they do not need to explain or describe the experience; allow them instead to flow directly out of it, even if they do not appear to make much sense.
8. Repeat the score (stages 2–7) twice more with a different person's movement 'seeding' the movement landscape each time.
9. When complete the small groups share what each person wrote in respond to the three different movement experiences. Go through the environments in turn, allowing the person who initiated the movement to read first. When everyone has read people may like to share their experiences more freely.

Discussion Points

■ What do you understand by the term non-stylised dance?
■ What is it that makes a series of movements dance, as opposed to just movement?
■ How can a technical training in dance impact on a performer who is practising non-stylised dance?
■ Compare Helen Poynor's method of facilitating dance with Rosemary Lee's approach (see Chapter 8).

Notes

1. This term is borrowed from the writing of theatre practitioner Eugenio Barba, for a full explanation of his ideas about 'extra-daily' technique see Barba and Savarese (1991, p. 9). Briefly, it indicates that the use of our bodies in performance is different from their use in daily life. Performers in many of the world's traditions use what Barba refers to as 'extra-daily' techniques. This would apply equally to ballet and classical Indian dance.
2. This reflects Anna Halprin's three level of awareness (Worth and Poynor, 2004, pp. 59–60). Anna Halprin is an American choreographer, dancer and teacher whose radical approach over the past 60 years has been a significant influence on dance both as a performance and a community art. I trained with her in the 1980s. She is an enduring influence on my approach; the integration of drawing and writing with movement work is one example of this.
3. Movement Ritual is a fluid sequence of floor movements encouraging flexibility in the spine and fostering in-depth kinaesthetic awareness as it works through the whole body. It can be used as a daily practice, a warm-up/work-out, a physical meditation and a springboard for movement explorations.
    Feldenkrais Awareness Through Movement Lessons® are another good source. There are many registered Feldenkrais practitioners in the UK.
4. For more detailed information on the RSVP cycles, including practical explorations, see Worth and Poynor (2005, pp. 68–74, 111–26, 175–9 and Halprin (1969).

10 Meetings with Strangers

Adam Benjamin

*Adam Benjamin is an inspiring practitioner who is probably best known for his contribu-
tion to integrated dance. As co-founder of CandoCo Dance Company he has played a
major role in changing and challenging the nature of the involvement of disabled people
in dance.*

*In this chapter he outlines his own journey as a dance artist, and explores the ten-
sions that exist between accessible practice and professional performance.*

I began writing this chapter in Cape Town during the making of *Second Time
Broken*, my second work for Remix Dance Company – South Africa's first professional integrated dance company. My previous commission for Remix had been
when they were still struggling to gain recognition. Since winning the Award for
Cultural Development in 2002, they had secured funding and made the transition
from part-time community-based company, into the professional arena. Now,
with an office, an education team, a company manager (and van!), what is it that
makes them 'professional' rather than 'community'?

They still have the same artistic director, Nicola Visser, and continue to include
disabled and non-disabled, black and white dancers. Is it simply a question of
finance that distinguishes them from what they were four years ago?

In considering this question I looked back on my own journey in dance. I was
27 when accepted to study Dance and Fine Art at what was then Middlesex Poly-
technic; a late career change made possible by the openness of the course and the
flexibility of the teaching staff. Graduating in 1990, I started work on my first
exhibition as a painter and scrambled to take on any dance work in order to buy
paint and canvas. This was how I entered community dance, saying 'Yes' to every
class I was offered, often busking my way through, learning on the hop as well as
teaching part time at a local college.

One of those community classes, co-taught with Celeste Dandeker, was to
evolve into CandoCo Dance Company[1]. Celeste had been a rising star in the

London Contemporary Dance Theatre of the 1970s until an on-stage accident and the resulting spinal injury left her using a wheelchair, and to all intents and purposes put an end to her career in dance.

By 1993 I had given up all hope of a quiet life as a visual artist to become a full-time dancer/maker/teacher/company director – straddling both community outreach and professional performance. At this time Celeste and I were already touring the UK and Ireland, and though we didn't know it, we were about to take off around the world.

Development of CandoCo

CandoCo's early years illustrate the nature of the boundary between community and professional dance, for while we started as an open-to-all, 'Everybody can dance' class, we quickly began to set ourselves performance and choreographic standards. Raising the game in this way also imposed a new kind of selectivity. Before long we had to reduce the numbers of dancers so that a smaller group could be maintained on a limited budget. As directors we made decisions in the way that any professional company must. We needed dancers who would fit into a newly defined team, which involved rehearsing, performing and delivering workshops. Touring was an integral part of our first funding agreement, so it needed to be a company small enough to move around the country. This painful process of selection was certainly one of the defining elements that distinguished the CandoCo of 1990 from that of 1993 and marked the company's journey into what is referred to as the 'dance industry' and a world of financial balance sheets and employment responsibilities.

With this shift the ethos changed from 'Everyone can dance' to 'Everyone can dance, but not necessarily with us'. Professional companies like CandoCo move away from immediate accessibility as they seek more accomplished performers and pursue higher levels of excellence, while hopefully continuing to spread ideas of participation and involvement to an ever-widening audience[2]. CandoCo developed an education program, as did Remix in South Africa, in order to sustain community links, develop audiences, satisfy funders and build training opportunities for previously excluded members of the dance community. Thus professional dance fosters community dance development, which in turn feeds the professional scene[3].

As CandoCo emerged in the mid-1990s it radically altered the way disabled people were viewed – not just in dance but on a societal level too, through exposure on stage, in film and in the written word. CandoCo's shift to professional touring meant that its education team were able to take integrated dance to communities throughout the UK. In an incredibly fertile period between 1994 and 1997 the education work helped launch (amongst others) Blue Eyed Soul, Velcro, StopGap, Independance, Tardis and HandiCapace Tanz Kompanie (Germany). It also influenced a generation of young dancers and dance students who have since made their way into significant positions around the world, amongst them Nicole Richter, who reinvigorated the artistic direction at Axis Dance Company in the USA, Katie MacCabe in Cambodia, Vicki Fox who worked in Poland, and Nicola Visser who established Remix in Cape Town.

With support from the British Council, CandoCo was able to participate in the world dance community, forging links with countries where inclusion had barely been broached, and in some, where it was not even on the agenda. Success on such a large scale, however, does not always promote creativity, and by 1996 my own journey as a choreographer with the company had faltered and I had begun to seek other settings to develop my work and restore my vision. On leaving the company in 1998 I began to create again, and found that there was an enormous demand for inclusive work worldwide.

In the years that followed I continued to develop my performance, improv and choreographic skills, collaborating and researching notably with dancers like Russell Maliphant, Kim Itoh, Jordi Cortes and Rick Nodine, and with companies like Vertigo and Scottish Dance Theatre. Throughout this time I maintained strong links with non-professional dance/dancers. Community involvement linked to professional work has been the balancing act at the centre of my practice since my first meeting with Celeste Dandeker in 1990, when the field of dance and disability was still in the process of throwing off the therapeutic and the charitable interventions of the previous decades, and had only just set about the task of defining a new aesthetic[4].

Dance by Disabled Performers – Some Issues and Debates

Aesthetics in dance are constantly being questioned, and although we have come a long way, there is much that continues to confuse. The debate is as vigorous and vital as any in the arts today. I was recently asked by a disabled performer for feedback after a show. The most interesting part of his performance for me had been some invented text which I felt would have been better used live rather than recorded. It was recorded because of his dislike of speaking on stage. My feedback was that if he wished to work professionally then he would need to broaden his range and draw on a wider range of performance skills.

If work is shown under the community banner we are not necessarily expecting highly developed skills. It is acceptable for the choreographer/director to derive material in the face of limitations and reservations and, as in this case, use recorded text rather than spoken text. The moment we enter the professional arena there is a realistic demand that performers will demonstrate exceptional skills and qualities, and (particularly in the case of disabled performers) transcend or take us beyond physical difference. This issue of performance capabilities weaves through the fabric of professional/community dance; the skilled choreographer working in the community will find ways of utilising whatever abilities the individuals on the project possess, certainly pushing and encouraging performance standards and bringing out the best in everyone, but at the same time not making unrealistic demands on individuals and not expecting high-level performance knowledge or skills where they don't exist[5]. Choreographing for community requires a particular sensibility about where people are in their lives as well as in their journey as performers. It is, as often as not, about creating the best situation in which all these different, and differently skilled, people can thrive.

Malcolm Black is a striking and skilled disabled dancer who performs in Remix's *Second Time Broken*. In the four years since we had last worked together his physical range and focus (as a result of Friedreich's Ataxia) had, despite his continuing commitment to performance and training, declined. After the first week in the studio it seemed important that we discuss whether he was still able to perform; whether he could bring sufficient resources and energy to this new production; no small topic for those who have worked together over so many years. The talk was emotional and crucial for all of us and hinged around just this issue: being able to merit one's presence on stage in a professional setting. Malcolm made it clear that he wished to continue, and with the company's full support also clearly expressed, it was then my responsibility to create a piece in which he could coexist with the other dancers on stage. By coexist I mean feel validity in his presence on stage as an artist, without excuse or apology.

Figure 10.1 Adam Benjamin: *Second Time Broken (Tania Scott)*

The answer came via an overheard conversation in a Kalk Bay café. Local artist Katherine Glenday was creating ceramic vases that could be struck, albeit carefully, to create sound. I had already decided on the title *Second Time Broken*, so this snippet of conversation immediately caught my attention. Introductions made, Katherine invited us to her studio and then loaned us her pots to experiment with, for which generosity of spirit I am eternally grateful! We immediately began (literally) to break new ground in the studio. The fragility and danger of dancing with ceramic vases added a layer of meaning that spoke to me both of Malcolm's condition but of something far greater and universal. The work now united us in a common task, a shared question about the risks we choose to take and the implications involved. In the end, Malcolm proved as robust as ever, but the issue, once addressed, led me to deeper consideration about the human condition.

The sounding of the pots held a particular resonance when struck by Andile Vellum, a deaf dancer, and different significances again when carried by Nicola Visser (who is white) and Mposteng Shuping (who is black). Katherine, whose work usually carries with it metaphors of fragility and care, was able to witness her pieces in a completely new light. 'Lurched off their pedestals', handled by dancers, on occasion thrown, dropped and toyed with. The vases also became central to the music created by Neo Muyanga, leading him into an entirely new range of percussive sound. As so often is the case in inclusive work, it is the most fragile link, the most vulnerable spot, which provides the opening to new understandings and new perceptions.

Challenges for the Choreographer

As a choreographer I need to take real note of the physicality of my dancers, to respect and learn from each in order to understand what they might offer that is unique, and that might add to our understanding of dance. The world that is spun from these distinctive qualities is what takes us, with luck, towards a new aesthetic. Simply thinking that a company is 'professional' and should therefore be able to handle technical work, is to create a potentially disabling environment – or an environment in which only physically strong and technically capable disabled dancers can thrive. Here, the more profoundly disabled dancer is once again handicapped by the physical language employed by the choreographer. This fault is most often seen in 'one-off' or first encounters between professional choreographers and inclusive companies. An experienced eye can see the rift opening between dancers with more severe impairment and his or her colleagues – this subtle unravelling of the ensemble reveals a void at the centre of the work.

If current trends are anything to go by, it seems that we want our disabled dancers fit, lean and mean, and although the sight of highly active and virtuosic disabled performers *is* thrilling and inspiring, it seems to me that we are at risk of losing sight of the essentially poetic principles at the heart of the work; the question of how different things – really different things – connect. Beauty is an elusive bird and if disabled dancers are only employed because of their athleticism or their passing proximity to the classical dancer's body, we may yet have to return to community dance, where the net is cast wider in order to see how the challenge of difference is really met,. If there is one undeniable challenge in the world today, it is to understand what different cultures and people have to offer each other, and dance remains one of the most exciting and immediate mediums through which this can be demonstrated. Over recent years community dance has been considered a less elevated and less sophisticated branch of the art form, but perhaps that should now be questioned. The challenges to our understanding of aesthetics is, if anything, greater in community dance than it is elsewhere and it is without doubt there, away from the glare of the spotlight, that real creativity and innovation can take its first uncertain steps, throwing up new possibilities that may shape the dances of the future.

The pivotal figure in this complex picture is the choreographer/director. This is the person who invites and inspires disparate individuals into a unified and unifying whole, into people proud of their achievements and confident of their capabilities. Increasingly this is a professionally trained dancer/teacher, for their skills must be multiple, they must be dancers first and foremost, but then also educators, communicators, negotiators. They must bring with them the experiences of a life lived, not theorised. They must be 'hands on' and detached at the same time; they need to understand people and the arts, for their interventions are not simply with the academically gifted or the dance trained but with people of all abilities and backgrounds.

Community Dance/Professional Dance – is There a Difference?

Reflecting on 20 years of continued involvement in dance, and watching the ebb and flow of companies and dance organizations, I am more than ever convinced that the real difference between community and professional dance is not one of aesthetics. I have seen work by professional companies which for me satisfies few aesthetic criteria, and I have seen work by non-professional groups which has held me spellbound. Nor is the difference any longer solely about body type, for there are now ample professional companies and choreographers whose work has included widely different bodies, notably DV8, Alain Platel and Michael Clark, and while it is true that companies like StopGap, Remix, Axis and CandoCo maintain a far greater commitment to inclusivity, the balletic mould has most definitely been broken. Disabled people are embedded within the UK dance scene in a way unimaginable in the 1970s. Perhaps this is one of the most remarkable cultural shifts that has taken place in recent years and one that has begun to have repercussions throughout dance education and training as disabled people, now visible, exercise their rights and educational institutions scramble to make sense of the new order.

Defining Features of Community Dance

So how can we define community dance – if no longer through body type, age or the presence of a wheelchair user? It may have been a long and very winding road to reach such an obvious conclusion, but it seems that the defining element of community dance is its relevance to local people, to the people who live next door to you – perhaps at this moment unknown. Community dance is made in a neighbourhood and performed by neighbours (some of whom may even be professional dancers). It might be seen in one or two venues around that neighbourhood or borough, and even make the odd excursion further afield, but it rarely tours and does not often place itself on the market shelf (even though it might dream of being there).

I am more than ever attracted to this defining feature of community dance; dance that is conscious of its role in nurturing creativity and contributing to the cultural life of its locale, aware of its potential for educating and enlivening the imagination, perhaps most importantly, of opening channels of communication between strangers. Community dance in many ways is dance that knows its place[6]. I never once imagined when I trained as a dancer that I would spend so much of my life overseas, nor that I would have the privilege to work in South Africa – a country which, under apartheid, exemplified all that community dance opposes. Strange that a principle, so much to do with 'neighbourhood', should have taken me so far from my own backyard!

Today's community dances in all their astonishing profusion are melded from the lives and multicultural experiences of neighbours *and* strangers, linking people who may hold little in common, either with each other or with the place in which they find themselves living. In an age of mobile populations, refugees and shifting demographics, dance has the capacity in the right hands to connect people in the most immediate and compelling of ways and to forge links across cultural and political boundaries. It is worth remembering that even 20 years ago there were two no more diverse populations than those of disabled people and professional dancers, poles apart, suspicious and mistrustful of each other's worlds. Now there are disabled people who *are* professional dancers. Once the door has been opened, how far we travel and what connections we make are restricted only by our imagination; when a mind is attuned and informed as to the possibilities that the world holds, the choices and possible journeys are endless.

Discussion Points

- All the chapters in this section include some reference to community dance and professional dance. Do you think it is helpful to see them as different aspects of the dance world?
- What does Adam Benjamin say characterises professional performance?
- Compare Adam's defining features of community dance with the definitions in Chapters 1 and 2.

Notes

1. CandoCo was the first professional company for disabled and non-disabled dancers
2. It was just this facet of CandoCo's approach that caused many dance institutions to reconsider their attitudes to integrated work. See 'The problem with steps', *Animated* magazine, Autumn 1999.
3. CandoCo began its Foundation Course for disabled dancers in 2005.
4. See In Search of Integrity. *Dance Theatre Journal*, **10**(4), Autumn 1993.
5. See http://www.adambenjamin.co.uk/directory.html.
6. For discussion of the relationship of choreography to place see Benjamin (2002, p. 36).

Part 4
Community Dance Practitioners

Introduction

Part 4 focuses on community dance artists:

- what they actually do
- how they acquire their skills
- routes into the profession and possible career options
- the other people and agencies that they work with

If you have recently become involved in participatory dance work or are considering a career as a community dance artist the following chapters will give you an insight into what these people actually do. You will realise, as you read through this section, that it isn't like other professions which have a clear route from universally recognised initial qualification through to well-defined roles and progression opportunities. There *are* qualifications and there are various career options once you get started, but people rarely follow the same pathways. This is what excites me about belonging to this world. I enjoy the flexible, unpredictable, open-ended nature of the work. My ongoing contact with community groups nourishes me and helps me refine my skills.

I also have a real sense that I can shape my career as an artist. I can choose which work to accept and I can create opportunities to work with individuals and communities where I think I can make a positive contribution. Yes – I imagine emerging practitioners thinking 'It's all right for people like Diane – they've been around for ages so it's going to be easier for them to find work'. This may be so, but my approach now is the same as it has always been: I have an idea for a project and I explore funding opportunities, find participants and create partnerships with people who are interested in working with me. If there is something that inspires and challenges you as an artist, you will find a way of making it happen. As community dance continues to develop into an established profession I believe there will always be opportunities for practitioners to be proactive in engaging others in the art of dance.

There are specific skills and knowledge which help with this process and these are discussed in Chapter 11 together with leadership behaviour which supports person-centred practice. In the following chapter Sue Akroyd sets out ways that dance artists can acquire these skills and engage in continuing professional development. Keyna Paul's chapter will give you an insight into what employers are looking for, and in Chapter 14 I look at the artist's role in building effective relationships with the various people involved.

When you take account of the needs of the different stakeholders it is not surprising that community dance practitioners often act as intermediaries: they are artists, but, as they have connections with a number of different 'worlds', they need mediation skills to help members of these different worlds meet and understand each other. They can be the 'glue' that binds together diverse elements of the same community. Sometimes dance artists on participatory projects help groups by creating links between 'officialdom' and local community issues and aspirations. They can use their knowledge of the health service/arts council/voluntary sector/local authorities/education/criminal justice system to demystify bureaucracy, translate jargon into everyday language and help communities identify possible sources of funding.

As you read through these chapters think about your own skills and the kind of work you would like to be involved in. Make notes of areas which interest you and find out about opportunities for gaining more experience. You don't have to wait for a formal course of training – perhaps, for example, you can find an opportunity to shadow an experienced artist who is working in a context which interests you.

Further Reading

Adams, P. (1998) *Gesundheit.* Healing Arts Press, Rochester.
Cameron, J. (1994) *The Artist's Way: A Course in Discovering and Recovering Your Creative Self.* Pan Macmillan, London.
Thompson, N. (2002) *People Skills.* Palgrave Macmillan, Basingstoke.

11 The Dynamic Role of the Community Dance Practitioner

Diane Amans

This chapter explores what it means to be a community dance worker. It includes:

- *Case studies showing how different dance artists have become involved in community dance*
- *Skills needed to lead participatory dance workshops*
- *Leadership behaviour and the way this connects with person-centred practice*
- *Personal Effectiveness – and making time to 'nourish your artist'*
- *Some thoughts on the needs and agendas of the various people and organisations associated with a community dance project*

The accompanying exercise will help you audit your own strengths and identify areas for development. You can follow these up in Chapter 12 where Sue Akroyd outlines a flexible approach to continuing professional development opportunities for community dance practitioners.

WANTED – an enthusiastic, imaginative, well-organised dance artist with exceptional people skills, boundless energy and the ability to cope under pressure. (Must be flexible and able to work unsocial hours.)

The job vacancies advertised in dance journals and associated web sites continually reflect the great variety of work that is being delivered by dance practitioners in community contexts. Community dance practitioners are engaged in a range of different activities: they teach classes, create dance pieces, organise showcase events, liaise with partner organisations, write reports, produce dance resource materials, manage budgets, deliver training, carry out administration tasks and develop new audiences.

Some practitioners are employed full-time by a dance agency: others work in community dance on a part-time or freelance basis. Freelance dance artists may spend some of their time in community work and the rest of their time in other aspects of dance work – for example choreographing and performing with a dance company. The following case studies illustrate the working lives of four very different community dance practitioners.

Emma

Emma has been working for two years as a community dance artist. After graduating with a degree in Dance Studies, she took up an apprenticeship with a dance company and now has a full-time permanent post with them.

Emma currently runs 14 sessions a week in a variety of community and education settings. These include youth dance groups, after school dance clubs, over 50s group, classes in a primary school and early years family sessions. The company employs one other community dance artist (part time three days a week) and five freelance dance artists who deliver a variety of community classes.

When she is not leading classes Emma's time is spent doing administrative tasks, attending meetings, planning and coordinating her portfolio of work and preparing for the community dance showcase. She has fortnightly mentoring sessions with the artistic director of the dance company. She is surprised how much of her time is spent on administrative tasks and meetings. She has just been asked to hand her youth dance groups over to freelancers as the company want her to spend time developing projects with the local health and social care team.

Emma's role is defined for her by the dance company she works for. She was recruited to carry out specific duties outlined in a clear job description, although she is encouraged to contribute ideas for new projects. Any changes or developments are discussed at team meetings.

Ashley

Ashley has a portfolio of freelance dance work. He developed his passion for dance after being involved in a youth dance project when he was 15. The touring company which led the project inspired Ashley to train in dance at a professional level and he is now keen to provide positive dance experiences for young people. He is concerned about the rather pot luck nature of dance education in schools, which varies considerably according to the skills and interests of the teachers at any given time.

Ashley combines regular weekly sessions in schools, colleges and day centres with choreographing and performing dance pieces with a dance company he founded with two other dancers. Most of his community dance work is passed on to him by the local authority dance development officer, who keeps a register of freelance artists.

Ashley has considerable autonomy in deciding how he spends his time. He usually finds that there is no shortage of freelance work although sometimes, for example in school holidays, he has several weeks where he has less work (and consequently less income) than he would like.

Lynne

Lynne initially trained as a secondary school modern languages teacher and became involved in community dance after she attended classes in belly dancing. She enjoyed it so much she enrolled on a part-time training course for teaching dance and now runs her own classes.

Three years ago she began with one class in her local community centre and now runs weekly classes in three different venues over a fairly large rural area. She has just been awarded a local authority voluntary arts grant to develop a performance piece for the local community dance showcase event. She has invited a guest choreographer to lead the project and hopes to involve participants from all three groups.

She meets up with other dancers at Forum meetings organised by her local dance agency. She enjoys being part of the performing arts world but is rather self-conscious about the fact that most of the other dancers are much younger and many have dance degrees. Her local dance agency supports her with mentoring sessions and she regularly attends class.

Jerome

Jerome is a choreographer and artistic director of a dance company. In addition to making work and touring with his own company he choreographs work for other companies in the UK and Europe. Four years ago he was commissioned to create a dance piece for a community dance festival. The dance involved participants from different community groups and included dancers of all ages. Since then Jerome has been involved in other community projects and works on these alongside his own company's work.

He enjoys using his skills as a choreographer in new and different contexts and finds that what he has learned from making dance with community groups is nourishing him as an artist.

These pen pictures illustrate the very different journeys which lead to working in community dance. Lynne had done very little dance until she was in her early forties, whilst Ashley has danced every day since he was a teenager. Many dance artists, like Emma, choose to work in community contexts from the outset. Others, such as Jerome, take on community work to supplement their 'main passion' – as a performer or choreographer. Most community dance artists find that the experience of working on participatory projects offers unexpected rewards, including the opportunity to develop new skills.

What Skills Does a Community Dance Artist Need?

The 'wanted' advert at the beginning of this chapter is a lighthearted summary of actual comments made by directors of dance agencies (Amans, 2006). Recent interviews with these directors and other managers who commission work from community dance artists revealed that the following are particularly valued:

- Organisation skills
- People skills
- Knowledge of contexts
- Respect for and sensitivity to the contexts in which they work
- Putting participants at the centre of their practice
- Demonstration of good practice in teaching
- Skills as a dancer and choreographer
- An inclusive approach
- Awareness of diversity issues
- Able to manage and balance individual and group needs
- Ability to evaluate
- Creativity
- Enthusiasm
- Professionalism

The extent to which the above skills and knowledge are considered to be essential will differ according to the priorities of the organisation employing the artist. The job description in the box on the next two pages was for a post with Green Candle Dance Company in Autumn 2005.

This job description is clearly aimed at recruiting a dance graduate with an extensive range of community experience. It is important to Green Candle that their community practitioner is an *artist* with additional skills. Green Candle has a commitment to 'working in a way which is inclusive and creative' and, like many dance companies involved in community dance work, they have a commitment to work in a person-centred way.

Person-Centred Practice

The term 'person-centred' is used in a Rogerian sense to emphasise the value of the individual and to promote the development of the individual within the group[1].

Community Dance Artist Job Description

This new post will be largely practical, involving teaching, facilitating and choreographing dance with children and adults within a broad range of education and community settings.

The Community Dance Artist will be part of a small team working to the Associate Director.

She or he will:

- teach dance sessions, both solo and with other artists employed by the company, including the creation of choreography
- assist the Associate Director in planning, administering and evaluating education projects
- produce written project outlines and session plans
- write documentary and evaluation reports on educational and community work (for partner organisations, funding bodies and the Green Candle Board of Directors etc.)
- create dance resource materials for INSET sessions and teachers' packs etc.
- assist with supervising student and work placements
- attend regular meetings with company members and Board meetings as required
- possibly assist in the devising and performing of small-scale performance for particular contexts
- fulfil any other reasonable task in the furtherance of Green Candle's work

Person Specification

The Community Dance Artist will:

- have completed professional training in contemporary dance (to degree-level or equivalent)
- have professional experience as a dance artist
- have additional skills in popular or non-western dance forms
- have at least three years regular teaching experience in schools and community settings
- have excellent teaching ability with children, young people and adults of diverse ages, abilities and backgrounds
- be able and willing to teach older people (60+), children and adults with learning disabilities, deaf young people, people with

> physical disabilities (some training will be provided if needed in
> particular areas
> - have experience and skills in devising/choreographing work for
>   educational and community contexts
> - a strong commitment to community dance practice and the com-
>   pany's values and ethos
> - be committed to working in a way that is inclusive and creative
> - have strong project leadership skills
> - have sound and up-to-date awareness of child protection, equal
>   opportunities, health and safety and safe dance practice
> - have good awareness of educational issues in schools including
>   knowledge of the National Curriculum at all key stages
> - have basic office and IT skills (word processing, filing etc.)
> - have a good standard of literacy including the ability to write
>   reports
> - be a good communicator and advocate for the work
> - have good skills in working as part of a team
> - cope well with change and challenge
> - be of cheerful disposition
> - be willing and able to travel occasionally

These extracts from the Foundation for Community Dance booklet *Dancing Nation*, highlight the impact on the participants of working with a leader who establishes a collaborative relationship with the dancers in the group (FCD, 2001):

Shaun and Roy work in a special way because they don't teach you as a group but as an individual, they let you do your own style – and they suit your abilities to the moves – instead of teaching one move to all the group

It's not just a teacher–pupil relationship. You go to school and there are teachers who teach you, but Gail and Ian are different, that's why our work is so effective because the atmosphere we work in is so great

In creating a dance, Wolfgang allows us to express ideas through a piece of music, or through words and improvisation and uses them to contribute to a production. So a production doesn't come solely from him, it comes in many ways from us

Rosemary Lee, in the introduction to *Dancing Nation*, says of the leaders:

Their belief that participants can dance, are worth listening to and their respect for their students and the art form itself unquestionably have a profound effect on their group. It is what makes an inspiring teacher – some-one who believes in you utterly and your potential as a creative individual (*ibid*)

Leadership

The leadership behaviour of the artist delivering the session determines whether or not the experience of the participants reflects the core values of community dance (see Chapter 1). Ideally the leader will have knowledge and understanding of group dynamics and excellent people skills. John Adair, whose action-centred leadership theories are often used in team development training, stressed the importance of leadership which supports the needs of the task, the group and the individuals in the group. He distinguished between task-oriented and mainte-nance-oriented leadership actions (Adair, 1998).

Task-oriented functions are concerned with the achievement of goals, seeking and giving information, and successfully completing activities. Maintenance-ori-ented actions focus on the emotional life of the group, offering support and encouragement and promoting effective relationships. Although members of the group may contribute to task and maintenance functions it is the leader's responsi-bility to ensure that both sets of actions are carried out and the right balance is achieved between them.

Table 11.1 shows some aspects of community dance artist behaviours which illustrate the different leadership actions:

Another way of looking at leadership behaviour is to consider leader interven-tion and participant autonomy as a continuum. In a group which is very 'leader-centred' the dance practitioner makes the decisions and implements them with little or no opportunity for participants to make choices. At the other end of the spectrum the group has total freedom to control all aspects of the session. This is

Table 11.1 Leadership actions.

Task-oriented leadership actions	Maintenance-oriented leadership actions
Lead warm up activities	Help participants communicate ideas
Teach movement phrases	Encourage participation
Teach steps and set routines	Offer support and/or praise
Suggest starting points for choreography	Motivate and inspire
Give feedback after improvisations and sug-gest additional/alternative movements	Facilitate interaction between group members
Suggest solutions to choreographic problems	Use humour to relieve tension
	Spend time on relationship building activities
	Allocate time for break/refreshments
	Provide refreshments
	Containment/'holding' a group safely

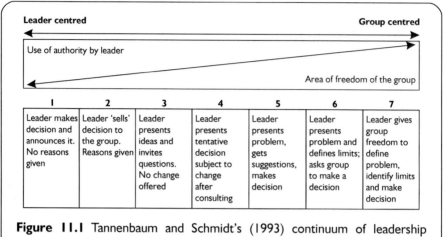

Figure 11.1 Tannenbaum and Schmidt's (1993) continuum of leadership behaviour.

illustrated by Tannenbaum and Schmidt's continuum of leadership behaviour (Figure 11.1).

Although many participants in dance projects appreciate some freedom of choice, most want clear leadership and a definite structure to the sessions. In a mixed ability community dance group it takes ingenuity and flexibility on the part of the practitioner to manage sessions which stimulate and challenge the more confident group members whilst ensuring that those members who prefer to 'play safe' and be told what to do are encouraged to take risks.

Artists working on performance projects acknowledge that their leadership style changes according to the context in which they were working. For example, in the sessions leading up to a performance the area of freedom of the group is reduced as the leadership style becomes more task-oriented. This leadership behaviour corresponds, unsurprisingly, with situational and contingency theories of leadership (Johnson and Johnson, 1991) (different situations require different leadership styles). The existence of an 'end product' inevitably means that the leader has to take control and ensure that the group is ready to perform. For a short period the task is all-important and may take more of the leader's time and energy than attending to individual and group needs.

Community Dance – Whose Needs is it Meeting?

This is a fundamental issue to be considered in any discussion about the role of a community dance practitioner. In person-centred community dance practice it is important to ensure that the needs of the participants are met, but there are other people and agendas involved. Consider the needs of the following:

- the organisation commissioning the work
- the funding body
- host organisation staff such as teachers/support workers
- family members of the participants
- dance artist leading the project

Members of each of the above groups have their own needs and priorities, some of which are listed in Table 11.2, together with participants' needs.

These needs are not necessarily incompatible, but occasions will arise where there is conflict. For example, the commissioning organisation may want an 'end product' in the form of a performance, whereas the participants want to enjoy exploring creative ideas and making art without the pressure of a performance. Who decides which needs have priority?

Another example of conflicting needs is where an artist wishes to teach a dance style with carefully choreographed routines and is working with participants who attend the class mainly for social and recreational reasons. They just want to enjoy moving and are not interested in 'getting it right'. How far is it the responsibility of the dance practitioner to promote skills development in order that people are better able to engage with the art form?

In his critique of cultural imperialism in community arts practice Owen Kelly asserts that 'directive professionals' are fulfilling 'their own professional needs' rather than those of the community (Kelly, 1984). Is this true of community dance professionals? To what extent are dance artists *aware* of their needs and the way these are influencing their practice? Sometimes dance practitioners have not

Table 11.2 Needs and priorities.

Needs of participants	Needs of funding body	Needs of commissioning organisation
Access to dance activities	Policy implementation (e.g.	Meet targets
Skills development	social inclusion)	Provide access to dance
Social activity	To be seen to support 'wor-	Introduce new activities
Making art/being artists	thy causes'	To be seen to introduce new
Exercise	To monitor how money is	activities
Sense of achievement	spent	Fulfil requirements of the
New challenges		national curriculum

Needs of dance artist	Needs of staff in host organisation	Needs of family members
Paid work/job security	A break from usual routine	To know participant is happy
Job satisfaction	To see participants enjoying	and safe
To create work/choreograph	themselves	To have regular respite from
To perform	Professional development	caring
New challenges		To find enjoyable leisure
To help others/feel useful		activity for participant
Sense of achievement		

considered their own needs and lack the awareness to realise that they may be allowing those needs to influence their practice. What is important is that all needs are taken into account in the planning and implementation of projects and that dance practitioners have the necessary skills and awareness to work in a collaborative way. They also need skills in assessment, observation and evaluation so that they can be sure the dance sessions are meeting the agreed needs of participants and other appropriate stakeholders.

Personal Effectiveness – and Making Time to 'Nourish Your Artist'

The challenges presented by community dance require artists to have both skills and stamina. It can be exhausting work which needs to be managed efficiently if the dance practitioners are to avoid burnout and retain their enthusiasm for the work. There are some basic skills in organisation and self-management which are essential for both freelance dance practitioners and those who are employed by a dance agency or other community organisation (see Resources section for tips on making the best use of your time).

Effective time management and skills in prioritising tasks will mean that dancers are able to fit in time for *themselves* – for reflection, reading, going to see performances, attending class and continuing professional development. Dancers who do not make time to nourish themselves as artists are likely to lose motivation and may

Figure 11.2 Freedom in Dance Salford Elders Project *(Matthew Priestley)*

experience stress-related illness. Dance agencies have a duty of care to the dance art-ists they employ. A number of organisations help practitioners manage their time and set up opportunities for them to discuss their practice. This may be in individ-ual mentoring sessions or in group forum events which focus on sharing good prac-tice and discussing areas which are problematic. These opportunities for developing reflective practice are an important investment in the professionals who deliver community dance.

Many freelance dance artists, such as Ashley in the case study above, find it dif-ficult to prioritise time for reflection and attending networking events, as they see this as time which does not generate income. Others, like Jerome, have success-fully applied for a grant to fund their own CPD activities. Jerome has identified an experienced practitioner whom he pays for mentoring sessions. He also costs in development time for each project that he undertakes. This means that he is paid for the time spent in planning and evaluation and Jerome sees this as an essential part of his practice.

Conclusion

The role of the community dance practitioner is dynamic and wide-ranging; it can vary considerably according to the context of the work and the needs of the stake-holders. Some dance artists have full-time posts with clearly defined roles set out in a detailed job description. They may work for a community dance agency or other organisation which takes responsibility for monitoring their practice. Other dance artists have a portfolio of freelance work which includes participatory com-munity projects. Whilst they are accountable to the various organisations which contract them, they have more freedom to define their own roles. This autonomy for practitioners and the rich diversity of practice is part of the attraction of working in community dance.

Does it matter that the roles of different practitioners vary considerably from one organisation to another? There are certainly some significant differences in relation to expectations and conditions of service, but perhaps the differences are not impor-tant as long as community dance work is underpinned by the same core values.

Discussion Points

- Do Emma, Ashley, Lynne and Jerome share the same core values? What information do you need in order to answer this question?
- Consider the needs model in Table 11.2: what is the dance artist's role in managing the needs and priorities of these different groups?

Exercise

Complete the self evaluation audit on p. 142 and list your strengths as a community dance artist. Make a note of your continuing professional development priorities.

Notes

1. See Kirschenbaum and Henderson (1990) for a discussion of person-centred practice.
2. See Resources section for time management techniques and tools.

12 Getting to Where You Want to Be

Sue Akroyd

Sue Akroyd is Head of Professional Development at the Foundation for Community Dance. She has worked as a community dance artist and as a dance lecturer at Liverpool John Moores University. In this chapter Sue focuses on the knowledge and skills that dance practitioners need to work in community settings and the way in which these can be acquired and developed. She gives an overview of the various training courses and opportunities available to emerging and established community dance practitioners and outlines key principles and features of continuing professional development for community dance artists.

The idea of 'becoming' a professional community dance artist is a curious thing.

There's nothing to tell you when you've made it – no finishing line, no certificate on the wall, no letters after your name, no professional licence. So how do you – and others – know when you *are* one? In the simplest terms, it's when you begin to earn a living working in dance in community settings. But beyond that, what makes you a professional community dance artist? How do you know when you are ready to do the job? If you want to be one, how do you go about it?

The answers to these questions are not straightforward.

In community dance, there are no formal or universally agreed criteria that determine an individual's 'readiness' to practise as a professional. Expectations around standards, competence and 'professionalism' have evolved organically, over time and in tandem with the nature and demands of the work, so there is no prescribed route into the profession and few 'must haves' or 'must dos' on the way to becoming a professional practitioner.

In fact, a key characteristic of the community dance profession is the variety of routes people take into it, and the range of people who do it. Individuals come from diverse backgrounds, training and experience, and practise different styles and forms of dance. This is one of its strengths: different people bring different things to the work, which enables the profession as a whole to engage with a wide range of individuals and communities, each with different needs, interests and ambitions. Community dance is an inclusive profession: it values difference and individuality and supports many interpretations of what it is to be a dance artist.

So Can Anyone Be a Professional Community Dance Artist?

Yes and no. Yes, in that you don't have to be any particular age, gender, race, size, shape and so on. Nor do you have to work in a particular dance style or have had a specific type of training. But there are fundamental values and principles that underpin community dance practice and define the community dance artist, regardless of background, training or experience. Community dance artists:

- share a belief that dance can make a unique and positive contribution to the artistic, creative, educational, social and physical wellbeing and development of individuals and communities
- are committed to enabling access to, and participation in, dance for people of all ages, abilities and backgrounds
- possess specialised skills, knowledge and attitudes/qualities (competencies) that make it possible to deliver high quality, safe, enjoyable dance experiences that meet the creative, learning, physical and social needs and ambitions of a wide range of participants, in a wide range of settings and contexts.

To be a community dance artist is to hold particular beliefs about the relationship between dance, people, and people dancing, and to possess the skills, knowledge, commitment and motivation to put these beliefs into practice.

And How Does this Come About?

Values can be imparted and nurtured and individual beliefs and attitudes are shaped by an awareness and openness to experiences and environment. But essentially you are either driven by certain beliefs, and committed to pursuing them through your choices and actions, or not. So in some ways, community dance can be seen as a 'calling' or a way of working that 'clicks' with certain people. However, that is not all there is to it – passion and commitment are not enough. Skills and knowledge, the ability to put ideas into practice, to know what to do, when to do it, and to be able to do it effectively – these are crucial aspects of being a professional, and the good news is that these things can be learned, nurtured and developed.

So Where Do I Begin?

Most people's first exposure to dance will be through watching or participating – at school, as a hobby or socially. Your early dance experiences are the beginning of your learning: watching dance gives you a sense of the form and can expose you to different dance styles, techniques and aesthetics. Participating in dance gives you a crucial understanding of what it feels like to dance, how your own body works, learning about making dances, as well as the beginnings of transferable skills such as communication, cooperation, listening, observation and problem-solving.

Your experiences as a participant and a watcher may continue and develop through your personal and professional life, but if your professional goal is to work in community dance, you will need to expand your dance experiences to include some more focussed learning. This could take place in several ways, ranging from formal, mainstream training and education, to self-directed, experiential learning.

1 Mainstream Education (School, College and University)

Many artists currently working in community dance have not had access to the study of community dance as part of their initial education – for many mature or long-standing practitioners it did not exist as an option. These days, it is possible to pursue dance qualifications from secondary school right through to doctorate level. The study of community dance within mainstream education only really becomes an option post-16, on courses offered at colleges of further education or universities.

Further Education Courses and Qualifications

There are several colleges of further education in the UK that offer a Higher National Diploma in community dance – a two-year course that is roughly equivalent to the first year of study on a university degree.

> To find research courses in UK colleges and universities, visit the web site of the University Central Admissions Service (UCAS) at http://www.ucas.ac.uk/ and do a course search.

University Courses and Qualifications

Most university dance courses involve the study of community dance in some form or another, and many include independent or negotiated study units that can be tailored to individual interests, such as community dance.

A degree course that has a focus on community dance is likely to place emphasis on those areas of study connected to dance teaching, working with different groups of people, project planning, dance management, work-based learning and historical and contextual studies relating to community dance that is its purpose, place and identity.

If you are interested in studying community dance within a broader context of community arts, arts management, physical activity etc. then you may wish to search for Joint Honours degree courses which offer the opportunity to study dance in combination with another subject.

 The Foundation for Community Dance has produced an Information Sheet entitled 'Community Dance in Higher Education' that provides background information and contacts for university courses that feature community dance in their curriculum. Downloadable from the Foundation's web site: http://www.communitydance.org.uk/.

Postgraduate Qualifications

If you already have a first degree, or its equivalent, you could stay in higher education and continue your study through one of the following options:

- a higher (Masters) degree: at the time of writing there are no courses in existence that focus purely on community dance, but it may be that you are able to pursue community dance as a specialism within a negotiated Masters programme.
- a postgraduate degree: you can study for a Post Graduate Certificate of Education (PGCE), which qualifies you to teach in schools. There are dance specialist PGCEs, and whilst this is training you specifically to work in schools, much of the knowledge gained is transferable to community settings.

 To find research masters and other postgraduate courses in UK universities, visit the Prospect graduate careers web site (http://www.prospects.ac.uk/) and do a course search.

- the Post Graduate Certificate: Dance in Community, at Laban Centre London. This is currently the only full-time, accredited vocational course specialising in community dance at this level. It is a well-established course, offering an intensive programme focussing on building essential skills and knowledge for community dance practice. You don't necessarily need to have completed a dance degree to be accepted onto the course, but need to demonstrate relevant prior learning or experience.

 To find out more about the PGC:DC visit Laban's website: http://www.laban.org/.

What Will I Gain from Studying Dance at University?

A great deal of what you study on a dance degree – particularly art-form skills, knowledge and appreciation – will provide a useful foundation for working in community dance. On those courses that offer specialised study of community dance, you will have the benefit of exploring how to apply your art-form skills in the area in which your career goals lie. In addition, you are part of an education framework that enables you to achieve a nationally recognised qualification. Many, if not most, employers in the dance sector (and most certainly in other non-arts sectors) will recognise – or be reassured by – attainment of a first degree.

2 Vocational Dance Training

As well as mainstream colleges and universities there are specialist or 'vocational' dance training schools across the UK that offer a range of qualifications at Further and Higher level. The vocational schools provide a general training in dance with accreditation in the form of Diplomas or Certificates of Higher Education.

Traditionally, they offer a progression route for young people who have studied dance at a local dancing school – working to a syllabus and taking graded examinations – or those whose initial dance studies may have taken place at school, in a youth dance company or at a local dance, and want to pursue a career as a performer, choreographer or dance teacher in the professional performance, commercial and private sectors.

While it is not the most direct route into community dance, more of the vocational schools are beginning to broaden their curriculum and recognise community and participatory dance as a potential career route for which students need to be prepared. It might be your choice to do your initial training in dance in this setting, and focus on the development of specialised skills for community dance at a later stage.

For information on vocational dance training, visit the web site of the Council for Dance Education and Training: http://www.cdet.org.uk/.

3 Other Ways in

A college, university or dance training school might not be right for you. It may not offer you the kind of learning experience you want or need, or it may not be an option for other reasons.

Outside of mainstream education or vocational training settings, various dance agencies and organisations within the professional sector offer foundation courses, apprenticeships and other types of training course, some of which are accredited. Some courses are offered at age 16 and upwards as vocationally based training, that is an addition, an alternative, or an access route to further and higher education. Other courses might be part-time, occasional or 'one-offs' allowing you to build an individual, flexible programme of training and study according to your needs and circumstances.

This is a slightly more complicated route to take, as it means organising your own learning programme and piecing together your training – rather like a jigsaw – to ensure that you are getting what you need to progress towards your career and learning goals. This can be daunting, especially if you are in the early stages of your 'education'. Finding out what opportunities exist, where, and what they will offer you, can be confusing. But there is help at hand:

- The Foundation for Community Dance offers information and advice about professional development and training opportunities in community dance. It can also signpost you to other organisations for information about training opportunities in community dance.

 Visit the Foundation for Community Dance web site at http://www.communitydance.org.uk/.

- It is always a good idea to familiarise yourself with your local and regional dance organisations: get onto their mailing lists, visit their web sites, drop them an email and stay informed about opportunities in your area.

Even if you are just starting out in your training and education, it is really valuable to 'get networked' early on. Make the most of organisations that are there to help you – they will be a valuable support through your career, so why not make friends with them right from the start!

So Which Is the *Best* Route Into Community Dance?

No one route is 'best' and in reality, most community dance artists have gone through a combination of education, formal training, experiential learning and personal and professional experience – and not necessarily in that order. A survey of the profession, undertaken by the Foundation for Community Dance in 2007*, asked practising community dance artists about their training, entry routes and career progression. The responses revealed that, whilst there is no 'standard' route into community dance as a profession, there were some commonalities:

- The majority have a 'grounding' in dance (through practical experience, formal training, or academic study, or a combination of all three).
- Many, but not all, have got a qualification in dance (and some have a qualification specifically in community dance).
- Most have done some form of additional learning beyond their initial education or training – either formally, through professional courses and the like, or informally by such means as observing, assisting, or volunteering with more experienced professionals

From this we discover that no single learning experience – or type of learning experience – is necessarily sufficient to teach you everything you need to know. The learning required for a career in community dance doesn't happen up front, all in one go. Just as eating one bowl of cereal at 8.00 a.m. won't give you all the energy and nourishment you need to get through a whole day, three years' dance training – however thorough – will not sustain you through your whole career.

Your initial training may make you competent to begin practising professionally as a community dance artist, and qualifications may help open the doors to employment, but it is your ongoing learning as a professional, working person that enables you to fulfil your potential, sustain a career and continue to gain satisfaction from your work.

Ongoing professional learning is commonly referred to as Continuing Professional Development, or CPD for short. Its benefits – not just to the individual, but also to employers, the practice and the profession as a whole – have seen CPD increasingly recognised as playing a central role in professional practice, not just in community dance, but across all professions.

As a professional community dance artist, if you are committed to doing the best that you can do, and being the best you can be, then CPD will have a central role to play in your professional life.

About CPD

All our personal and professional experiences offer us the opportunity for learning, but CPD is a conscious and systematic approach to maintaining and extending one's professional skills, knowledge and expertise. It means that our learning is planned, rather than *ad hoc* or incidental.

What defines an activity as CPD is that it is done in order to reach a particular personal or professional goal. We work towards achieving a specific personal or professional outcome, or enhancing an aspect of professional practice.

CPD and You

As a practising professional, you have a responsibility – to yourself and others – to invest in your own learning and actively engage with your own professional development in order to:

- maintain a baseline level of competence in your professional role
- ensure that your knowledge and skills are relevant and up to date
- enable your own progression and future employability

It is important to acknowledge that no one can do everything, or is equally good at all the things they do, and that we all have different strengths and weaknesses. But there is always room for improvement, and as a professional practitioner you should be committed to getting better at what you do. This is where CPD comes in.

CPD is the vehicle that enables you to:
- focus on your existing competence in your professional role
- identify the development you need to improve your performance
- reflect on your learning and progression
- work towards achieving your future professional ambitions

The whole process centres on you. It demands self-awareness, rigour, and a considered and developmental approach to learning. It means getting to know yourself personally and professionally, making informed choices about how, when and where your learning takes place, making time for learning, and reflecting regularly on the outcomes of your learning.

Without your investment and engagement, CPD becomes a superficial exercise; *with* your investment and engagement, CPD enables you to take control of your own learning and professional choices.

By putting CPD at the heart of your professional practice, you value and demonstrate a commitment to both your own professional progression and to meeting others' expectations of you as a responsible, capable and committed practitioner.

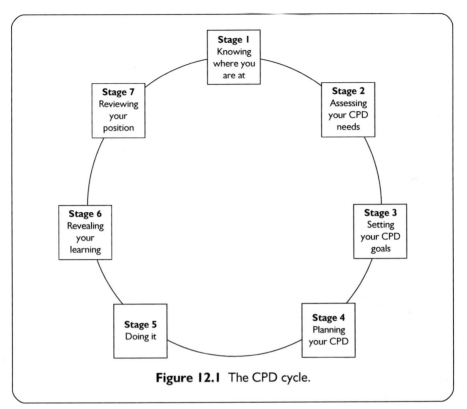

Figure 12.1 The CPD cycle.

So How Does CPD Work?

Regardless of what stage you have reached in your career, the cycle of CPD is the same (Figure 12.1).

Stage 1: Knowing Where You Are At

Before you start planning your CPD, you need to have a clear sense of where you are at now. Getting to know yourself in a professional context is crucial to making informed decisions about how to proceed with your CPD: the more information you have about yourself and your needs, the clearer you will be about what to do next.

Ask yourself:

- What skills do I have?
- What is the current breadth and depth of my knowledge and understanding?
- What am I able to do?

Your answers to these questions start to reveal your professional competencies.

Now ask yourself:

- How do I like to learn?
- When do I learn best?
- How do I learn best?

Your answers to these questions start to reveal your preferred learning style.

Reflecting on what you can do now, how well you can do it, and understanding how you learn best, is the starting point for making the right choices about how to proceed with your CPD.

SUGGESTION: If you find it difficult to answer these questions, or you don't feel fully confident in your responses, this in itself will tell you something about where you are at. Self-reflection is a skill (and gets better and easier with practice), but initially you may benefit from some help. Make use of other people around you who know you – a teacher or tutor, your peers or work colleagues. In addition, there are a multitude of self-assessment tools and learning styles questionnaires available on the Internet that will take you through the process step by step.

Stage 2: Assessing Your Professional Development Needs

Your professional development needs are particular to you, and will change over time as you develop, deepen and extend your professional competencies. You need different knowledge, skills and abilities at different times and for different purposes, but broadly speaking your professional development needs will be determined by two key factors:

- the demands of your current professional role
- where you want to be and what you want to do in the future

The Demands of Your Current Professional Role

Sometimes, your professional development needs can be obvious. Starting a new job, or being offered work in an area of practice that is new to you, can reveal obvious gaps in skills and knowledge that need to be addressed.

- It may be a condition of employment that you are able to evidence competence in a specific area of practice (which may or not be dance-related), or in working with a particular group.
- Some work might require you to undertake particular training, or to be tested, or to have evidence of your competence in order to fulfil a legal requirement of employment.
- Some qualifications – first aid for example – need to be updated regularly. Employers in some contexts are increasingly bound by sector policies that demand that practitioners be suitably developed to a prescribed level. These

include the criminal justice sector, health and social care, and any other context where practitioners are working with children, young persons or vulnerable adults.

Throughout your career, the demands of your employment or your employer will continue to guide or even dictate a certain proportion of your CPD needs.

Beyond this, your awareness of what it takes to be an effective practitioner in any given context can be heightened and informed by taking care to keep yourself updated about current trends in what is considered best practice. Learning from experienced practitioners, witnessing their practice, and reading about their work in industry journals, can all be useful ways of revealing your own learning needs.

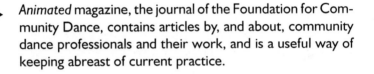

Animated magazine, the journal of the Foundation for Community Dance, contains articles by, and about, community dance professionals and their work, and is a useful way of keeping abreast of current practice.

Where You Want to Be and What You Want to Do in the Future

Having a clear sense of what you want to do in the future will help you to decide what you need to do now.

It may be that you have a detailed and ambitious career plan mapped out ahead of you, or you may just have an idea that you would like to work in a certain way or explore a new area of practice. Either way, it is likely that to achieve this goal will require some additional learning on your part. Taking time to research the demands, expectations or requirements of your future professional role/s and mapping those against your current knowledge, skills and understanding will reveal the competency gap and consequently the learning needs.

Stage 3: Setting Your CPD Goals

This stage is about making an explicit commitment to your learning. Remember that CPD is a systematic and planned approach to learning, so you need to know what you are aiming for and when you have achieved it. A popular mechanism for articulating goals (or objectives) is the acronym SMART, which stands for:

- Specific
- Measurable
- Agreed
- Realistic
- Timed or time-specific

If we apply this to setting your learning goals, it works as follows:

- Specific – being clear and definite about what you will achieve:
  'I will be able to do a risk assessment for my parents and toddlers group that meets the requirements of the playgroup leader' rather than 'I will be better at risk assessment.'
- Measurable – being able to tell when you have achieved the goal:
  'I will know that I can do a group-appropriate risk assessment because the playgroup leader will accept my risk assessment as satisfactory.'
- Agreed – shared with/agreed by appropriate others:
  'I have the support and agreement of my employer and the playgroup leader in working towards this learning goal to meet the requirements of my professional role.'
- Realistic – achievable given your current position, the learning required and the resources available:
  'I have the capacity to learn how to do risk assessment and there are resources available to enable me to achieve this learning whilst fulfilling my other professional responsibilities.'
- Timed – setting a deadline by which the learning goal will be achieved:
  'I will be able to independently undertake a risk assessment on the parent and toddler group by the time the new term begins.'

Stage 4: Planning Your CPD

In many ways this is the simplest stage of CPD, but it can also be the most time-consuming and most difficult to manage. This is because it may depend on other people and the availability and cost of appropriate activities.

The main thing to remember is that your choice of CPD activity should be based first and foremost on what you need or want to learn and how you learn best:

1. What you want to or need to achieve/learn
2. Your learning style
3. Resources (time, money, transport, energy)
4. What's available

In other words, work from the inside outwards: what is the point of all that self-reflection and goal setting if you then resort to jumping randomly from one training course to another – just because they happen to be there? This is not only inefficient (and potentially costly), it is also ineffective. In the long term it will not satisfy your needs and won't necessarily move you forward – or at least not in the direction you had hoped!

Of course, you shouldn't deprive yourself of a great opportunity just because it doesn't fit into your learning plan. Generally speaking, you should first decide what you need, and then go out and look for it or make it happen, rather than the reverse.

So What Kind of Things Could I Do?

CPD is often mistakenly presumed to be restricted to formal off-the-job training courses, seminars or workshops. On the contrary, CPD can take many forms and can involve a wide range of activities and processes, depending on your personal and professional needs, your preferred learning style and the particular demands of your employment or working life. So whilst nothing *automatically* counts as CPD, almost anything *could*, and there is a huge range of possibilities, including:

- Learning from experience:
  - Keeping a reflective journal
  - Self-evaluation
  - Observing others
- Independent learning:
  - Research
  - Reading
  - Using learning/CPD tools: paper-based, online, audio/video/multimedia
  - Writing for a professional journal
  - Attending events, conferences, performances
- One-to-one learning:
  - Peer appraisal
  - Mentoring
  - Co-mentoring/buddying
  - Counselling, life-coaching, development needs analysis, career advice
- Peer or group learning:
  - Peer group/action learning sets
  - Artists forums/practitioner support groups
  - Networking events
  - Working with a new partner in your team
- Work-based learning:
  - Apprenticeships, work placements, shadowing, job swaps
  - Sabbaticals and secondments
  - Experimenting with a new activity, approach or system in your work
  - Learning through being taught
  - Professional or academic courses leading to qualifications/accreditation
  - Professional-level classes, workshops and courses
  - Lecture-demonstrations and seminars

Figure 12.2 Ruth Spencer CPD Day (*Brian Slater*)

Your capacity to reap the benefits of any given CPD activity is dependent on making informed choices: whilst your *learning needs* will dictate the *subject content* of your CPD activity, the *type* of activity you choose should be informed by your preferred *learning style*. There's no point doing a theoretical course by distance learning if you are an experiential learner. Equally, if you find it frustrating to sit and listen to other people speak for long periods of time without making a contribution yourself, you may choose small discussion groups and seminars over a formal conference.

Once I Know What I Want, Where Do I Get it and How Do I Fund it?

Finding the right CPD doesn't automatically mean giving up huge chunks of your time, spending loads of money and travelling half way across the country.

Organising your own learning opportunities from what is already in place and available around you is a real option – and an attractive one if cash and time are in short supply. Opportunities for CPD can be found in the workplace, amongst your peers or colleagues, by reading a book for an afternoon, or by finding one day a month to be in the studio. But you should not settle for something that is irrelevant, inadequate or of insufficient quality to satisfy your learning needs just because it is cheap and available.

Sometimes it will be necessary or desirable for you to seek CPD opportunities further afield. There are numerous individuals, companies and organisations that provide CPD opportunities for professional dance artists. Again, these are not necessarily costly training courses or time-consuming commitments. The CPD provision on offer can be anything from mentoring schemes, and opportunities for volunteering, to toolkits, resources and advice surgeries.

Some organisations specialise in offering CPD activities that are specifically targeted at dance artists working in community settings. Courses, resources, information, advice and guidance are increasingly being developed to support particular specialised areas of practice or to ensure that community dance artists are able to fulfil the legal requirements of employment in specialised contexts.

When looking for CPD opportunities, don't limit your research to the dance sector – a great deal of relevant, useful and high-quality CPD is offered through other types of organisation. There are training organisations and CPD providers in other art forms, for example visual arts, writing, theatre and music. Organisations representing and supporting specific sectors – young people, health, sport and so on – may also offer training and CPD that is transferable to the context of your professional practice.

There are also voluntary sector training organisations that offer courses geared to the specific needs of the arts and voluntary sectors. Again, this training is not dance specific, but offers CPD in aspects of professional activity that are common to most, if not all sectors: everything from time management and communication skills to project management, ICT, finance and fundraising.

Financing Your CPD

Finding the cash to pay for your CPD can be difficult, and for many professional dance artists, being able to invest financially in their professional development requires an ongoing and delicate balancing act between income and expenditure.

But there are sources of additional help, and here are some of the possibilities:

- If you work for an organisation, you may have access to a staff development or training budget that may meet your CPD costs without needing to raise additional funds.
- Some dance (and non-dance) organisations occasionally offer bursaries or training funds designed to support artists who work in a particular genre or context or who are at a particular stage in their career.
- Individuals can apply to the UK Arts Councils (England, Scotland, Wales and Northern Ireland) for funding to support their professional development and training.

To find out more about funding available through the UK Arts Councils, visit their web site: http://www.artscouncil. org.uk/.

- There are some Trusts and Foundations and other grant-giving organisations that provide grants to support individuals to undertake professional level training.

 To search for UK trusts and foundations, visit the web site of the Association of Charitable Foundations: http://www. acf.org.uk/.

- Career Development Loans (CDLs) are available through an arrangement between the Learning and Skills Council (LSC) and three high street banks. You can use a CDL to fund a variety of vocational (work-related) courses with a wide range of organisations.

 To find out more about Career Development Loans visit http://www.direct.gov.uk/ and follow the link to the Education and Learning page.

Part of the balancing act between earning and learning is being creative in your approach to how you fund your CPD. Prioritise your CPD needs and identify the best and most cost-effective solutions for them. Consider different ways to harness the 'investment' of others – can you offer something in return for their time or expertise? Can you share the cost of some training by inviting other practitioners to participate?

Not all your CPD will have a direct cash cost, but do be aware of hidden or indirect costs. For example, work-based learning or attending peer-learning groups might not have a fee attached to them, but giving your time does have financial implications: when you are training, you are not earning. This is an important consideration, particularly if you are an independent, freelance, or self-employed artist. In the overall planning of your CPD you need to balance out the demands on your time made by CPD against the need to earn a living.

CPD always uses some resources, be they time, money, energy or headspace. What is important is that you use your available resources appropriately and wisely. It is easy, given the pressures of work and the need to earn a living, to neglect CPD. But its importance to your current work and to your overall career development is considerable. In the longer term, CPD will increase your earning potential, so you should see it as an investment rather than a drain on your resources.

Stage 5: Doing Your CPD
Enjoy!

Stage 6: Revealing Your Learning
One of the most difficult things about CPD is identifying, articulating and evidencing the outcomes. The impact of your CPD will not always be immediate, or obvious. At a gathering of members of the Foundation for Community Dance in 2005[1], experienced practitioners identified the gradual 'emergence' of the impacts of CPD within their practice and their overall confidence and growth on a holistic and long-term basis.

But remember the M for Measurable from your SMART learning goals. It is important for your own sense of progression – and also to others who have a vested interest in your CPD (especially if they have funded it) – to be aware of the learning that has occurred and how it has, or will, impact on your work.

It can be hard when you return to your day-to-day working life to find space and time to think about how to process the things that you have learned. But there are a number of things you can do to clarify and share your learning and integrate it into your work:

- Keep a CPD journal or log book to record what you have done and your thoughts and experiences whilst you are doing the activity.
- Make an action list, noting interesting or useful ideas, and how you might begin to put them into practice.
- Set aside time after the activity (or at regular times during the course of your CPD) to go through your notes and summarise the main points (this could turn into a CPD report later if this is beneficial or required).
- Set aside time to share your experiences (or knowledge and skills) with others in your organisation or peer group.

Work hard to articulate your learning. It is important to place value on what your CPD has given you and to be able to articulate the value to others. In an unregulated profession where training, qualifications and experience are not standardised, being able to be clear about what *you* know, have learned, and can do, is even more important.

Ask yourself direct questions, such as:

- What do I know now that I did not know before?
- What can I do now that I could not do before?
- What do I understand more fully?
- What new things can I bring to my practice as a result of this CPD?

More importantly – *answer them*! And not just in your head – write them down, speak them, share them:

- Write them in your CPD journal
- Share them with a colleague
- Build them into your curriculum vitae and job applications
- Find a way to articulate them in your marketing materials, funding applications and project proposals
- Practise how you will say them to others when discussing your work, seeking employment or in formal appraisals

Stage 7: Review Your Position – Knowing Where You Are At

This brings us neatly back to Stage 1 in the CPD cycle – knowing where you are at. Engaging in CPD will – or should – move you forward in terms of your skills, knowledge, abilities and understanding. Your learning changes you and puts you in a new place, so it is important, before you start on your next phase of CPD, to review where you are starting from. Preferred learning styles can also change over time, so it is always important to revisit the self-reflection phase before you embark on a new phase of learning.

Even if you are not planning any CPD, it is never a waste of your time to revisit the key questions as a means of noting and affirming, for yourself and others, where you are at, at any given point in your professional life.

CPD in the Bigger Picture

This chapter makes the case for the value of Continuing Professional Development in terms of your own practise and progression as an existing, or aspiring, professional community dance artist. But the impacts of your engagement in CPD will be felt much more widely – take a look at the list below.

Who Benefits From Your CPD?

- You
  Continuing Professional Development:
  – Promotes confidence in your work

- Maintains or increases your level of competence
- Develops new areas of expertise
- Enables you to make links with fellow professionals
- Increases your employability and career options
- The Public (Your Participants)
  Your engagement in CPD will enable them to benefit from:
  - Working with a skilled, confident, dance artist
  - Up-to-date ideas and practices
- Employers
  Your engagement in CPD will enable them to:
  - Trust in you as a responsible and engaged professional
  - Have confidence in your technical competence and professionalism
- The Profession
  As you develop your knowledge and skills, you help to:
  - Increase the shared body of knowledge and expertise
  - Raise professional standards
  - Ensure that the profession remains dynamic
  - Enhance their profession's public image

Taking a Firmer Stance

The working environment is constantly changing as cultural, educational, legal, social, political, commercial and environmental policies and practices develop. The demands made on professionals and organisations develop equally quickly. Since these changes are inevitable, so is the need for continuing learning and development.

Professionalism relies increasingly on an ability to respond quickly to changing conditions and we are all being encouraged to embrace change and foster innovation. No longer can keeping up to date be optional; it is increasingly central to professional and organisational success. The response of many professions to this challenge has been to embrace CPD. Community dance is no exception.

With the growth of community dance, the increasing diversity of settings in which dance artists are working and employers' expectations around quality assurance and legal compliance, it has become increasingly important for individual community dance artists to be able to communicate and evidence their professional credentials, and for the profession as a whole to achieve recognition on a par with that of other professions.

That means taking a firmer stance around standards, competence, and professionalism; quality assurance and accountability; and training and professional development.

Leading the way is the industry's membership organisation and development agency – The Foundation for Community Dance. Since its inception in 1986, the

Foundation has represented community dance professionals and their practice, lobbying for greater recognition of community dance and providing support that enables practitioners, their employers and organisations at local, regional and national level to undertake their work better, with greater satisfaction and with greater benefit to the communities they work for and with.

Making a Move

In 2005, the Foundation began an initiative called Making a Move, with the aim of developing a UK-wide professional framework for community dance: a comprehensive and integrated model of support for the community dance profession, consisting of people, organisations, networks, systems, resources and information.

The idea behind the framework is to address the professional needs of people and organisations working in, or with, or in support of community dance, enabling the profession as a whole to move towards a more confident and resilient future by:

- achieving professional recognition for community dance artists and their practice
- helping to ensure that community dance artists are equipped to deliver high-quality, safe, enjoyable dance experiences for participants
- assuring employers of an individual's ability to deliver safely, legally and effectively against their agendas, be they health, learning, social or artistic
- providing clearer guidance for those entering the profession and better signposts for progression
- supporting provision of, access to, and engagement with opportunities for ongoing professional development

In order to achieve this ambition, the proposal is to build a framework that consists of two main strands of support: professional standards and professional support.

Professional Standards

The framework will provide benchmarks for community dance practice: agreed standards for those choosing to work in the profession, a code of professional conduct, guidelines on competency requirements for community dance practice, research and debate around professional standards in community dance and guidelines for employers and providers that help them in the recruitment and support of community dance artists.

Professional Development

The framework will set in place practical measures to enable professionals to progress their practice through engagement in CPD: information about CPD opportunities in community dance, 'How to?' guides, resources and toolkits to support professional development and progression.

It will offer a matrix of different elements that will create a flexible, yet rigorous framework of support, allowing people to engage with it according to their individual professional needs and pathways. Rather like a climbing frame, the framework is robust and sturdy but open, with many possible points of contact and routes through – supporting people to get from one place to another: from where they are to where they want to be.

At the time of writing, the professional framework for community dance is in development. By the time you read this book it may well be in place, but in one very positive sense it will never be 'complete'. The framework will respond to the changing demands of the world of work and to the ambitions of community dance artists themselves. As the profession and the practice develops, so will the framework.

The Making a Move initiative represents a significant shift for the community dance profession – and looks towards a future where the answers to the questions posed at the start of this chapter:

- What makes you a professional community dance artist?
- How do you know when you are ready to do the job?
- If you want to be one, how do you go about it?

will be more straightforward.

To discover the answers will be an exciting and important journey – and one in which the community dance artists of the present and future will play a key part.

Exercise
- If you have not already done so, complete the self-evaluation audit on p. 142 and make a note of your continuing professional development priorities.
- Reflect on your preferred learning style by talking it through with someone who knows you or by completing a learning styles questionnaire[2].
- Start to keep a CPD journal in which you log your activities and note any action points.

Notes
1. This contribution was made during a discussion about CPD in 2005 at a consultation meeting for the Foundation's Making a Move initiative.
2. Learning Styles questionnaires help you understand about your preferences when it comes to learning new things. You can find out more from the Campaign for Learning: http://www.campaign-for-learning.org.uk/.

Community Dance Artist: a Self Evaluation Audit

Use this audit tool as a focus for considering your strengths and any areas you may need to develop. If possible discuss it with a colleague (you could use it as a focus for peer appraisal). Do you think all the items are relevant and important? Is there anything missing?

Rate yourself on the skills, knowledge and experience listed below

0 = non existent/don't know   1 = hardly any   2 = insufficient   3 = adequate
4= above average   5 = excellent

	Score	Notes/Action points
Dance skills		
Technical skills as a dancer		
Skills in devising/choreographing work		
Dance appreciation		
Teaching skills		
Skills in planning and evaluation		
Range of methods to engage participants in dance		
Leadership/Group management skills – including balancing individual and group needs		
Ability to teach different ages and abilities		
Extent to which practice reflects core values of CD		
Communication skills		
Verbal communication (one to one/teaching groups)		
Verbal communication (presentations/meetings)		
Telephone skills		
Initiating contact with new people		
Assertive communication skills		
Active listening skills		
Ability to read non verbal communication		
Literacy skills e.g. ability to write reports		
Knowledge		
Knowledge – community dance contexts		
Knowledge of wider dance world		
Up to date knowledge about safeguarding and duty of care issues		
Awareness and understanding of equality and diversity issues and legislation		
Personal effectiveness		
Time management		
Ability to prioritise tasks		
Keep records up to date		
Manage own business affairs (marketing, invoices, dealing with correspondence)		
Information retrieval systems		
IT and office skills		
Nourishing your artist – How often do you:		
– attend dance performances?		
– make 'playtime' for yourself?		
– find time to be creative?		
– engage with other art forms?		
– go to exhibitions?		
– daydream?		
Continuing Professional Development		
Do you engage in regular CPD activities? (reading, going on courses, mentoring, peer observation, attending networking events) Which are most enjoyable? What do you get out of them?		

In which sections did you get 4s/5s? Where were your 1s and 2s? Did you score 0 for anything?
Did you make any action points? Make a diary note to revisit these action points in 6 months' time.

13 Career Pathways and Employers' Perspectives

Keyna Paul

*Keyna Paul is director of **lincolnshire dance** and was project manager for the initial Dance Links programme as part of the PESSCL (PE, School Sport Club Links) strategy. She has had a key role in supporting both emerging and established dance artists and is particularly interested in continuing professional development. In this chapter Keyna discusses dance artists from an employer's point of view and includes case studies from arts, health and sports sectors. These comparative studies highlight the skills, knowledge and attributes that employers are looking for in community dance practitioners.*

The community dance profession has developed rapidly from the first animateur posts in the late 1970s to a group of professionals connected by a set of values and supported by an umbrella body, The Foundation for Community Dance. However, there is little comprehensive research into the relationship between how dancers are trained and the skills demanded by employers. This gap has been addressed with a key piece of research 'Mapping Dance' which was funded by National Council for Graduate Entrepreneurship (NCGE) The key purpose of the research was to 'assess the scale of dance provision in the higher education sector with reference to how this provision developed employability and entrepreneurial skills in the student dancer' (Burns, 2007, p. 3).

This work is significant because it offers comprehensive data (Table 13.1) about how individuals involved with dance earn a living. The data is extrapolated from several sources and includes some estimation, but provide interesting information for those who work in dance and their employers.

The research also looks at a range of degree courses and compares the relative time allocated to different aspects of dance. The results show that by far the greatest proportion of time is spent on choreography/composition, theoretical skills, dance techniques and improvisation. Interestingly, from the employers'

Table 13.1 People earning a living from dance (Burns, 2007, p. 12).

		Source
Total employed in dance sector	30,000	Dance UK
Total performers	2,500	Equity Members' Survey
Total teachers	22,500	75% of total: of which FCD estimate 4,500 are engaged in community dance
Total 'supporting' dance – management, choreology, notation, therapy, history/archive etc.	5,000	Assume that remainder are engaged in this sector

perspective, teaching/workshops skills receive less time – even though 75% of dancers find these skills essential in their employment.

This research provided evidence for why I, like many other directors of regional dance agencies, have contributed to the development of many continuing professional development opportunities for dancers working, or wishing to work, in different community settings. These opportunities have included curated commissions, chorelabs, performance opportunities, shadowing and mentoring relationships, as well as one-day or short training courses developing teaching, health and safety and communication skills for working with different community sectors. Many of these programmes have been devised to give dancers the skills needed to address the particular needs of local communities or to deliver the aims of regional dance agencies. Local initiatives such as these contributed to a patchwork of training opportunities across the country – with much duplication but little standardisation.

Some agencies have further developed their courses into more comprehensive programmes or certificated courses and have achieved accredited status with a number of awarding bodies. Many of these accredited programmes are recognised to be of high quality. However, the growth in employment areas beyond the immediate arts and art education fields has led to increased demand, resulting in employers calling for standardisation and clarity within dance qualifications and for dancers to operate within a professional code of practice. The precise nature of this is a source of debate, and the Foundation for Community Dance is developing a framework for professional practice which will provide some professional standards and clarity about what constitutes 'high-quality' dance experiences in community dance.

Many employers have become interested in working with dance artists because of government initiatives and policies, particularly around creativity and healthy lifestyles. These include:

- a focus on creativity as an essential characteristic for future employees in the 21st century
- concern with increasing the level of physical activity undertaken by individuals
- a shift in the health sector from a focus on ill health to an emphasis on promoting wellbeing
- acknowledgement that we in the UK are faced with an ageing population.

Four very significant initiatives are:

- Every Child Matters: Change for Children
- Creative Partnerships
- PESSCL – Dance Links
- Choosing Health

Every Child Matters

The Children Act (2004) provides the legislative framework for the government Green Paper 'Every Child Matters: Change for Children'. This wide-ranging paper provides a comprehensive focus on many different aspects of a more cohesive approach to supporting the development of children from birth to 19 years of age.

Central to the legislation is the requirement that organisations which provide services for children and young people have to find new ways of sharing information and working together. In addition, children and young people must be given far more say about issues that affect them both as individuals and collectively. This means organisations supporting the development of self-advocacy and recognising the need for quality assurance systems.

All aspects of Every Child Matters are linked to five separate but interrelated outcomes that the government believes are most important for children and young people to thrive:

- be healthy
- stay safe
- enjoy and achieve
- make a positive contribution
- achieve economic wellbeing

The impact of this legislation has been far reaching for everyone who works with children or with local authorities. A key impact for community dance artists is that they must have enhanced clearance with the Criminal Records Bureau (CRB) and their own public liability insurance. They also need to be familiar with the particular health and safety procedures of different employers. All the strategies and initiatives which follow relate directly back to Every Child Matters.

Creative Partnerships

Creative Partnerships was established in 2002. It is managed by Arts Council England and funded by the DfES and DCMS. Over one thousand schools are involved with the initiative, which aims to develop:

- the creativity of young people, raising their aspirations and achievements
- the skills of teachers and their ability to work with creative practitioners
- schools' approaches to culture, creativity and partnership working
- the skills, capacity and sustainability of the creative industries

This programme has shifted the focus for artists who work in schools: instead of merely sharing their own art form skills they are now required to find ways of using these skills to nurture the creativity of pupils and teachers, developing creative approaches to teaching and learning in all aspects of the curriculum.

Creative Partnerships has enabled dance artists to develop long-term sustained relationships with schools, rather than the more traditional short-term 'quick fix' approach of one-off or short-term experiences. The Ofsted inspection in 2006 identified that Creative Partnerships programmes were contributing to all five of the Every Child Matters outcomes:

> Convincing evidence was provided in all Creative Partnerships areas about the contribution of the programmes to Every Child Matters outcomes. The vast majority of pupils directly involved enjoyed their education in and through Creative Partnerships; good behaviour, cooperation, enthusiasm and pride were common outcomes. Skills that were consistently improved – literacy, numeracy, ICT, self-confidence, team working, and an ability to show enterprise and handle change – are likely to contribute to pupils' future economic well-being. The nature of particular initiatives enabled some pupils to develop good regard for the safety and well-being of others; they showed high levels of responsibility in potentially high-risk situations such as handling different materials. In a smaller proportion of projects pupils showed that they could manage personal stress, contributing to a healthy lifestyle. Opportunities for pupils to make a positive contribution to the community through Creative Partnerships programmes were valued by pupils; in community-based projects, pupils displayed high levels of social responsibility. (Creative Partnerships web site)

The Creative Partnerships web site is at http://www.creative-partnerships.com/aboutcp/.

PE School Sport Club Links (PESSCL)

In 2002 the government launched the PE School Sport Club Links (PESSCL) strategy. In Learning through PE and sport, a guide to the Physical Education,

School Sport and Club Link Strategy it stated the overall objective to enhance (DfES, 2002, p. 4):

> the percentage of 5–16 year olds in England who spend a minimum of two hours each week on high quality PE and school sport within and beyond the curriculum from to 75% by 2006 and to 85% by 2008

The strategy has eight interlinked work strands:

- Specialist Sports Colleges
- School Sport Partnerships
- Club Links
- Gifted and Talented
- Professional Development
- QCA PE and School sport Investigation
- Step into Sport
- Swimming

The first two – Specialist Sports Colleges and School Sport Partnerships – are central to developing the concept of building a national infrastructure for school sport. The remaining six provide the tools that schools can use to help pupils achieve at least two hours a week of high-quality PE and school sport.

In 2004, in recognition of its unique position straddling both the arts and sports, dance was identified as a separate initiative within the Club Links section of the strategy.

Central to Dance Links was the need to establish a shared language between professionals working in schools (particularly Specialist Sports Colleges) and out-of-school dance providers developing and delivering activities in those schools.

The resulting document *Dance Links – A Guide to Delivering High Quality Dance for Children and Young People* was published in November 2005. This document provides clear guidance for schools, helping them to identify high-quality dance provision and supporting effective access to such provision for children and young people within and beyond the school curriculum. It provides dancers with specific language and criteria with which to approach schools for employment.

Choosing Health: Making Healthier Choices Easier

The focus of this 2004 white paper is to provide support structures which encourage individuals to make healthy choices about how they live their lives. It details six priorities for action:

- reduce numbers of smokers
- reduce obesity
- increase exercise

- support sensible drinking
- improve sexual health
- improve mental health and well-being

In August 2006 ACE, in partnership with Department of Health and DCMS published the 'Dance and Health' folder. The pack contains brief case studies which exemplify how dance can be used as an activity within the range of healthy and active lifestyle options available to people. It suggests ways that potential employers can find dancers and how dancers could identify potential employers through contact information about key providers.

As employers seek ways of delivering government agendas, community dance practitioners are finding new markets for their work. There is a growing awareness of the skills, knowledge and attributes possessed by these artists and the following section illustrates how these meet the needs of employers.

Meeting the Needs of Employers

In these four case studies employers from the arts, health and sports sectors were asked to provide an outline of a successful project under the following headings:

- Purpose of the project
- Structure
- Outcomes

To enable some comparison the skills, knowledge and personality traits of the dancers employed in the case studies have been considered against the composite list of Table 13.2 which I use at *lincolnshire dance* when assessing the employability of dancers. The table forms the basis of a benchmarking exercise which occurs as part of an initial meeting between dancers who want to work in community contexts and myself. The task is completed following a workshop in which I observed the dancers leading and informs discussions between the dancer and myself about the types of work they would like to undertake.

Case Study 1: *lincolnshire dance*

This project was devised to raise the profile of the contribution which dance makes as part of a healthy lifestyle for older people. It was coordinated by *lincolnshire dance* and comprised one dancer and a support worker leading sessions with individuals attending a day centre in Lincoln.

The programme comprised hour-long weekly sessions held over a ten-week period in a room within the centre. Each week participants took part in a number of creative chair-based and standing dance tasks. Staff from the centre also took part in the sessions.

Table 13.2 Dance skills and knowledge desired in those employed by *lincolnshire dance.*

Dance skills/knowledge
Dance technique, preferably more than one
Choreographic skills
Understanding of social, cultural, political dance history
Broad knowledge of the dance sector

Teaching methodology
Able to develop creativity in others
Able to work creatively themselves
Able to collaborate, both when leading sessions and as part of a team planning projects
Use a range of teaching skills
Knowledge of learning styles
Understand and meet the needs of participants of varied abilities, ages, backgrounds and
stages of development including those with special needs and disabilities
Understanding of group dynamics
Knowledge of child and adult development, physical, cognitive

Business skills
Good verbal and written communication skills
Project management including planning, scheduling, coordination of people, delivery and
evaluation
Self-management skills
Able to fundraise
Budgeting skills
Basic office skills
Knowledge of relevant legislation in related fields such as education, health, and sport
Duty of care/relevant legislation
Knowledge of first aid

Communication skills
Place people at the centre of their work
Interest in people

Personality traits
Want to share their enjoyment of dance with others
Cope well with change and challenge
Positive outlook on life
Open and receptive to feedback
Reflective practitioners, able to self-appraise

The participants themselves undertook the evaluation. It showed that positive
outcomes were achieved not only in relation to physical health but that the laugh-
ter and fun had improved their sense of wellbeing.

Case Study 2: Dance For Life
Dance for Life delivered this project through 'Stance Dance company', in partnership with Arts Council England, Yorkshire and local schools in response to
demand from local teachers who had identified social issues, such as bullying, peer

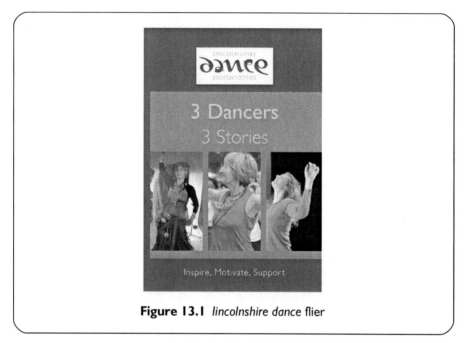

Figure 13.1 *lincolnshire dance* flier

pressure and identity as being of most importance to children's health. 'Stance Dance' comprises four dancers and is led by the Project Director of Dance for Life. For this project one dancer acted as a team leader who liaised with schools, led rehearsals and organised evaluation of the project.

The project comprised half or full days delivering a performance and workshops to groups of up to thirty pupils aged 9–18 years. Each performance was followed by a discussion with the audience about the content of the piece and how it dealt with different aspects/health issues.

Evaluation showed that both staff and pupils felt that the project was a success in terms of engaging and inspiring the pupils to dance and be involved in the creative process.

Case Study 3: Lime

The project was devised by 'Lime' to bridge an identified gap between inpatients and the community setting within secondary mental health services. The workshops were aimed at both inpatients and those in community services. Strong partnership with Manor House Recourse Centre (MHRC) meant that inpatients were given frequent encouragement to attend the sessions and if necessary transport provided to MHRC.

The programme comprised weekly two-hour sessions, led by a dance artist, using drama and dance activities for a period of ten weeks.

The workshops achieved their aims, and feedback from service users was very positive, identifying fewer feelings of isolation and increased confidence as key outcomes. The group continues to meet and this is an additional measure of the projects success.

Case Study 4: Tynedale School Sports Partnership

The programme was developed to raise the level of interest in dance within Haydon Bridge High School. Towards the end of the summer term the school holds an activities week which included dance as one of the options.

Pupils in Years 9 and 10 experienced a variety of dance styles, including, jazz, contemporary and rock and roll. Dancers from Dance City and the local area led workshops each afternoon. This gave the pupils and staff ideas to develop their own work in the morning sessions.

Evaluation showed that the pupils and staff enjoyed the sessions and dance was offered for a second year as a curriculum subject but with a more structured approach.

Each of the case studies presented had a different purpose and involved different client groups. However, there is a strong correlation between the skills, knowledge and personality traits which the different employers required from the dance artists who they employed.

It is clear to see that the greatest variation in the requirements of the different employers is within the range of business skills used by the dancers. Tynedale School Sports Partnership required very few business skills for the case study cited. However, as the dancers were employed to deliver a session as part of a bigger project, perhaps this was understandable. Similarly, in the case study cited by Dance for Life where the dancers were involved in overseeing a longer term, complex project at many different venues some project management skills were required. This simple comparison suggests that the different demands of employers may relate to the project rather than employment sector.

Further discussion about the requirements of each employer showed a variation in the value which each employer placed on the range of skills, knowledge and personality traits they required. Isobel Davison, Assistant Partnership Development Manager at Tyneside Schools Sport Partnership, emphasised that understanding group dynamics and meeting the needs of each pupil within a class of varied abilities were vital skills for dancers who she employed. She also identified the flexibility to cope with change as very important because of the timetable pressures within a school situation. In contrast, Brian Chapman, director of Lime, stressed that high-quality artistic skills coupled with sensitivity to individual needs and social and cultural contexts were paramount when he recruited dance artists. Whilst there is variation in emphasis on the skills and knowledge needed the

Table 13.3 Evaluation of the case studies.

	Case study			
	1	2	3	4
Dance skills/knowledge				
Dance technique, preferably more than one	x	x	x	x
Choreographic skills	x	x	x	
Understanding of social, cultural, political dance history	x		x	
Broad knowledge of the dance sector			x	
Teaching methodology				
Able to develop creativity in others	x	x	x	x
Able to work creatively themselves	x	x	x	
Able to collaborate, both when leading sessions and as part of a team planning projects	x	x	x	
Use a range of teaching skills	x	x	x	x
Knowledge of learning styles	x	x	x	
Understand and meet the needs of participants of varied abilities, ages, backgrounds and stages of development including those with special needs and disabilities	x	x	x	x
Understanding of group dynamics	x	x	x	x
Knowledge of child and adult development, physical, cognitive	x	x		
Business skills				
Good verbal and written communication skills	x	x	x	x
Project management including planning, scheduling, coordination of people, delivery and evaluation	x	x	x	
Self-management skills	x	x	x	
Able to fundraise				
Budgeting skills				
Basic office skills	x			
Knowledge of relevant legislation in related fields such as education, health, and sport	x		x	
Duty of care/relevant legislation	x		x	
Knowledge of first aid	x	x	x	
Communication skills				
Place people at the centre of their work	x	x	x	
Interest in people	x	x	x	
Personality traits				
Want to share their enjoyment of dance with others	x	x	x	x
Cope well with change and challenge	x	x	x	x
Positive outlook on life	x	x	x	x
Open and receptive to feedback	x	x	x	
Reflective practitioners, able to self-appraise	x	x	x	

employers who provided case studies are all looking for a complex range of skills used in different combinations depending on the purpose of the project and client group. Whilst this represents no more than a snapshot of the types of work opportunities for dancers the strong similarities between the requirements of different employers may mean that dancers do not need new skills to work in the increasing range of markets looking to employ dancers, rather that they need to identify the priorities of different employers for particular projects.

Undoubtedly it would be helpful to have a simple guide about how the many qualifications available in dance relate to the requirements of employers, particularly those who lack the confidence to gauge the quality of dance work. In addition, employers would be assisted in matching dancers to particular projects if dancers themselves developed a clear rationale for their work and were able to articulate clearly how they want to use their dance skills and how this addresses the needs of employers for particular projects.

It is clear that there are increasing employment opportunities for dancers in a variety of markets. The complex range of skills and knowledge required indicates that employers have very high expectations of the dancers they employ. This suggests the need for the dance sector to address the skills and knowledge developed during training, as identified in 'Mapping Dance' and also engage employers in debates about their requirements so as to develop a shared language and understanding of these.

Information About Organisations Providing Case Study

lincolnshire dance is a regional dance agency established in 2000. Since then it has prioritised the development of a skilled cluster of dancers and dance organisations creating, facilitating and performing dance within the county. Continuing professional development has been and continues to be central to all activities, which the organisation undertakes.

Lime is a Manchester-based arts charity and was established in 1974. It has a core team of seven employees who act as a channel between the arts world and the health world. Lime works through a number of partnerships, using a range of art forms, including dance, to develop, coordinate and implement a wide range of arts projects in healthcare settings.

Tynedale School Sports Partnership was established in 2002 and now comprises over 40 schools in Tynedale, Northumberland. The partnerships is hosted at Haydon Bridge High School and Sport College. It encourages a wide range of activities but two of the School Sport Coordinators have a major role in supporting schools across the partnership so that yearly dance festivals can be organised across the partnership for age ranges from five to eighteen.

Dance For Life was set up in 1992 by representatives from both Bradford Council and Bradford health to address the health concerns of young people, particularly teenage girls from black and ethnic minorities. It works through educational and community contexts to increase young people's confidence levels and sense of self; increase their knowledge about health issues and encourage them to make the right lifestyle choices to improve their health.

Exercise

- Keyna Paul mentions several government initiatives relating to creativity and healthy lifestyles. Can you find any recent examples of government policies which are impacting on community dance practice?

14 Partnership working
Diane Amans

There are many different examples of joint working – with considerable variation in the size and purpose of partnerships. Some strategic partnerships involve dozens of people working together to tackle an issue that affects a large geographical area. At the other end of the scale smaller partnerships focus on a single community problem or plan a local festival. In this chapter I look at how dance artists have been involved in partnerships and the innovative ways in which they help organisations achieve their objectives. I also discuss some of the challenges and opportunities presented by collaborative working.

> Successful partnerships can achieve goals that individual agencies cannot (Audit Commission, 1998).

As partnership working has become widespread in the UK, community dance artists have already worked successfully with public authorities such as health and social care, criminal justice, housing and education. Working with different partners is challenging, but it can offer exciting opportunities for dance practitioners, whether they are independent freelancers or part of a dance agency team.

There are formal partnerships, with service level agreements between two or more agencies, and there are more informal arrangements which might involve networking between professionals with similar objectives. Whether the partnerships are formal or informal, the skills needed for effective joint working are very similar, and community dance practitioners often possess these skills.

Formal Partnerships
In formal agreements between dance agencies and their local authorities. a dance development worker is sometimes directly employed by the local council and works as part of their cultural development team. In other areas a local authority may contribute funding towards a post which is managed by a dance agency.

Figure 14.1 JABADAO conference 2005 Diane Amans and Penny Greenland (*Linda Neary*)

There is usually a service level agreement which sets out, in broad terms, the agreed areas of work together with any action points.

Partnerships with local councils can result in benefits for all concerned. Individual artists and dance agencies have access to a wide network of support and advocacy opportunities. The councils have access to skilled dance practitioners who will help them implement their cultural strategies. All partners are able to share information and resources and they may be able to collaborate in joint training/ professional development opportunities.

There are various ways in which the dance development posts are line-managed within partnerships. Some dance artists have an office base in a local authority venue and a line manager from a dance agency. Others are managed by a cultural services manager with secondary or indirect supervision from an arts development officer. Provided the nature of the relationship is discussed and agreed by all partners the dance artist should have plenty of support. In practice, the success of any joint working initiatives will depend on effective communication, agreed objectives and good working relationships.

Informal Partnerships

Partnership working on a more informal basis may be associated with something which has a specific time frame. For example, a community health project might involve a regional dance agency, freelance dance practitioners together with school teachers, the health promotion team, leisure services, a local business sponsor and community volunteers. For a short period of time they will work in partnership with each other and, although some of the partners might be involved in more formal long-term service agreements, others join them on a more temporary basis.

In my experience, it is sometimes the dance artist who acts as a catalyst and brings together different people who might otherwise not have worked together. This is one of the joys of community dance work; it offers an opportunity to create partnerships so that we can do what we want to do. I have often started with an idea and then set about bringing together people who can help me make it happen.

Engaging with Other People's Agendas

Some artists worry that collaborating with other agencies means that the dance work is somehow diminished. Interestingly, this concern is not shared by the young dancers who took part in consultation during 2007 for the North West Youth Dance Regional Development Plan[1]. The research revealed they just accept

Figure 14.2 Freedom in Dance *At My Age* project 2004 *(Matthew Priestley)*

that dance is linked with other parts of their lives: 'of course it's good for health, yes it helps us understand ourselves and others'. The reality is that the Arts *do* satisfy other agendas. We can see this as an opportunity to develop new relationships and learn to speak other people's languages.

Community dance practitioners need to be able to talk about the benefits of dance in terms of other people's agendas. It doesn't dilute the art form. It doesn't mean that dance is in some way less important – but it could be that some of the partners/stakeholders/other agencies don't realise how important it is. We need to understand *their* priorities and help them understand how dance could become part of their action plan.

If we can explain how what we do connects with Health and Social Care priorities, for example, we are more likely to be approached to run community dance projects in different settings. In fact, we don't have to wait to be approached – we can be proactive in connecting with other people's agendas.

However, some practitioners question why we *should* be proactive in connecting with Health and Social Care agendas. What about community dance agendas?

This is an understandable point of view. Dance professionals don't want other professions to dictate what they do. It reinforces the notion that dance is something to be used to help other professionals achieve their aims and objectives. But we can do something to change this perception. We can choose to see ourselves as equal partners in collaborative working, which benefits everyone involved. After all, the agendas are not very different. Take the example of Table 14.1, from a Freedom in Dance 'mature movers' project which connects with the standards in the Department of Health's *National Service Framework: Older People* (Department of Health, 2001).

The agendas are very similar – we just use different language. We need to draw attention to the similarities in our aims and build relationships based on mutual respect. It makes sense to do this if we want to open doors to new work opportunities and stimulating challenges. If we can create alliances with other professions this will strengthen funding bids and bring more resources into community

Table 14.1 Comparing different agendas.

Health and social care agenda	Community dance agenda
Active older age	Engage people in dance activity because it is
Promote good mental health	life-enhancing and it makes you feel good
Reduce age related disease	Make new choreography which challenges
Improve balance and coordination	age stereotypes
Reduce social isolation	Build relationships with others by sharing
Challenge stereotypes	pleasurable activities
Root out age discrimination	Create opportunities for self-expression
Treat people as individuals	Celebrate the diversity of each unique indi-
Recognise and manage diversity	vidual participant

dance. It will also create new opportunities for dance with groups and individuals who currently don't dance.

How Do We Create Alliances with Other Professions?

Partnership working with other agencies is like working at partnerships in any area of life. It's about building relationships. Whether we're part of a multi-agency initiative to set up a community dance project or getting to know a new circle of friends, the relationship building skills are very similar. They include:

- finding out what the other people are interested in
- learning to speak the same language
- identifying things you have in common

These are the 'people skills' which are necessary in any effective relationships. It is also very useful to find out about the wider contexts in which our partners work – the government's national frameworks, present and future funding sources, legislation and local authority priorities. We are more likely to be listened to if we can outline proposed projects in language which connects to other people's agendas. This will help our partners understand our aims and priorities and might lead to unexpected sources of funding or in kind support.

When I am planning a dance project I have clear ideas about the artistic content. In my mind there is no ambiguity about the aims. It's an arts project. But there's more chance of my getting other partners involved if I can profile other elements of community dance – such as its contribution to arts and health, its impact on social inclusion, its potential for addressing citizenship and diversity issues. Even if I'm not working in collaboration with other professions on this project it's a useful exercise to consider how it *could* connect to other agendas. You never know – I might want to do a follow-up project with this group and I might need partners to get involved.

Partnership Case Study

Here is an example of how a dance project was made possible through totally unexpected resources. I was invited to demonstrate Freedom in Dance methods to members of South Manchester Healthy Living Network. The audience included representatives from Health, Social Care, Housing, Transport, Leisure and Regeneration. Volunteers from the audience took part in a creative dance workshop whilst I described how the various activities linked to falls prevention and healthy ageing. I didn't need to point out that people were having fun and enjoying social interaction as well as creating dance which engaged performers and audience.

After the event I had two phone calls. One was from a housing manager who wanted me to set up similar sessions in a sheltered housing unit, and did I know how he could raise funds for this? The other call was from a leisure services manager who had a budget and a remit for engaging more over 50-year-olds in exercise – did I know of any groups who might be interested in participating? I put them in touch with each other and we set up a dance project. We were delighted to work with partners from health, housing and leisure services.

Challenges of Partnership Working

It isn't always this straightforward, though. You sometimes find yourself in partnership relationships where there are tensions because the partners want different outcomes, or there's a shared vision but no one wants to lead on it, or there's no funding and all the partners are too busy to write funding applications. This can be really frustrating if you are a freelance artist who has been invited to put together a proposal, and three meetings later it still doesn't seem to be going anywhere.

This is where the dance practitioner may need to take the initiative in pushing for some decisions because the partnership seems to be just a 'talking shop'. If you're the only one at the meeting who is not on a salary it's in your interest to get things moving. Occasionally I have taken the lead in suggesting that a project is not viable because the partnership does not have the resources to achieve what it has set out to do. I don't think we've anything to lose by taking the initiative in this way. Sometimes a project does not get off the ground, but then I don't have to go to any more unfocused meetings in my own time and I can move on to more promising ventures.

On the other hand, an artist's intervention might nudge people into action. In one memorable meeting between members of a Health Strategic Partnership we really seemed to be going nowhere and I questioned whether it was worth continuing. Suddenly one partner excused himself from the meeting to return minutes later having made a hurried phone call which resulted in a firm funding offer. Then another partner disappeared and returned with match funding. All this happened within twenty minutes of the artist suggesting we call it a day because there was no funding to continue the dance project!

Conclusion

Most dance artists will be involved in joint working at some stage of their career – either as part of a public sector partnership or by contributing to a small-scale community collaboration. Before becoming involved in partnership working it is worth taking the time to clarify what your role will be and checking that all prospective partners have a clear idea of what the partnership hopes to achieve. It may be that there is not a shared vision, but you feel it is worth joining a group anyway because you have the chance to contribute ideas and influence possible outcomes.

The following questions might help you decide whether or not to become involved in a partnership:

- What is the purpose of the partnership?
- What would your role be?
- How much time would be involved?
- Will you be paid for the time?
- What opportunities does it offer you? (Artistic/professional/personal development?)

As long as you are realistic about the amount of time you are prepared to allocate, and you feel there is an opportunity for meaningful involvement, there is no reason why it should not be a positive experience.

Certainly community dance artists can offer considerable potential benefits to any collaborative work. Partnership working needs people who can build relationships and that's something we're very good at in community dance. They're the skills we're using every day. Community dance practitioners are creative, resourceful people with leadership skills and experience of communicating with a diverse range of people. As flexible professionals who can 'think outside the box' we can work with other stakeholders to develop joint visions and deliver change.

Exercise and Discussion Points

- Find out about regional partnerships in your area – which organisations are working together and what are their objectives? The following have been common topics in the past: health, community safety, social inclusion, regeneration, housing and crime prevention.
- Can you think of ways in which dance artists could become involved in helping partnerships deliver their objectives?

Note
1. Research carried out by Deb Barnard as part of Youth Dance Regional Development Plan, 2007.

Part 5
Community Dance Delivery

Introduction

In this final part of the book I deal with the practical aspects of planning, delivering and evaluating our practice. I set out to share what I have learned and offer some guidelines and samples of resources. If you are new to community dance you may find it useful to use these as starting points, which is exactly what they are. I hope you will continuously reflect on your practice and that of others as you develop your own leadership style and your own approach to planning and recording your work. I suggest you seek out opportunities for observing other artists at work and discussing your own projects with others. This will help with reflective practice – and, as you gain experience, you will feel able to depart from your session plan when you sense that something different would better meet the needs of the group.

In Part 3 Rosemary Lee describes how she starts with a plan but is constantly noticing and reading feedback from the participants and checking in with herself – her observations and feelings about the session. She talks about responding to the present, being in the here and now. Similarly, Helen Poynor highlights the importance of self-awareness and being open to what we can learn from participants (see Chapter 9). Both these artists are *reflexive practitioners*. They combine sensitivity to the needs of the participants, awareness of their own needs and the ability to respond in the moment.

Think about your own practice and your experience of being a participant in someone else's session. Are you a reflexive practitioner? Have you experienced dance leaders who seem to be engaging in an ongoing process of reflection? What was it like to be a participant in their group? At the end of most chapters there are exercises or discussion points. I suggest you read through them, select those which particularly interest you and discuss them with colleagues. Tutors responsible for community dance studies may wish to use these as a focus for classroom discussion or written assignment.

Further Reading

Blom, L. A. and Tarin Chaplin, L. (1989) *The Intimate Act of Choreography.* Dance Books, London.

Dunphy, K. and Scott, J. (2003) *Freedom to Move: Movement and Dance for People with Intellectual Disabilities.* Maclennan & Petty, Sydney.

Gough, M. (1993) *In Touch with Dance.* Whitethorn, Lancaster.

Langford, S. and Mayo, S. (2001) *Sharing the Experience: How to Set Up and Run Arts Projects Linking Young and Older People.* Magic Me, London.

Lerman, L. (1984) *Teaching Dance to Senior Adults.* Thomas, Illinois.

Lynch Fraser, D. (1991) *Playdancing: Discovering and Developing Creativity in Young Children.* Dance Horizons, Pennington.

Smith-Autard, J. M. (1994) *The Art of Dance in Education.* A&C Black, London.

Tufnell, M. and Crickmay, C. (2004) *A Widening Field: Journeys in Body and Imagination.* Dance Books, Hampshire.

15 Planning a Session
Diane Amans

This chapter will help dance artists consider the practical aspects of leading community dance sessions. It is aimed primarily at those who are new to the profession, but experienced community dance workers may find the material useful in helping them reflect on their methods of planning and delivering sessions. The prompt questions will help the reader to clarify aims and objectives and select activities that will achieve these. The chapter also includes practical advice on timing, writing a session plan, risk assessment, use of resources, group management and methods of documenting the impact on participants.

Before You Begin
The following questions are a useful starting point for any intervention – whether it is a one-off taster session, a regular weekly programme or a month long residency, the questions that need to be asked are:

Who?   Where?   When?   What?   Why?   How?

Who?   Find out as much as you can about the participants. Who will you be working with? Is it an established group or a group formed especially for this project? Have they chosen to take part or has someone else made that decision? What are their interests/expectations/needs? Who says so? How many people will you be working with and what are their ages? What is known about their previous experience of dance?

What do you know about participants' health and movement ability? Sometimes you may be briefed by other people (for instance in schools and hospitals). In other contexts it will be up to you to find out what you need to know to keep people safe and plan an appropriate session. Many adults will happily chat about their health. Take particular note of any medical conditions and check up on contra-indicated activities. (NB: Think about confidentiality and data protection when you record this information.)

If you are working with children, young people or vulnerable adults what are the duty of care issues[1]? Who is the carer?

Who else will be in the session? If you are working with other artists, co-leaders or support workers, are your respective roles clear? Will there be teachers/parents/carers in the room? Do you want them to join in or watch?

Where? What is the venue like? Do you have any choice of room? Look at floor surface, ventilation, whether there are any fixed hazards like pillars or cupboards with sharp corners. If your session is for a seated group, do the chairs provide support? Is there plenty of room for free activity? Is the room a thoroughfare for other people? What happens in the space before your session? (For instance, will the floor need sweeping if it's been used for dinner?) What are the arrangements for tea/coffee making? How do you access the space?

Do you need to find out who holds the key? Who else will be working nearby? Will they disturb you or ask you to turn the music down?

When? What happens just before/after your session? How long will the session last? Do you have any say over when the session takes place and how long it lasts? Have you got a particular deadline for being out of the space?

What? What will you include in your session? Have you taken account of previous evaluations/feedback? If this is a newly formed group how will you 'break the ice'? What activities will you use to warm the group up? What is the main focus of the dance activity? Has this already been decided or will it be negotiated with the group? If you are working towards a performance, who decides on the theme? Do you need any props or other resources? Will you be using music?

Why? Why have you chosen these activities and how are they linked to your aims and objectives for the session? How were these decided?

How? How will you know if you've achieved your aims? What indicators will you use to determine success? Have you thought about how you will evaluate the session? How will you document the work? (Do you just need a record for your own use or will you be expected to produce a report?)

Finally, *how* do you find out the answers to these questions? If it is the first session or a one-off workshop you need as much information as possible beforehand. Whenever possible try to arrange a briefing meeting with the organisation who has commissioned the work and even meet the participants if this can be arranged. Prepare for the meeting by making a checklist of the questions you need to ask.

Some questions will not be answered until you begin the first dance session. If this first session is planned carefully it can be a useful opportunity to assess the participants and check out the approach that will best match the skills and interests of the group.

Writing a Session Plan

If you are delivering a session for a school or college there will be a standard format for lesson planning. This is likely to include a scheme of work and session plans which take account of the different needs of individual learners. Some dance agencies also provide a standard *pro forma* for their dance artists to complete[2], whilst others leave practitioners to devise their own systems. Community dance work which does not involve conforming to a prescribed formula leaves dance artists free to write the session plan in their own style. It is a matter of personal choice and you may find it useful to experiment till you find a system that works for you. Some artists just have brief handwritten notes in a small notebook; others prefer to type plans which they keep in a loose leaf file together with other documentation, such as meeting notes and risk assessments.

I find it helpful to use colour to highlight different elements in session plans. For example, if resources, such as music and props, are highlighted or written in colour it is easy to check and make sure nothing is forgotten. Coaching points/ reminders about safety issues could be a different colour which will make them stand out as you glance at your notes. It is also worth paying attention to how much time you estimate each activity will take. If you find you have five minutes remaining and you are only half way through your hour-long plan you need to know where the time went. Did the session start late? Did you spend too long talking about the dance before you began moving? Was the plan realistic or had you included too many activities? In the above example the plan includes the estimated start time for each activity with the actual times written on the plan. This helps with planning future sessions.

An experienced practitioner does not need to continue to write notes out in full – particularly if the activities are tried and tested 'old favourites'. Many artists find a short-hand version of the plan is sufficient. The actual process of writing out a session plan – however you choose to do it – is a significant part of any preparation. If the plan is well thought through the dance artist may find that the session flows naturally without frequent reference to the written notes. On the other hand, if something unexpected happens or your mind 'goes blank', it can be most reassuring to have a well-structured plan with you.

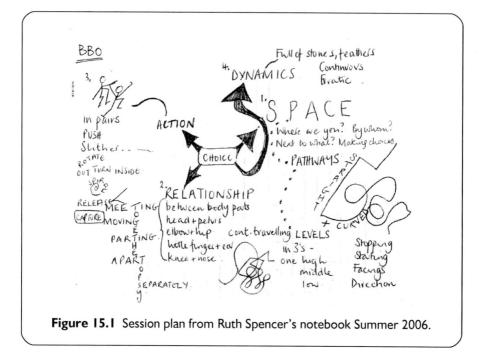

Figure 15.1 Session plan from Ruth Spencer's notebook Summer 2006.

Alternative Approaches to Session Planning

The approach I've described so far is only one way of preparing to lead community dance work. Some highly effective and inspiring practitioners do not plan their classes in this way. Ruth Spencer is an independent dance artist working with many different community groups. She records all her work in a spiral bound notebook and prefers to create a diagram as she plans her session. Look at her plan in Figure 15.1 and see if you can follow Ruth's thinking.

Risk Assessment

Assessing risk is an element of duty of care and is part of any planning process. It needs to take account of all aspects of the session – the environment, the activities, the people involved and any equipment or resources which are used. Risk assessment means thinking ahead and identifying anything which might cause an accident or injury to people involved in the session. A dance session is not going to be completely free from risk, but dance artists can identify possible hazards and take steps to control these.

It is important to document risk assessment procedures and retain these records. Some organisations expect you to use their risk assessment methods and forms; others assume you will take any necessary precautions. In any case it is worth having your own system and taking the trouble to file your notes. The Resources section includes examples of risk assessment forms taken from community dance projects.

Music and Accompaniment

Choice of music – and whether or not to use music at all – is a personal matter. If you like to include accompaniment in your sessions there is a huge variety of sounds to choose from. Experienced community dance artists usually have a wide range of recorded music and participants sometimes appreciate the chance to bring a piece of music that they particularly enjoy. As you listen to music you will find your own way of categorising the different types and the movement possibilities suggested by the sounds. It may be that you prefer to work without sound or with voice and other sounds that you can make with the group – experiment and see what works for you.

Percussion instruments and other live music can add an exciting quality – if you work with improvisation you could invite a musician who will improvise along with the dancers. Participants who have difficulties with hearing may find live music preferable to recorded music (which can cause problems with some hearing aids). Live musicians can add a very special quality to a dance session. Make sure they have directions to the venue and a briefing about what you expect of them. Check out their access needs and what they need in terms of space, time for set-up and so on. Naturally there is a cost to be considered, but I have always either found funding for a musician or, in some cases, found that the host organisation has a member of staff who plays an instrument. On one memorable occasion, in hospital, a therapy assistant brought in his violin to accompany a gentle duet as I led a session with very frail older people.

If recorded music is to be included in the dance sessions whose equipment will be used? If you are using your own, is it appropriate for the space? Where are the electric sockets? Will you need an extension lead? Will this need to be taped down to ensure it is not a hazard? Some organisations require visiting artists to have any electronic machines checked by an electrician to ensure they comply with health and safety standards[3]. If you will be using equipment provided by the host organisation have you allowed time for familiarising yourself with their machines? Have you checked out music copyright and performing rights laws if you are using recorded music?

Props and Materials

There are numerous commercially produced props to support dance work[4] – for example scarves, parachutes, ribbon sticks, feathers, lengths of fabric and masks. If you enjoy craft work you can easily make your own versions of these. Ordinary everyday objects such as chairs, hats, balls and walking sticks also offer exciting possibilities. If you have the chance to block out light you can create a totally different atmosphere with torches, lasers or glow sticks. There are some practical considerations when using props in dance sessions. Apart from making sure you have sufficient for all participants you need to check to ensure they do not present a health and safety risk. Some percussion instruments are not suitable for use with children; scarves can cause an accident on a slippery floor; parachutes are best used in rooms with high ceilings and unbreakable light fittings. When working in health settings it is important to consult relevant staff, as there will be policy guidelines relating to materials which can be used with people who are unwell.

Personal Preparation

This may take any number of different forms. Some dance artists like to go into the space and spend time moving and preparing their body and mind for the session ahead. Others like to quietly organise their music and props and read through the session plan. It may be that you have little time for personal preparation, but at least take the time to focus yourself, think through the aims of the session and be available to greet your group.

People Management

Being able to engage with people, build relationships and 'hold' a group is essential in leading participatory dance sessions. There are a number of strategies that help us 'connect' with other people and encourage them to engage in activities in their own individual way. Some of these are very simple and, whilst they may seem too obvious to mention, it is surprising how often they are forgotten.

- Greet each participant individually (smile, eye contact, touch where appropriate).
- Make sure you arrive in good time so you are available if someone needs to ask you anything/let you know about an injury etc.
- Use people's names and help them learn each others' names.
- Time spent on an icebreaker (such as a name game) will pay dividends later on when you want them to do partner and group work.
- Incorporate some interactive warm up activities which have a social element as well as serving as a physical warm-up.
- An activity in a circle – such as a parachute game or a circle dance – is often useful in helping a group 'gel'.
- Be sensitive to situations where there are participants who are new/different/ just don't seem to be very popular with other members of the group. You can

manage this effectively if you are careful how partners and groups are selected. Move people around and be prepared to partner someone who needs extra help.

In addition to the participants in a community dance session there are sometimes co-leaders, support workers and diverse other people who may have a reason for being in the space where the activity takes place. In planning a session the dance artist needs to consider how these people will be managed. Co-leaders and other artists should have a copy of the session plan and a clear understanding of their roles in the session.

You may encounter the occasional support worker who decides to become an additional co-leader. If a staff member's well-intentioned 'helper behaviour' is too interventionist the dance practitioner needs to manage the situation so that the participants are not denied opportunities for personal growth and self expression. This is not easy – particularly in organisations where the prevailing culture is to be fairly directive and to limit opportunities for individuals to make decisions.

One solution is to enlist help with documenting the impact on participants. I have found it very useful to prepare an observation checklist for support staff to complete as an 'outside eye' whilst I am working with a group. This serves a number of purposes; I acquire some valuable evidence to help me with evaluation; the support worker has a meaningful role; and I retain control of the nature and frequency of any interventions.

Methods of Evaluation

The results of evaluation help with planning future sessions, and the selection of appropriate evaluation methods is an important part of the planning process. Time will need to be allocated for feedback discussions, written questionnaires or any other activity involving participants. It may be necessary to devise evaluation tools which are less word-dependent if the participants are not able to use language easily. Chapter 16 considers evaluation in more detail and includes examples of different methods of gathering evidence and documenting evaluation.

Conclusion

Careful and thorough planning will usually help practitioners deliver effective participatory dance in community settings – provided that the dance artist is flexible enough to adapt the plan, or abandon it altogether if necessary. The key aspect here is to remain 'present' and aware of what is happening. It is more important to notice reactions and feedback from participants than to stick rigidly to a timetable of activities. From time to time even very skilled and experienced artists find that a session just does not work very well. It may be, after evaluating the session, that the cause of the problem becomes clear; but occasionally there just doesn't seem to be any explanation when things go wrong. On these occasions I usually talk it through with another practitioner and, if I still can't work out what happened, I just accept that it was disappointing and try to forget it. I aim for high standards, but I have learned not to punish myself if I do not always achieve them. Planning is very important, but it does not guarantee that every session will be an unqualified success.

Exercise

Imagine you have been asked to lead an introductory dance session for one of the following groups. Write a session plan and make notes on any action you would take before this session.

- An after school dance club for 15 Key Stage 2 children
- A youth dance group
- An adult community group (mostly women) who have been meeting for an exercise class and have decided they want to do something more creative
- A group of adults with learning disabilities who attend a community centre to take part in a range of activities
- Residents in a home for older people. This will be a taster session and about 12 participants are expected

---

Notes

1. See Chapter 6 for more discussion on duty of care.
2. Spiral Dance Company, for example, includes a blank lesson plan in its dance artists' pack, together with policies, codes of practice, risk assessment forms and guidelines on many aspects of practice.
3. The government Health and Safety Executive (HSE) issues guidance in relation to electrical compatibility. Most public organisations have a health and safety policy which requires all portable electrical appliances to be tested.
4. JABADAO and Rompa are just two who produce excellent catalogues. See Resources section for contact details.

16 Giving Value?
Diane Amans

Evaluation is working out the value of something – 'making judgements, based on evidence, about the value and quality of a project' (Woolf, 1999). As community dance artists we are expected to understand the impact of our work on the participants and to be able to demonstrate the extent to which aims and objectives have been achieved. The evaluation process also has the potential to contribute to an artist's own professional development and can be an important part of developing skills as a reflective practitioner. The challenge is to find reliable ways of gathering evidence of quality and meaningful methods of evaluating it.

> *Evaluation is about calculating worth. Its difficulty arises from the essentially relative nature of worth...Evaluation is not, despite being widely used in this way, shorthand for 'How did we do?' though answering that question is a step along the way. (Matarasso, 1996)*

The dance worker leading a project is often responsible for determining its value and reporting on the outcomes. This chapter discusses the ways in which dance artists engage in critical reflection and examines the validity of evaluation processes.

Why Do We Evaluate?
1. So we can be better practitioners?
2. So we can use evaluation in our planning?
3. So we can check out the extent to which we have achieved our objectives?
4. To measure ourselves against quality standards/targets?
5. To demonstrate to funders and other stakeholders that we're delivering what we said we'd deliver?
6. To get evidence for more funding?

These are all valid reasons for evaluating, but it is likely that some have a higher priority depending on the context of the work and the viewpoint of the various stakeholders. It is important to be clear about *why* we are evaluating so we can decide on the evaluation methodology. Arts Council England (ACE) asks artists for information about proposed evaluation methods before they award grants for projects. In their guidelines on evaluation (see the box below) ACE outlines the benefits to artists of evaluating their work.

- Evaluation helps with planning, as it makes you think about what you're aiming to do, how you will do it and how you will know if you've succeeded
- Ongoing feedback keeps you on track and helps to avoid disasters
- Evaluation helps you to adapt and change as your project continues
- Evaluation is a good way of dealing with 'quality assurance' – you keep an eye on things to make sure quality is maintained
- Evaluation helps prove the value of what you are doing
- Evaluation records your contribution to the field you are working in
- Your evaluation can help others working in the same field
- Information you collect can also be used for reporting back to those with an interest in the project (e.g. participants, funders) and telling others about what you've done
- The evidence you collect can support future applications

(Arts Council England, 2004)

Evaluation is part of our professional practice – the process of evaluation helps artists engage in the debate about what constitutes good practice. But who decides what is good practice and what criteria are being used?

Who Makes the Judgements?

If the artist leading the project is also responsible for making judgements about its value, it requires considerable detachment and objectivity to ensure that the evaluation process is well balanced.

This example in the box below illustrates what can happen when an artist does not realise the extent to which he is influencing the feedback he is receiving. He may genuinely believe that he has evaluated the project in a thorough and professional way. There were many positive aspects of the work, but there were also areas which could have been better. The artist missed an opportunity for some valuable feedback.

Practical Example

The dance artist gathered his group together for feedback at the end of their week-long community dance project. He asked each individual if they wanted to say anything. When someone made a positive comment the artist's encouraging non-verbal responses invited further contributions. When someone made a negative comment or no comment at all he acknowledged it briefly and moved quickly on to the next person. This was an integrated group with a non-disabled workshop leader facilitating the discussion. Some of the disabled dancers were not able to communicate verbally and their support worker was out of the room making telephone calls (she had asked if she was needed at this point and the artist had said 'no').

One of the disabled participants later remarked to a friend –'I don't think he's really interested in us as individuals – just as a vehicle for making him look good'. She did not feel able to voice this view publicly as she felt that the artist did not want to hear negative comments.

The artist wrote a positive evaluation report quoting the excellent feedback from participants. The host organisation invited him back for the next year's project.

It is the responsibility of dance artists to make sure that the work is evaluated effectively, but this does not necessarily mean that they are the only ones who make these important value judgements. Everyone involved in a community dance project should have an opportunity to contribute to the evaluation process. This includes participants, support workers, other partners and members of the audience. They all have their own values which will influence how they define quality – one person's high-quality project can be seen, by someone else, to be a waste of resources. This subjectivity is an inevitable factor in evaluating arts activities, but, as Matarasso argues, it need not devalue or invalidate the process. We need to devise evaluation procedures which 'take account of the legitimate subjectivity of different stakeholders'.

Sometimes stakeholders do not have a clear idea of what outcomes are possible or appropriate. This can often be the case when dance is a new activity with a community group and the dance artist is expected to suggest project goals. Despite the fact that aims and objectives focus on intended benefits for those who take part, it is not always possible to involve potential participants in the planning stages of a project. However the project is set up, the challenge for the dance artist is to make sure that methods of evaluation are flexible, inclusive and accessible. There will need to be effective strategies for encouraging feedback and it may be useful to involve other people in the evaluation.

Some community projects have external evaluators who can provide excellent additional evidence. The questions asked by someone who is not very close to a project offer interesting food for thought. Naturally there are resource implications here; an external evaluator has to be funded. This is why it is important to think about evaluation *before* a project begins. A framework needs to be agreed with all stakeholders and, if an external evaluator is necessary, then the fee can be costed in at the beginning.

What Are We Evaluating?

1. The impact on participants?
2. The extent to which we achieve our objectives?
3. The artistic content in the work?
4. The skills of the artist?
5. The final performance?
6. The processes involved in creating work?

Good practice in evaluation means being clear and *specific* about what is being evaluated – however, some aspects of community dance are easier to measure than others. We need to find a way to measure those aspects of our work that we and the participants find significant. But who decides what is significant? It may be that the participants think one thing is significant and the facilitators or funders find something else significant. Whose significant aspect is the one that counts?

There are no easy answers here but, if the evaluation is to be meaningful, there needs to be agreement about what outcomes are going to be measured. The indicators have to be thought through beforehand, together with ways of measuring progress towards the agreed outcomes. There is no point claiming that participants in a dance and health project demonstrate a greater confidence in movement if we have no record of what 'less confident' looked like. Evaluation involves comparison; we need to have something to measure against.

Methods of Evaluation

Answers to the why, who and what questions all inform the methodology. How is the work evaluated? There are many ways of collecting evidence to help evaluate community dance projects – interviews, questionnaires, video, feedback discussions, photography, diaries, tape recordings, observation, 'graffiti walls' and final performances. In choosing the appropriate methods for collecting evidence and documenting the work the evaluators need to consider, among other things, whether the methods are accessible and user-friendly for all the participants.

These judgements require evaluators to have the necessary awareness and skills to ensure an inclusive approach. For example, if the participants don't use words to communicate, how can dance artists check whether their own beliefs about a project's value reflect the experience of the participants? The *At My Age* project (see box below) illustrates different ways of documenting a dance project.

Making Judgements

Each of these questions – why, what, who and how – raises more questions. If we consider these in a practical sense now, how do we actually work out the value of community dance work? How much information or involvement do we need and what criteria are we using to make judgements about value? Are we going to look at aesthetics or the extent to which people are engaged in dance? Are we going to judge the quality of the relationships or look for evidence of participant enjoyment?

Clearly these questions cannot be answered without reference to the aims and objectives of the project – but the questions have to be asked before the work begins. If we don't think it through and cost it in before the project starts we may severely restrict our options when it comes to selecting methodology.

Personally I use a range of different methods to collect evidence and document projects. The following example illustrates how these are used in evaluation.

As project coordinator I had overall responsibility for evaluating this project, but there were many people whose judgements were incorporated into the

At My Age – an Intergenerational Dance Project

In Spring 2004 Freedom in Dance, a UK-based community dance company, completed a video project called *At My Age*. Over 30 children, young people and older adults worked with choreographers and a film artist to create a short video which explored intergenerational relationships and perceptions of youth and ageing.

Aims of the Project

- To promote better mutual understanding between people of different generations
- To challenge stereotypes of youth and ageing
- To increase skills and creativity of participants
- To extend access and participation in community dance

Impact of the Project
The impact of the project was documented using a range of methods.

Project Log for Participants' Comments and Drawings
This was an A4 sketch pad which was prominently displayed during each dance session with the invitation: 'Please make comments/words/pictures in this book'. Most participants contributed to the log and sometimes parents sent in pictures that the children had made when they went home and talked about what they had been doing (see Figure 16.1).

Matilda dancing in the park.

Figure 16.1 Freedom in Dance project log *At My Age* 2004.

The project log also included photographs and feedback from members of the audience who came to the video screening.

Photographs
A photographer attended four out of the seven days and the photographs were a useful focus for discussion.

Video
A video artist filmed the dance workshops and this visual record helped participants to contribute to an evaluation of the work in progress. The feedback discussions were also filmed, giving an opportunity for the project coordinator to reflect on participants' comments after each session.

Questionnaires
Participants were invited to complete simple questionnaires. If the participants were too young to read, an adult asked the questions and recorded the responses to the following questions: What did you enjoy? What did you not enjoy? How did it make you feel? What did it make you think about?

Feedback Discussions
Throughout the project there were informal discussions with small groups and individuals.

Project Coordinator's Log
This contained session plans with observations and reflections during and after sessions.

evaluation process. I had regular discussions with the other artists on the project and took account of participants' responses as I planned each new session. Some of the most valuable feedback came from people who were not directly involved on a daily basis but had a link with the project. Parents, costume makers,

Figure 16.2 Freedom in Dance *At My Age* Freedom in Dance project 2004 (*Jackie Mellor*)

photographers, providers of refreshments and transport, guest artists – all made interesting and thought-provoking comments which fed into the evaluation. I noted down comments I overheard when visitors were watching the end of rehearsals. I stored up the little observations like 'I was really surprised when my husband joined in – he only went to drop the children off'.

External Evaluator as 'Critical Friend'

In my work as a community dance artist I try to involve an 'outside eye' whenever possible. This may be a member of staff, if I am working in a health and social care setting, or it may be an arts worker. Often I bring in an external evaluator. I feel this adds rigour to the evaluation process – and it keeps me on my toes. It's an invaluable source of professional development for an artist. In addition to discussing evidence for evaluation there's nothing quite like being asked to justify decisions and talking through alternatives with an experienced practitioner. On one memorable project the external evaluator gave me some very useful feedback about my communication style. I was working with deaf and hard of hearing young people and I had adapted my methods to keep verbal prompts to a minimum. I learned some basic sign language so that I could lead the introductions and initiate simple activities. I also involved signers to help with more complex communication. What I hadn't realised, until I read the gentle feedback from the external evaluator, was that my well-intentioned communication methods contained a significant flaw. I continued to use my habitual arm gestures – often fairly exuberant – thus introducing the visual equivalent of considerable 'background noise'. The rest of the evaluation report related to the impact on participants and was extremely favourable, but most memorable for me was the comment about arm gestures. This feedback was an unexpected 'gift' to help me evaluate my practice.

Self-evaluation

As artists involved in participatory dance activities with different community groups we have plenty of scope for personal development if we are open to receiving feedback. Alongside an evaluation of the dance activity we have an opportunity to evaluate our own practice and raise awareness of our strengths and any areas for further development. We will only receive this essential feedback, though, if we establish relationships based on trust and openness – where participants, colleagues and observers feel comfortable in sharing value judgements which may not always be easy to hear. We need feedback if we are going to understand the impact of our behaviour on others. The Johari Window[1] (Figure 16.3) is a useful model to illustrate how feedback can help increase our self awareness.

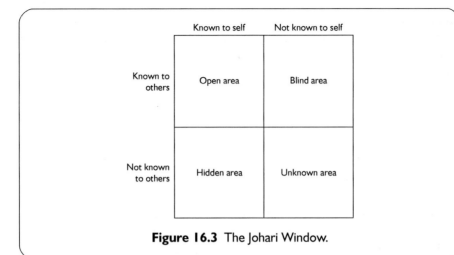

Figure 16.3 The Johari Window.

In evaluating community dance projects we have an opportunity to increase the size of our open area by inviting others to give us 'feedback presents'. If we have a good level of self-awareness and understand our own values and behaviour we are more likely to be able to be able to make objective value judgements about others.

Conclusion

The questions and issues discussed in this chapter illustrate the complex nature of measuring quality and value. Evaluation is too important to be left to the end of a project. Although the last-minute questionnaire is still a feature of some community dance activities, it has limited worth if this is the only method used to evaluate the work. Careful planning, imaginative documentation and appropriate methods will result in more effective evaluation.

Discussion Points

- What is the difference between documentation and evaluation?
- Read the Chapter 7 comments by audience members and participants who had taken part in performance events. How useful are these in evaluating community dance work?

Note

1. The Johari Window is a tool for understanding and developing self-awareness. Further information can be found at http://www.businessballs.com/.

17 Project Coordination
Diane Amans

If you are a community dance artist who also acts as project coordinator you will find that this chapter gives a comprehensive overview of your responsibilities in managing the work. There is a checklist with prompt questions and details of two actual projects showing the very different ways in which practitioners develop projects from an initial idea through to delivery and evaluation. The chapter includes:

- *Writing a proposal and developing the project*
- *Costing and managing budgets*
- *Publicity*
- *Risk management and duty of care*
- *Administration and record keeping*
- *Partnership working*
- *Documentation and report writing*
- *Managing endings*

Delivering community dance involves far more than writing session plans and carrying out evaluations. The project coordinator has to manage all aspects of the work from the beginning through to writing a final report. Sometimes practitioners take on both roles – they are dance artist and coordinator. In other cases, for instance when artists are working for a dance agency, they may have a line manager who acts as project coordinator.

The following questions will usually have to be answered before any dance project takes place, though in some cases the questions have been dealt with before the project coordinator becomes involved. Even so, it is important to be clear about your 'ideal situation' so that if you are involved from the beginning you know what you are aiming for and where you are prepared to compromise. If the project structure has already been established it may still be possible (or necessary) to suggest changes. This checklist will focus your planning and signpost you to sources of help.

Project coordinator checklist

- **Aims** What is the purpose of the project? Who decides? Are you working for an organisation which has set clear aims for the project or will you need to suggest aims? Perhaps the project is your idea and you have aims in mind. Why have you chosen these?

- **Participants** Who will take part in the project? How many? Is there an existing group? If so, what are their interests? How active are they? Do you have any say in who takes part? What criteria will you use to decide on the make up of the group?

- **Schedule** How many sessions? How long is each session? What time of day is best? If it is a health/social care/residential setting, check for clashes with established activities (such as bingo) or community visitors such as hair-dresser or chiropodist.

- **Venue** Have you a choice? What type of floor/furniture/ventilation? Can you get into the venue before the start time? What happens just before/just after the session? Will this impact on your work? Are there facilities for refreshments?

- **Content** It may be that the project aims determine the dance form, but, if that is not the case, what type of dance would be most appropriate? How will you decide what to do/where to start? Will the participants prefer set dances or improvisation? Will there be icebreaker activities? What is the best way to warm up the group?

- **People management** As project coordinator you will need effective people skills to manage interactions with a wide range of people. You are responsible for ensuring that everyone directly involved in the project is clear about roles and understands what will take place in the sessions. If you are not actually leading the dance sessions, how will you liaise with the lead artist? How much support does he/she need? Who else is involved? Who are the partners you will be working with? Have you established clear lines of communication? The people skills that are important here are the ability to build relationships, listen effectively and be able to adapt your communication style to suit various situations.

- **Equal opportunities/inclusion** Does the planned project take account of the different needs of those involved? Have you taken steps to make sure you are not excluding any potential participants without good reason? Will you accept all comers? Are there any issues relating to access/diversity/inclusion? Sometimes we can unwittingly exclude people by the way we recruit partici-pants for a project. Think about how people find out about your activities and have a look at the make-up of your group. Does it reflect the diversity of the local population? Perhaps it doesn't, and you have made well-considered decisions about targeting a particular section of the community. Check the dates to make sure there are no clashes with key faith festivals or other important events. Make sure that you are aware of any considerations relating to dress, food and drink. The Shap Calendar of Religious Festivals has information about key dates for different world religions – see contact details in the Resources section.

- **Publicity** Are you responsible for this? If so how will you publicise the project? Do you need to make any presentations? Is there a budget for leaflets or adverts in newspapers? Is information written in clear, jargon-free language? Will you be using images? If so, do you have consent to use them?

- **Duty of care** What do you need to do to take care of the people on the project? Will you carry out a Health and Safety questionnaire? Who will take responsibility for this? Will it be done before the project or at the first session? Where will the information be stored? Have you done a risk assessment on venue and activities? Have you discussed existing controls and precautions with all staff involved? It may be that the host organisation has carried out a risk assessment on the venue, but you still need to look at possible hazards in the context of dance sessions. Will you be working with children, young people or vulnerable adults? If so you will need to consider **safeguarding** issues. As project coordinator you have a duty of care to participants, staff, yourself and the general public. The Resources section has sample Health and Safety questionnaires and Risk Assessments, and Chapter 6 has further information on duty of care issues.

- **Insurance** Does the project have adequate insurance cover? Have you seen artists' certificates of insurance? Does the venue have **public liability insurance** cover?

- **Resources/music/materials** Do you need to buy/borrow any resources? Will you be using music? If so do you need a licence? (See Resources section for information on music copyright.) If you want to use your own CD player you may need to check whether the venue requires it to be PAT tested by their health and safety staff[1].

- **Liaison with partners** How will you report on the project? Do you need to have meetings with host organisation/arts officers/funders/anyone else? Have you allowed time for this and costed it into the budget?

- **Documentation** As with all other aspects of the project, documentation needs to be considered at the planning stage because there are resource implications. Part of your role is to discuss this with your partners and suggest appropriate methods of documentation to suit the budget. If you decide to involve photography or video you will need to organise consent forms (see Resources section for an example consent form.) If the documentation is to be shared with participants it needs to be in a format which is accessible for them. On the other hand, if it is to accompany an evaluation report to demonstrate that the aims have been achieved, it will need to bring the project alive for funders and others who may not have witnessed it. You may decide to involve a visual artist to make paintings or drawings of your project. Bisakha Sarker, a dancer working in a wide range of community contexts, often involves artist Noelle Williamson who paints as participants respond to Bisakha's dance ideas. The paintings in Figure 17.2 were made during a dance session in a hospital waiting room. Bisakha used the paintings in her illustrated report of the project. There was no problem with gaining consent as patients can not be identified in the paintings – and works of art have been created in the process. (Many patients came back to see the paintings when they were finished).

■ **Monitoring** What records will you be keeping? How will information be collected? Who needs to receive monitoring information? Where will you store the information? Many organisations which fund projects ask for information about participants – such as gender, ethnicity, age, postcode, and whether there are any disabled people involved. It is worth knowing as early as possible which details are needed for a final report.

Figure 17.1 Bisakha Sarker (*Simon Richardson*)

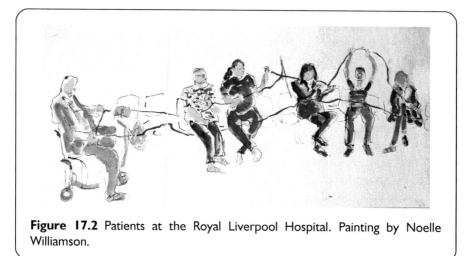

Figure 17.2 Patients at the Royal Liverpool Hospital. Painting by Noelle Williamson.

- **Evaluation** What will you be evaluating and what methods will you be using? Will there be an external evaluator? Have you costed this into your budget? Chapter 16 looks in some detail at evaluation methods.
- **Celebration/final session** Is this definitely the end or might there be a follow-up project at some future date? Whatever the circumstances, the challenge for the project coordinator is to find a way to make the last day special and end on a positive note[2].
- **Mentoring/support for you** Do you need any specific help/advice? Will you need support? Have you created opportunities to discuss the practice with a mentor? Do you think this is important? Have you costed it into the budget?

Case Study 1: Project with Older People

In this first case study the artist leading the dance sessions was also the project coordinator. Amanda Rosario, a dance artist, was approached by Tamesbridge local authority arts officer James Sheikh, who wanted to set up a pilot community dance programme for older people in the borough. James was keen to promote arts and health programmes and was very proactive in developing partnerships with health, social care, charities and voluntary agencies. Amanda had recently completed a training course in leading dance activities with older people.

After an initial meeting Amanda prepared the following proposal and presented it to a meeting of the local Healthy Living Partnership who were interested in funding the venture.

Proposal for a Pilot Community Dance Programme in Tamesbridge

Aims
1. To create opportunities for older people in Tamesbridge to join in dance activities regardless of ability
2. To document and evaluate benefit to participants with particular reference to the impact on health

It is proposed that this community dance project be delivered in 3 × 6 week blocks to three different groups of older people in Tamesbridge. For example:

1. Fit over-fifties living independently
2. More dependent older people who attend a day centre but still live in their own homes
3. residents in sheltered housing or similar

The project will include 18 dance sessions for up to 45 local people. The sessions will be facilitated by a lead artist and a co-leader, both of whom have attended training courses in leading dance with older people. Sessions will include warm-ups, breathing exercises, relaxation and a range of dance activities. The objectives of each session will be to improve mobility and strength and to offer opportunities for individuals to express themselves creatively through dance. At the end of the dance sessions there will be light refreshments; artist and co-leader will take responsibility for organising these and facilitating the social interaction between participants.

The programme will include a range of activities and dance styles and the evaluation methods will incorporate feedback discussion and the completion of simple wellbeing questionnaires to monitor the impact on participants.

An illustrated evaluation report will be provided within two weeks of the end of the project.

In her presentation Amanda showed a brief DVD of dance work with older adults and described some ideas for recruiting participants – running taster sessions in day centres, circulating leaflets and fliers to GP surgeries, supermarkets, churches, bingo halls etc.

The members of the partnership were impressed with Amanda's presentation and they offered to provide assistance with marketing and other support where possible. They agreed a budget and requested that the project be launched with three taster sessions in the town hall as part of the Falls Prevention Awareness Day which was due to take place in a month's time. Weekly sessions would begin two weeks after the taster sessions.

Costing and Managing Budgets

The costing for the project included fees for artists and co-leaders, costs of materials, publicity, photography and refreshments. Amanda also included a fee for coordinating and managing the project and charged for time to produce an illustrated evaluation report. Venue hire was supplied as in-kind support by the Healthy Living Partnership.

Amanda was responsible for managing the budget, which came from a local authority grant. The fee, in two instalments, was paid direct to the artist who trades under the name 'Horos Dance'. All costs, including the co-leader's fee, were paid from the Horos Dance account[3]. In costing the project Amanda allowed for the development time which took place before the work was even agreed:

One month to go till the project begins – the artist coordinator has so far spent 14 hours on the project:

Initial phone call with Arts Office, including 10 minutes writing notes	0 h 30 min
Preparation for proposal	2 h
Presentation to Healthy Living Partnership (inc. travel)	2 h 30min
Development work – recruiting a co-leader, visits to venues, liaison with Health and Social Care staff	7 h
Preparation and circulation of publicity material, writing copy for newsletter	2 h

Publicity

The project was publicised via leaflets, announcements in the local press and posters on community notice boards. Amanda provided copy for all the publicity material; the arts officer and other members of the Healthy Living Partnership took responsibility for circulating information amongst sheltered housing associations and other organisations which provide services for older people. At the Falls Awareness Day people were encouraged to take part in or watch the taster sessions and everyone attending received information about the forthcoming dance sessions.

Risk Assessment

Amanda carried out a risk assessment at the town hall and the three proposed venues: Sheltered Housing Complex, Day Centre and Leisure Centre. One of the proposed venues (a residents' lounge) had very limited space, large heavy chairs and a glass-fronted display cabinet. Amanda felt the room was not really suitable for a dance session, but the warden was very keen to motivate her rather frail residents to take part in some form of exercise. The artist agreed to run six chair-based dance sessions for a maximum of ten residents and the warden agreed to move the display cabinet into a different lounge.

At the taster sessions the falls prevention team took responsibility for asking each participant if there were any health issues that the artist needed to be aware of. Amanda delivered a very gentle session and whenever there were activities which were not chair-based – for example partner work – she divided the group into smaller groups which she and the co-leader could safely manage. The remaining participants watched until it was their turn.

Before the six-weekly project began at the three venues, all participants completed a health and safety questionnaire and signed to say they agreed to inform the artist of any issue affecting their ability to take part safely in the session. In the event there were a few extra people enrolling on the first day at each venue. The artist and co-leader went through the questionnaire with them before the session starts. At one of the venues there was a woman who had a number of health problems, and had recently been diagnosed with cancer. Amanda was happy for the woman to watch the session, but asked her to get her doctor's advice before taking part[4]. The woman took a copy of the questionnaire and her doctor countersigned it.

Administration and Record Keeping

Administration for the project included liaison with key partners, completion of forms for the finance division to release funding, sending a letter of contract to the co-leader and photographer, collecting details of participants (names addresses and monitoring information such as postcodes and ethnicity) and keeping a register of attendance. This was all carried out by Amanda who also recorded her risk assessment and the steps she had taken to reduce risk.

There also needed to be signed consent forms for the photographs which were taken during the fourth week of the project. The artist prepared the forms, which were signed during the refreshment break at the end of the sessions.

Partnership Working

During the course of the project Amanda had communication with the following people:

- Co-leader
- Arts Officer
- Healthy Living Partnership (nine members)
- Falls Prevention Team (four members)
- Warden and assistant warden at sheltered housing
- Day Centre Manager

- Leisure Centre Manager
- Caretakers and cleaners at two of the venues (four in total)
- 48 participants (including taster days and weekly sessions)
- Support staff to assist with refreshments (six in total, five of whom joined in the sessions)
- Photographer

So, in addition to the participants, there were 78 other people involved in this short project. As coordinator Amanda was responsible for making sure that individual needs and wishes were recognised and that everyone involved was satisfied.

Documentation and Report Writing

Amanda documented session plans and the evaluation which was completed in a short meeting with the co-leader after every session. Any comments by staff and participants were recorded in the project diary together with the results of feedback discussions which took place during refreshment breaks every week. There was a demand, from participants, for the sessions to be continued and the arts officer agreed to explore possible sources of future funding.

The illustrated project report was written during the week following the last sessions. It was a 10 page document detailing the background to the project, list of aims, evaluation of the sessions in each venue, comments by participants, final conclusions and recommendations for the future. Photographs were included in the main body of the report with additional photographs in an appendix.

Amanda was only asked to provide two copies of the report, but she decided to produce ten copies – one for the arts officer and one each for members of the Healthy Living Partnership. She did this because it was likely to be used as an advocacy document to promote the work and all members of the group had shown considerable interest during the project.

Managing Endings

Although it was hoped that the sessions could be started again at a future date, the original pilot project in each venue lasted only six sessions. Amanda made the last sessions special by introducing a celebratory circle dance and giving an opportunity for everyone to request their favourite dance activities from the project. She and the co-leader also brought cakes and fresh fruit kebabs to share with the group. Whilst participants clearly appreciated the efforts to create a special atmosphere, they expressed disappointment and frustration because the classes were ending after such a short time.

Case Study 2: Intergenerational Performance Project

Marco was commissioned to create a site-specific dance piece to be performed by cross-generational community performers at a July street festival. He decided to act as artistic director and project coordinator and invited a guest choreographer to create the dance piece.

The arts organisation which commissioned the work asked for a dance that challenged stereotypes and celebrated diversity. The project began in May when Marco brought together a new group of dancers from widely different backgrounds. He drew on his various contacts in the community and found ten dancers aged seven years to 82 years who were prepared to take part in something new. One of the dancers was a performing arts student and three of the children attended Saturday dance classes. The adults in the group had never performed for an audience.

Marco organised an intensive rehearsal week during the school half-term holidays and then seven evening rehearsals once a week. The intensive week took place in the dance studio of a college and the weekly rehearsals were held at a hotel close to the site of the summer festival. The week before the performance there was a dress rehearsal on site. The choreographer, Bernie, worked closely with both Marco and the participants, incorporating their ideas into a witty 12 minute dance which delighted the performers and everyone who watched it.

On the day of the street festival the group performed three times to large audiences who gathered in the town square close to the shopping centre. They had changing facilities in the upstairs room of a local bar and between performances they returned there to relax and eat lunch. During these rest times each performer was interviewed about their experiences on the project and their comments recorded using a digital camera. This was done as part of the project documentation organised by Marco.

Project Coordination

This was a complex project to organise – the coordinator's tasks included:

- recruiting participants and arranging for their transport to and from rehearsals
- carrying out risk assessments on venues
- liaison with participants, parents, choreographer, festival organisers, support worker, publicity staff, costume maker, video artist, photographer
- sourcing costumes and props
- ensuring the safety and comfort of participants
- ensuring security of props and participants' possessions during performance
- booking space for rehearsals
- securing signed consent forms for photographs and video use

- ongoing reviews with choreographer, including choice of music and costumes
- ongoing reviews with participants
- providing copy for publicity
- managing the budget
- documenting the project and writing an evaluation report

Marco attended most of the rehearsals and took advantage of opportunities to chat with the performers and their parents. This meant that he was aware of ongoing feedback about the project and was able to deal promptly with any queries and concerns. Bernie was free to focus on the choreography as she knew Marco shared responsibility for taking care of the individual and group needs.

Marco compiled an evaluation report using feedback from performers, parents, choreographer, audience members, festival staff and other artists who attended the festival. He illustrated the report with photographs taken by the photographer he had invited to attend the dress rehearsal. The report was sent to the arts organisation which commissioned the dance.

Challenges – Dealing with the Unexpected

Marco is an experienced project coordinator who plans his work well but, like most projects, this one presented a few challenges. These were mostly relating to risk management and duty of care. First of all there were safeguarding considerations, as the participants included children and young people under 18 years old. Marco met with parents before the first session and it was agreed that a parent or other carer would accompany the children at all times. Just before the third rehearsal a seven-year-old girl was dropped off at the front door of the hotel by a parent who returned to collect her two hours later. Another parent, who did accompany the child to rehearsals, was happy for her daughter to go unaccompanied to the public toilets in the hotel foyer. On both these occasions Marco had to deal with different expectations and boundaries with regard to duty of care. As project coordinator he had to insist that people complied with the safeguarding measures he had put in place.

Another duty of care challenge occurred in relation to managing the pace of rehearsals. The adults, some of whom were aged over 60, needed a slower pace and more frequent rest periods than the children. However, they did not always like to admit they were feeling tired, and Bernie, who led the rehearsals, assumed everyone was comfortable if they did not say anything to the contrary. After the first two rehearsals Marco insisted that there were more frequent breaks during which people rested, discussed costumes, made an entry in the diary or worked in pairs to talk through their duets. Several of the older adults mentioned that they were glad the practical sessions now included a chance to 'catch their breath'. They had all

Figure 17.3 Freedom in Dance Big Dance 2006 rehearsal (*Matthew Priestley*)

been struggling a little but had not wanted to be the one to ask for a break – despite the fact that Bernie had made it very clear she was happy to stop when anyone felt they needed to. In reviewing the rehearsals with Marco, Bernie said this was a valuable lesson for her. In future intergenerational projects she will take particular care to think of ways in which the different energy levels might be managed.

On the day of the performance Marco was disappointed that there was very little technical support from the festival organisers – despite the fact that they had promised two members of staff. In the event there were insufficient stewards and Marco was thankful that he had brought along his friend, Sam, who was able to move props on and off stage, look after performers' valuables and carry out various other last minute tasks.

Marco thought he had considered every possible hazard when he carried out the risk assessment for the project. He had not predicted that members of the public might show their appreciation by throwing coins at the performers! Fortunately no one was injured and, together with Sam, he was able to intervene promptly.

The End of the Project

After the final performance the group gathered for a drink in the changing room, where Marco gave Bernie a thankyou gift and each of the participants a celebration card containing photographs which had been taken at the dress rehearsal. They were all invited to come together in September and view a DVD of the performance. All but two of the performers attended this informal gathering, which took place in the dance studio where they had previously rehearsed.

Lessons Learned

Both these case studies are examples of successful projects which were well managed by experienced practitioners. However, in evaluating their work both Amanda and Marco identified areas where they could improve their practice.

Amanda now takes particular care not to raise any unrealistic expectations about projects continuing beyond the initial pilot period. Although she had told participants that it was a six-week project, she also mentioned that the Arts Officer was seeking further funding and it was hoped the sessions could continue. If a similar situation arose in the future she has decided to 'play down' the possibility of sessions carrying on. She also considered ways of helping the Healthy Living Partnership find funding, as the Arts Officer moved to another local authority shortly after the end of the project.

The main lesson that Marco learned was to recruit an additional 'pair of hands' for the performance day: someone who knows the dance piece and is available to carry out errands at short notice. Although he did have a number of people in his team – parents, choreographer and the costume maker – he and Sam found it exhausting to deal with the technical support as well as making sure the performers were in the right place. In future he will make sure he has funding to hire dedicated technical support for his project – regardless of whether the organisation hosting the event say that staff are available.

Conclusion

These two case studies offer a flavour of the very different types of work which are managed by community dance artists. In both these examples the projects were initiated by external agencies, but there are plenty of opportunities for practitioners who want to develop their own proposals. If you have an idea for a project you could approach a dance agency, your local authority arts officer or any appropriate community partnership. Alternatively, you could create your own project and apply for funding from one of the grant awarding bodies that fund community groups[5].

Exercise

Think about a dance project that you would like to run. Come up with a project outline describing the project. This would include aims, target group, duration, venue etc. Really let your imagination go and devise your dream project.

- How would you go about setting up this project?
- Who could you approach to fund it?
- Write a proposal with a timetable of activities
- Produce a costing for the project
- Identify key tasks and who would be responsible for carrying out these tasks
- Produce a draft flyer to market the project
- Identify any issues which need clarification

Notes

1. The government Health and Safety Executive (HSE) issues guidance in relation to electrical compatibility. Most public organisations have a health and safety policy which requires all portable electrical appliances to be tested.
2. The Resources section contains ideas for creating celebrations and special occasions.
3. The artist set up the dance company in order to be eligible for a wider range of funding. It has a management group of four and all cheques are countersigned by one of the named signatories.
4. Exercise is contraindicated for some forms of cancer.
5. Contact your local community and voluntary services group for information about funding opportunities; details from http://www.ncvo-vol.org.uk/.

18 Challenges and Tension Lines

Diane Amans

In this book I have explored some of the challenges and tension lines associated with community dance practice. There is the ongoing debate about terminology: should there be a separate term for community dance and, if we use the term, what exactly do we mean by it? Sara Houston argues that, provided 'there is identification with the ideals for which community dance stands', then the term 'community dance' is valid.

Several contributors mention the distinction between 'community' and 'professional' dance, with its implicit hierarchy of aesthetics and performance standards. For example, Adam Benjamin talks about 'accomplished performers 'and 'higher levels of excellence' when he describes how CandoCo developed into a professional company. Benjamin acknowledges that, although the company had moved away from 'immediate accessibility', it would, hopefully, go on to 'spread ideas of participation and involvement to an ever-widening audience'.

Rosemary Lee also refers to these labels ('professional', 'non-professional' and 'community') and explains that she tries to ignore such divisions as they influence the way the audience views the performance. Regardless of context, Lee wants all her work 'to be considered critically as art' and doesn't want people to look at it with 'different eyes'. The challenge for community choreographers is to present dance performance in such a way as to avoid perpetuating divisions between a community/professional aesthetic.

In reading about Lee's working practice I reflected on another tension line in community dance – the extent and nature of interventions by the dance artist. As community dance practitioners we *are* interventionist, and some chapters in this book give an insight into the kind of interventions dance artists make. Lee thinks carefully about the way she works with a group and talks of 'treading a line between responding to the participant and responding to my artistic imperatives'.

Similarly, Helen Poynor talks of tuning in to the mood of the group before deciding on an intervention – whether to support a quiet, gentle exploration or to initiate something more energetic. These are examples of flexible practitioners who are ready to adapt their plans in response to feedback from the group. Poynor highlights the importance of self-awareness: if practitioners have an awareness of their own 'preferences and blind spots' they are more likely to support individuals to engage in dance in a way which is meaningful for them.

How do people gain the skills to work in this way? Can we train people to have self-awareness? As Sue Akroyd points out, skills can be nurtured and developed throughout one's career as a community dance artist. Self-awareness skills, as described by Poynor and Lee, encompass observation skills, noticing one's own behaviours and impulses, and checking that one is 'reading' other people accurately. These skills can certainly be learned and practised; ideally they will be combined with a fundamental interest in other people and a commitment to support them in achieving their potential as dancers.

Louise Katerega's story illustrates how she helped someone achieve his potential – again by thinking carefully about her own interventions. She raises some interesting issues about power relationships in participatory dance practice. Community dance artists have considerable power to influence not only the content of the sessions' activities but also the extent to which people feel able to make connections with the dance, and with other dancers. The way practitioners use their power – in other words their leadership behaviours – will determine whether or not a community dance project reflects the core values outlined in Chapter 1.

One of these core values is inclusive practice, and Katerega and Benjamin both describe their roles in relation to integrated performance projects which involve disabled and non-disabled dancers. Benjamin talks of the choreographer creating the best situation in which all these diverse people can thrive'. He encourages high standards whilst making sure he doesn't make unrealistic demands of performers. Katerega reveals how she supported integrated practice by withdrawing and taking a 'back seat' with a group who were accustomed to her leadership. This made it easier for a disabled choreographer to work effectively with the group without ambiguities surrounding who was directing the piece.

Benjamin and Katerega have many years of varied experience in community dance. Alan Martin, a relative newcomer to the profession, has had a very different route into the dance world. As a participant and a workshop leader he describes his experiences from the perspective of a disabled man and challenges practitioners to think about planning inclusive activities in *all* their sessions. This doesn't mean we have to simplify everything in case it presents a barrier – we just need to have open structures and flexible delivery methods, rather than hastily adding on an 'accessible' activity if a disabled dancer turns up. Disability equality legislation requires us to be able to make 'reasonable adjustments'[1] – this is something that community dance artists are doing every day. We don't do it because the law says we should, but because it's consistent with our defining values.

These values and principles are shaped by contact with other practitioners, professional development activities and our openness to new experiences. They are the 'glue' which binds together a very diverse profession. As long as we have dialogue with other practitioners, and carry on debating our practice, we will continue to evolve a shared ownership of our professional standards and a broad agreement about what we mean by 'good practice'.

For me, the 'community voices' in Chapter 3 highlight some of the elements which characterise community dance:

- accessible opportunities for people to engage in dance in a way which is meaningful for them
- celebration of diversity
- the experience of feeling valued
- magical, 'transformative' moments

I expect many practitioners can identify with the so called 'transformative moments'. I wonder how many artists can also relate to the challenge of recreating these moments for an audience: supporting dancers to perform in the embodied way they did during the making process. Live performance can be a thrilling experience for the dancers and the audience. At the other end of the tension line it can be full of stress and anxiety, thus making it an inappropriate experience for some performers.

There are many ways of celebrating achievement and sharing work with others; performing to a live audience is only one of them. A resourceful practitioner will be able to consult with the group and find a way which best meets their needs.

Community dance is a complex activity and dance artists need to be able to tune in to the needs of individual participants and the demands of partners in other sectors. It is also important to retain the focus on dance as an art form and make opportunities for nourishing ourselves as artists. This is just as important as continuing to update our skills. I hope that this book will have provided food for thought and some practical guidance. The Resources section, which follows, signposts you to further sources of information and support.

Notes

1. This refers to the Disability Discrimination Act 1995. The Commission for Equality and Human Rights website has information on this: http://www.equalityhumanrights.com/.

Resources

Duty of Care Quiz Answers – Chapter 6, Exercise 1

1. You have a duty of care to:
   - the people who come to your activity session
   - anyone you work with (colleagues, support workers),
   - anyone you employ
   - yourself
2. A vulnerable adult is a person who is, or may be, in need of community care services because of mental disability, age or illness, and who is, or who may be, unable to take care of themselves or unable to protect themselves against significant harm or exploitation.
3. No – artists are advised that they should not act in loco parentis or work with children, young people or vulnerable adults without the appropriate teachers, youth workers carers or other legally responsible staff present.
4. Risk assessment is a technique for preventing accidents and ill health by helping people to think about what could go wrong and ways to prevent problems. Some structures for risk assessment and action are included in the Resources section.
5. Insurance is a complex area and you should satisfy yourself that you have adequate cover for your work. Most organisations expect freelance practitioners to hold public liability cover and will ask to see a copy of your certificate of insurance. Public liability insurance covers a legal claim being made by someone other than an employee for accidental injury or damage caused by defect in the premises or equipment which it is your (or your employer's) responsibility to maintain. If you are working for an organisation which has its own building (for example a school) you are likely to be covered by their insurance. If you are hiring a building it is likely that the letting body will want you to use your own public liability.
6. The CRB Disclosure is a document containing information held by the police and government departments such as the Department of Health and the Department for Education and Skills. The check is carried out by the Criminal Records Bureau and helps employers and voluntary organisations make

safer recruitment decisions for positions that involve regular contact with children, young people and vulnerable adults.

7. In youth work practice the ratio of legally responsible adults to children/young people tends to be 1:8 regardless of age. The Arts Council recommends that a minimum of two people with legal responsibility are present at all times and that children under 8 are supervised all the time.

The above answers are taken from the Arts Council publication 'Keeping arts safe' and the Duty of Care guidelines issued by Pathway of the Biscuit training consultancy.

Diane's Top Tips for Community Dance Artists

- Learn and use people's names.
- Allow time for icebreakers and name games – even when participants know each other.
- Check that you don't talk too much when trying to engage people in dance.
- Think about how you might make each of your activities easier or more challenging.
- Practise careful observation – we receive non-verbal feedback all the time. We need to become skilled at noticing it and checking out that we are reading the feedback correctly.
- Encourage people to give you feedback – see it as a gift.
- Collaborate with other artists – including those from other art forms. This will nourish your creativity and help prevent burnout.
- Make time for yourself to dance – whether it's in class or at home with the furniture pushed back.
- Go and see a wide variety of dance performances.
- If you haven't already done so, create a separate dance bag or box which stays packed with a range of music and props – a sort of emergency pack in case you have to lead a session at short notice.
- Always have a variety of music with you for when you sense the need to change the energy in the room.
- Be clear about what you can offer. Think about your skills and competencies – what are you qualified for and capable of doing?.
- Be proactive – make your ideas happen!

Inclusive Practice – Interview with Caroline Bowditch

Caroline Bowditch is a performer and choreographer who is renowned for making work which challenges and delights audiences. In 2006 she created *Elevation*, a site-specific piece for Trafalgar Square as part of Liberty, the UK's largest disability rights festival.

The following is an extract from an email conversation between Diane Amans and Caroline Bowditch in 2007.

Q What do you understand by 'inclusive practice'?

A I think inclusive practice is one of those things that we all strive for but have real difficulty in achieving, for very good reason. I think it is the idea that we are able to offer classes or sessions that are so open in their structure and

Caroline Bowditch (*Kenny Bean, courtesy of Scottish Dance*)

delivery that they are accessible to everyone – from beginners to people with loads of experience, for people of all abilities and backgrounds. And that these are the classes that every participant leaves feeling they've thoroughly enjoyed, been challenged by and have had their expectations fulfilled. There are some community practitioners that come closer to achieving this than others.

I think there are two main points that come to my mind when thinking about delivering in an inclusive way:

1. The practitioner runs the risk of losing the specificity of a session because they feel it has to be somehow made more general or simplified so that as many people as possible can participate.
2. Workshop session leaders, unless they have an on-going relationship with participants, are less likely to really push people that they feel may be struggling in the class for fear of offending them in some way – this happens frequently to disabled participants.

Q Should community dance classes be open to everyone?
A This is a hard question to answer but I suppose I would say yes and no. There are advantages and disadvantages on both sides. I also think that not all community classes are open to everyone even when they state they are, due to many of the points I mentioned above. People also self-select – they go where they feel comfortable. I think this is not only about who is delivering the class but also about the attitudes of others who attend the class.

The advantages of all classes being open to everyone is that people have unlimited choice – everyone has the option to try everything or at least what they are interested in. I know, as a disabled dancer, how frustrating it is to read that such and such a class is only open to a specific group of people and in the past many of my options have been limited due to inaccessible spaces or inflexible attitudes of session leaders – although this happens more in professional settings rather community classes it must be said.

Inclusive Practice – Information Form for Non-Readers

Developed by Diane Critchley for DIY Theatre Group in Salford

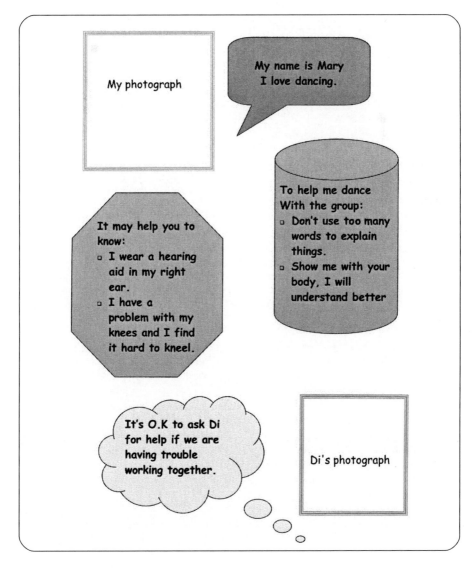

Time Management – Some Tips for Making the Best Use of Your Time

Make a 'to-do' list for your day and prioritise your tasks.

Start with a high priority task – even if you don't complete all of it.

Avoid putting off tasks that you find unpleasant or difficult.

They often turn out not to be as bad as you thought they were going to be. It might help to break them down into sections and treat yourself when you have completed a section.

Make time for tasks which are important.

Block off time in your diary and protect this time for its designated purpose.

Make time for you – to do the things you've always said you'd do if you only had the time.

Again, allocate time in your diary – and plan how you will spend this time. Protect this time, it is just as important as time for tasks.

Resist the temptation to spend time on non-urgent or trivial activities – unless that is how you have planned to spend your time.

Notice when you are engaging in displacement activities like rearranging the furniture, clearing out the top drawer, making unnecessary phone calls. If this is how you like to relax, allocate time for these activities and discipline yourself to stick to the task you had planned to do.

Organise your communication systems to suit your needs wherever possible

Switch your phone off if you need to focus on an important task. Plan time for people to reach you and for dealing with emails.

Give your self permission to say 'no'.

You don't have to please others or agree to take on another activity just because someone has asked you to.

Slow down and look at how you are spending your time. How could you make more time and reduce your stress?

Presentation Skills: Guidelines for Making An Effective Presentation

Prepare

Whether you are presenting to a large group or just describing your work to an individual think about what you want to say and structure it into a logical order.

Structure

Make notes and then condense these onto prompt cards/handouts/PowerPoint slides. (Even if you don't use the prompt cards you will remember your structure if you have written it down.)

Rehearse

Practise talking through your main points (in the car, in front of the bedroom mirror, to the cat!). You'll be more confident if you've talked it through a few times.

Relax

Practise relaxing and check your posture and facial expression for tension (it's really useful to see a video of yourself in these kinds of situations – you soon realise where your tension is).

During a Presentation

- Smile
- Make eye contact
- Modulate your voice more than usual (though not too much)
- Pitch your voice to the person at the back

- Pause at key points or visual aids
- Take less time than you said you would
- Use attention joggers (saying someone's name, change pace, have a short discussion)
- Get feedback from someone you trust

Suggestions for Music

Selecting music to use in participatory dance work is a matter of personal choice and experienced practitioners usually compile their own eclectic mix of music which works for them. It is important to have a range of sounds which can be used to support different styles and themes – it is also important to use music which you personally find inspiring. Participants are often happy to share their music choices and some will bring along music which makes them want to move.

The following music has been used by dance artists in a variety of community settings. I suggest you use this list as a starting point and add to it as you find music which works for you.

Discography

Guitar Music for Small Rooms	Warner Brothers WTVD 61360
The Dance of Heaven's Ghosts	EMI Premier 7243 8 55644 2 0
Buena Vista Social Club	World Circuit WCD 050 LC2339
Billy Cowie: *El Punal entra en el Corazon**	Divas Records
Philip Glass: *Songs from Liquid Days**	Sony SX2K89745
Pascale Comelade:	*Un Samedi sur la Terre**
Rondo Veniziano: *Odissea Veneziana*	BMG Music
Sacred Spirit	Virgin Records 7243 8 40945 2 2
Cirque du Soleil: *Quidam**	RCA Victor 0 90266 86012 8
Michael Nyman: *Drowning by Numbers**	Virgin Records
Erotokritos	General Publishing Company 5 202483 496621
Ludovico Einaudi: *Fuori dal Mondo**	BMG Classics
The Casablanca Steps: *Stepping Out*	BJP CD 008
Adam Bird: *Springs 1 &2*	Peanut Productions
Christopher Benstead: *Music For Dance*	
Michael Price: *Contemporary Dance Music* Vol.3	TCR- CD003
Portishead: *Dummy*	Go! Discs Ltd 828 522-2
Jean Michel Jarre: *Images*	Disques Dreyfus 01487378 2

Nina Simone: *Feeling Good*	Polygram 522 669-2
Funkrock Compilation:	Barely Breaking Even Records BBECD040
So Frenchy So Chic 2005*	Shock Records/Filter Music
JABADAO:	*Where I Be* (Music for Early Years) CD6
JABADAO Stepping Out	*Golden Oldies* CD7

*Film/Performance Soundtrack

Information on Use of Sound Recordings in Dance Work

Music Copyright

You are advised to check out music copyright and performing rights where you are intending to use recorded music. There are a number of issues which need to be considered, and you can find out further information from:

British Music Rights
020 7306 4446
http://www.bmr.org/

Performing Rights Society
020 7580 5544
http://www.prs.co.uk/

Mechanical Copyright Protection Society
020 7534 1245
http://www.ppluk.com/

PPL (Phonographic Performance Limited) deals with licence applications for the public use of sound recordings in dance classes. You complete a form giving details of the number of classes you teach and the average annual attendance at these classes. Your annual tariff is calculated based on the number of people you teach. Further information and application forms are available from Phonographic Performance Limited, 1 Upper James Street, London, W1F 9DE, +44 (0) 207 534 1000.

Celebrations and Special Occasions

Here are some cheap and simple ways of creating a special atmosphere. It may be that you want to celebrate the end of a project, a birthday, anniversary or special festival days celebrated by people of different faiths. Aim to surprise and delight – even if you just take one or two of these ideas.

Decorating the Space
Transform an ordinary room with some of the following:
- Unusual lighting – coloured lamps, fairy lights, candles in jars (careful if you have a very active group)
- Bunting flags made of crepe paper triangles stapled onto tape; make a more long lasting version by using fabric triangles and stitching them onto the tape
- Balloons and streamers
- Parachute suspended from the ceiling
- Fresh flowers – in jugs, petals in bowls, single blooms in glasses
- Posters – perhaps a theme which can be followed through in the dancing and food (e.g. a focus on a country such as Spain/India/Africa)

Food and Drink
- Exotic-looking fruit cocktails
- Bite-sized sandwiches with unusual fillings
- Cakes with a little message hidden in the bun case
- Food which celebrates a particular culture or country

If there is time you could involve participants in making some special food and decorating the tables.

- Make a display with fruit and salad – cut into fancy shapes if participants are safe with knives

- Have some messy fun decorating buns with tubes of ready made icing and a collection of tiny sweets and trimmings

Dance Activities

- Circle dance with all participants holding jars containing tea lights
- Improvisation with LED light sticks
- Dressing up clothes add that something extra – whatever the age group. Swirling circular skirts in bright satin fabric, feather boas, bells for wrists or ankles, silly hats, clown trousers and braces, boaters, walking sticks and bow ties

Little Gifts

Even with little or no budget you will be able to think of a way of giving everyone a small keepsake.

- Card with an individual or group photo
- Miniature box containing one or two chocolates
- Small plant or single flower
- Gift bag containing large cookie or piece of fruit with iced name on
- Poem rolled into a scroll and tied with ribbon

Celebrating Diversity and Making Sure Your Event is Inclusive

Check the dates of your special events to avoid clashes with key festivals and other important events. Find out about any considerations relating to dress, food and drink. Make sure your venue is accessible and user friendly – the project coordinator checklist will be helpful with this.

> The Shap Calendar of Religious Festivals has information about key dates for different world religions. Tel + 44 (0)20 789 81494 or search the net.

> The Festival Shop has an online catalogue of multifaith and multicultural resources which include DVDs and music together with fascinating ideas for activities: http://www.festivalshop.co.uk/.

Ideas for Creative Dance in Community Settings

My aim, in every dance session, is that the participants will enjoy movement and take pleasure in what their bodies can do. I also look for opportunities to 'make art' and I see it as part of my role to create an environment where people feel safe enough to try something different and express themselves without worrying about what it looks like to an 'outside eye'. If the group is going to perform their work at some stage I can support them to craft a piece which will be interesting for an audience to view. But first I want to help them enjoy *feeling* their bodies dance.

Sometimes I start in a fairly structured way and lead the group gently to more open-ended tasks. Whatever the context of my work – whether it is a one-off taster session, a regularly weekly group or a performance project – I try to establish a playful quality and a sense that there is no *wrong* way of responding.

Starting Points for Creative Dance Activities

Here are some examples of dance activities I have used many times. They are *starting points* and are not meant to be used in a prescriptive way. It is important to be prepared to share the leadership and pick up on ideas which come from members of the group.

I have divided them into the following sections:

- Introductory/warm-up activities
- Ideas for movement development
- Ideas for making dances
- Introduction to dance appreciation
- Ideas for closures

Each section begins with simple activities that are suitable for very young children and progresses through to ideas for older children and adults. With a few exceptions, though, I have used most of these ideas with dancers of all ages – with adaptations to suit different abilities and energy levels.

Introductory/Warm-Up Activities

Choose an activity that will focus group energy and help you gain the attention of all the participants.

- Walk into the movement space in a follow-my-leader line.
- Name game – roll ball to each child 'My name is Joe'.
- Name game – throw cushion/soft toy/puppet.
- Perform action rhymes, whilst seated round leader.
- Listen to music and encourage discussion. (What does it make you think of? Does it make you want to move slowly or quickly? Is it sleepy music/exciting music?)
- Talk about recent events (snow/bonfire night/a new pet) – all can be used as starting points for dance.
- Standing in a circle perform 'heads, tums, knees, feet' to rhythmic music (tap heads ×4, tap tums ×4, tap knees ×4, tap feet ×4). This activity can be extended to include other parts of the body and can be made more or less complex by varying the repetitions.
- Self massage – pat all over and focus on particular body parts.
- Circle clap – stand in a circle and establish a simple clapping rhythm (3 beats clapping, 3 beats rest). Leader encourages children to fill in rest pause by shaking different body parts.
- 'Beans' – leader calls out different beans runner/jumping/jelly/chilli/broad/baked beans and participants perform the actions: run/jump/wobble/shiver/make wide shape/lie down.
- Whole group makes an 'X' shape. Repeat with 'L' or any other letter – ending with 'O' if you want them in a circle for the next activity.
- Mexican wave with feet. All seated on the floor in a circle slowly lift feet one after the other round the circle. (Alternatively can be done using arms whilst seated.)
- Name game with rhythms. Clap rhythm of full name then say name. All join in and repeat rhythm.
- Name game move. Each person makes a gesture as they say their name. Everyone repeats name and gesture. This can be developed and used as a basis for making dances.
- Boogie Woogie warm up (with lively music). Leader demonstrates a move which is easy to copy and then passes on to the person next to them, who then leads a different move. It's OK to pass straight on to the next person if you can't think of a move or don't want to lead.

Ideas for Movement Development

- Small elastic – in twos skip round/jump up and down/make stretchy shapes.

- Statues – tiptoe slowly and freeze on tambourine beat.
- Statue shapes – as above but suggest 'wide/low/tall/twisted'.
- Circle statues – children tiptoe slowly and silently as leader taps triangle. When triangle stops children freeze.
- Movement to percussion – strong/shaky/still/melt. Leader beats rhythm on drum 1234 (fourth beat is stronger). Clap the rhythm so they recognise strong beat. Move around the room and stop in strong shape. Split into four groups in corners of the room. Move into the centre, one group at a time, making high and low strong shapes. When all groups are in the centre freeze and, on the beat of a triangle, melt to the floor.
- Newspaper accompaniment – tear the paper and make different moves to different sounds. Contrast sharp, jerky moves with longer, smooth moves. Let the children take turns at tearing the paper.
- Scarves – freeze and move. When the music plays make the scarf dance. Freeze like a statue when the music stops. Open fingers and let scarf fall to the floor. Create group dance by encouraging all those with blue scarves to come into the centre and make their scarves 'talk' to each other. Encourage dancers to improvise their own group scarf dances.
- Musical statues – adapt the rules to allow a dance structure to occur.
- Musical statues with a partner – A makes a shape and holds it. B moves around, over, under the statue. Change roles.
- Free movement around the space then one person stops in a shape. Everyone stops in same shape until all are still. After a moment's stillness any dancer can begin to move again.
- Mirroring – working with a partner, face each other and mirror movement without touching.
- Unison move – working in small groups, all face the same direction standing fairly close together in a diamond shape. Person at front begins to move slowly and others follow – as dancers slowly turn there is a new leader. Can be extended to include travelling.
- Floor patterns – move and stop. Move close to another person, round them, away from them. Move in straight lines, curved lines, zig-zag lines. Develop forwards/backwards/fast/slow/curved.
- Floor patterns from art work. Discuss lines and patterns in paintings, photographs, decorative arts and sculpture. Use these as a starting point for floor patterns in dance.

Ideas for Making Dances

- Dramatic themes – use a favourite story/poem/character as a stimulus for developing dance. Avoid asking children to *be* an animal/monster/Jack Frost

– encourage them to explore the movement qualities associated with the image.

■ Body shapes (angular, curved, twisted) – 4 counts get into shape/4 counts hold shape/4 counts travel in shape/4 counts return to neutral. Encourage clear transitions from one section to another.

■ ABC shape – working in threes, A makes a shape, B attaches to A and C attaches to AB shape. When all three are still A detaches and makes a new shape. B and C follow on as before. Develop by lengthening transitions.

■ Group sculpture – one person moves into centre and holds a shape, next person moves in and attaches to first. Continue until five or six dancers have formed a group shape. Give directions such as 'move only heads', 'slowly melt into a new group shape'. Participants can experiment in small groups to find different ways of moving in and out of a group sculpture.

■ Picture shapes – using paintings or photographs as a stimulus find two shapes and link them together. Work with a partner and learn each other's shapes. Move in unison... position 1 (4 counts), position 2 (4 counts) and so on.... Develop by changing levels, direction, size of movement. Try incorporating mirroring/question and answer moves

■ Encourage free movement in the space and then respond to the following suggestions: stop/go/floor/contact. This will encourage a more varied range of movement. Dancers can try it in their own time with their own 'inner commands'.

Dance Appreciation

If dancers are encouraged to observe and discuss dance this will help extend their movement vocabulary and help them with making their own dances. In addition to watching each other in dance sessions, try to watch live and recorded dance to develop skills of dance appreciation. The following questions will help: *What?*(Body Action) *Where?* (Space) *How?* (Dynamics) *Who?* (Relationships).

Ideas for Closures

■ Shoulder rub – sit in a circle facing the back of the next person.

■ Sleeping lions – an old favourite and very good for calming excited children. Just lie down as still as you can.

■ Listen to music or poems and discuss ways they can be used for dance next time.

■ Relaxation on the floor or sitting in chairs.

■ Feedback discussion of work created and how it could be developed.

■ Drawing on sheets of paper or in books – just free expression with pastels or felt tip pens.

- Farandole dance – a linked line of dancers making a snaking track across the floor. (Works equally well as an introductory activity.)

Early Years Dance Activities

Anna Daly, Ludus Dance

Ludus's 'Mini Movers' sessions give parents/carers quality interactive time with their toddlers. Together they experience creative and expressive movement play, which is aimed at helping young children move with confidence, imagination and awareness.

Each session lasts approximately 45 minutes and includes the following:

- **Circle** (10 min)
  Focus the group, meet and greet, movement introduction in enclosed circle, recognise the group
- **Warm up** (5 min)
  Physical warm up, standing in circle, bigger movements
- **Space and travelling** (10 min)
  Expanding movements to cover the space, more speed and energy, running, jumping, rolling, turning. Directed travelling through the space together
- **Creative and partner work** (10 min)
  More creative movement play. Exploring the theme. Concentrating on partner work, play, trust, imagination. Less led, more improvisation work between parent and child
- **Game/song** (5 min)
  A quick, fun group game or song – can be related to theme
- **Re-focus and cool down** (5 min)
  Bring the group back together, calm the energy, recognise the group once more, 'goodbyes'

Mini Movers ideas

Circle
- Hello song
- Squeeze the bear – pass round circle, squeeze and say your name

- Stretching your arms up few times – then waving up to ceiling
- Crawling finger up to ceiling like spiders – turns into raindrops – hear raindrops on floor
- Raindrops again – starting high, feel raindrops on your head, shoulders, knees, to floor
- Shakes – shake hands dry – up, down, up, down, to one side, to other side, behind you
- Magic hands – stretch and close jazz hands
- Shake and freeze – shake whole body like a jelly (with sound effects) and then freeze all together. Repeat 4 times!
- Rub down – rub hands together, work way up body rubbing as warm up – feet, legs, knees, tummy, back, chest, (do Tarzan noise here!) shoulders, arms, don't forget elbows, hands then cheeks, chin, nose ears and eyebrows
- Hide behind hands and after count of three, pull scary tiger face to everyone – repeat 4 times!
- Small curled up shape – changes to grow and stretch as tall as you can. Repeat 3 times
- Crouched down and after count of three JUMP up into the air – repeat 3 times

Moving and travelling with large elastic

- Shakes and freezes with elastic
- Lift high and then low
- Bounce it with your arms
- Wrap it on your belly, knee, toes, head
- Rubber knees (plies)
- Balance with one leg in the circle, other leg
- Jumping up and down
- Stretch circle big – creep in to make circle small. Repeat
- Holding on with one hand – all go round in a circle. Repeat other way
- Lay elastic on floor – jump inside elastic and then outside – repeat
- Tread on the elastic following it all the way round in a circle
- Make the elastic very small into the middle and put away

Races

- Start at one end of the room
- 'Point to the ceiling, point to the floor, point to the windows, point to the door' – we are going to .... to the end of the floor
- Crawl one way
- Slide backwards one way

- Jump one way
- Roll one way

Creative section – playground theme

- Try out these movements recreating rides in a playground, SLIDE, SWING, ROUND & ROUND
- Slide – small person lying on the floor being gently pulled along the floor by their big person. Can be held by their hands or feet depending on which feels safer for them. Sliding around the floor in straight lines, wiggly lines, circles. Exploring movements and trust
- Swing – be careful of backs with this one, remind adults to bend knees and take care. 1. Adults can carry small person in cradle arms and swing from side to side. 2. Can also hold small person round middle and swing forward and back through wide legs and then from side to side
- Round & Round – 1. On the floor turning round on bottoms. 2. Standing up and turning round on spot. 3. Holding hands and turning round together. 4. Holding on with firm hand grip, big person can swing small person round & round turning on the spot. The grip can be changed to under the arms if preferred
- Once these movements have been practised separately, introduce some music and direct creative work with voice and ideas. Standing back to allow interactions

Focus activity with parachute

- Spread out and keep low to the floor – sitting down around the edges the grown ups make the parachute ripple like water
- Minis walk, crawl, roll and move on top
- After a while… keep parachute very still and everyone off
- Team effort – to make parachute go up and down and little people run around underneath – keep parachute going up and down
- After count of three, make big tent – go into parachute, tuck it under and sit on it!
- When inside – wriggle fingers and toes – sing Goodbye song and wave goodbye
- Lift parachute up, over heads and into middle of floor to collect

Planning a Dance Lesson

Everyone has their own way of planning and delivering a dance lesson. Here is an example structure which follows the Ludus Dance format and can be used as a guideline.

Structure of a Dance Lesson
1. Aims of the dance lesson
2. Warm-up
3. Introduction of movement material
4. Exploration and development of movement material
5. Composition
6. Appreciation
7. Evaluation

1. Aims of a Dance Lesson
A Ludus Dance lesson includes dual aims: *Movement Aims* and *Cognitive Aims*.

Movement Aims refer to the selected physical material which is to be explored and developed during the lesson.

Cognitive Aims refer to the thematic content, which explores the intellectual and emotional development of the selected theme.

Selecting Movement Aims
As teachers, we select material which is appropriate to the age and experience of the students. Introduce movement material which enables individuals to build up a broad vocabulary of movement, including body actions and use of specific body parts; exploring the use of the body in space; changing dynamics and rhythmic qualities; and the varied use of relationships.

Selecting Cognitive Aims

The selected cognitive aims for dance lessons relate to the Ludus show themes. The themes also tie in with Programmes of Study for PSHE at the appropriate Key Stages of the National Curriculum.

2. Warm-Up

The warm-up is designed to prepare the body and focus the mind ready for the activities that follow. Selected activities should include both travelling through the space (using whole body actions) as well as focused exercises on the spot, working with individual body parts. The aim of a warm-up is to develop strength, suppleness and stamina through raising the pulse rate and body temperature, developing mobility within the joints, warming the muscles and developing body strength. Safe body management is essential including attention to posture and alignment and exercise should build in terms of energy and complexity.

Select warm-up activities that relate to other activities later in the lesson.

Pupils should be made aware of the effects of exercise on the body. (Programmes of Study for PE in The National Curriculum Guidelines)

3. Introduction of the Movement Material

It is in this section that the physical skills are introduced in depth. The chosen movement aims are explored through creative tasks, allowing the students to extend their own movement vocabulary.

It is important to move the students from familiar movement patterns to more unfamiliar ones. A lesson generally focuses on opposing movement actions and qualities building balanced movement vocabulary for the students. (Gough, M. (1993) In Touch with Dance. Whitehorn Books)

This section can include a combination of open-ended tasks plus teacher-led taught material if appropriate.

4. Exploration and Development of Movement Material

Adequate time should be given in this section, where the students can develop the work introduced in the previous section through extended tasks. Students should be encouraged to select, refine and repeat their work, building more complex movement phrases and sequences. Work can be explored and developed when working with others, in pairs or in small groups.

5. Composition

The students should work towards a finished composition, regardless of length, which they have had time to practise and repeat. The composition should reflect both movement and cognitive aims. The dances can be solos, duos, trios or larger groups.

6. Appreciation

The 'performing' and observing of the dance compositions is important in terms of consolidating and evaluating how much understanding has taken place. Students should be carefully led by the teacher offering suggestions in terms of how the class might observe the work.

7. Evaluation

Evaluation by the teacher is important in terms of assessing how the aims of the lesson were achieved and what could be improved upon. Observations will feed into the planning of the next session.

Resources for Teachers of Dance in Schools

Ludus Dance Touring Company has produced resources which include DVDs, schemes of work and session plans for dance teachers in schools . If you have little experience of dance in education you will find that Gil Graystone's introductory material helps you connect with the National Curriculum Guidelines for Dance. If you are an experienced dance teacher you could use the main themes and ideas from the framework and devise your own creative developments.

Further information about Ludus Dance and their teaching resources is available from the website http://www.ludusdance.org/ or telephone 01524 389901.

Sample Session Plan – Key Stage 2

KS2

Trapped – A Dance Framework and Scheme of Work for KS2 – Ludus Dance

LESSON 1 – RECOGNISING EMOTIONS

COGNITIVE AIMS	To recognise basic emotions.
MOVEMENT AIMS	To create a short dance sequence inspired by different emotions. To explore different dynamics and use of space to help communicate the emotions. To acquire skills of teaching and learning from peers. To work both alone and in pairs.
WARM-UP (1)	Begin in a circle. Warm up the face with expressions to represent the following emotions: HAPPY, SAD, PROUD and SCARED. Discuss each of the feelings and ask students to think of a particular situation that might make us feel each of these emotions. Talk through a variety of movements and shapes and try them altogether as a class. Take the children's ideas and also suggest some of the following for the children to improvise with in each of the following ways: SAD = rolling on floor slowly, hugging knees and hanging head low, stooped shoulders, slow, low, slouched, lethargic, circling HAPPY = wide shapes, big jumps, sprightly and elevated movements, stretched shapes, skips, gallops, bouncy, fast moving, energetic PROUD = big wide open shapes, heads held high, strong solid shapes, explore different levels, grand gestures SCARED = closed shapes, slow cautious movements, sudden gasps, wide hands, low level, (hiding), hesitant, 'creeping'
WARM-UP (2)	Identify the four main points of the compass (NORTH, SOUTH, EAST, WEST). You may wish to draw a symbol on the floor or label each point visually for each emotion point. Ask the children what move they could do when the emotion is called out, to represent this feeling. Select one of the movements suggested and practice it as a class. This could be a movement from before or a new idea presented by the children. Do this for the four emotions in the appropriate zone. Travel through the space and run to the allocated space when the teacher calls out the emotion. Whilst the children are travelling through the space, suggest that they explore some or all of the following: shoulder rolls, full circles with the arms, walking quickly, jogging, dodging, introduce turns, rolls etc.

225

KS2

Trapped – A Dance Framework and Scheme of Work for KS2 – Ludus Dance

LESSON I – RECOGNISING EMOTIONS

EXPLORATION

Give each child one of the four emotions: HAPPY, SCARED, SAD or PROUD so there is an equal amount of children working on each emotion. Working alone initially, ask the children to create 8 counts of movement for this emotion. Think about how this emotion makes us feel and think of a particular situation that makes us feel this way. The children can use new movements of their own or use some of the movements from the warm up.
Think about the dynamics of the movement and the use of different levels. Practice it so that it can be repeated.

DEVELOPMENT (I)

Working with a partner (who has been working on an opposite emotion) e.g. Happy paired with Sad people and Proud with Scared. Watch each other's SOLOS and give constructive feedback. What could make it better? Is it obvious which emotion is being portrayed? Think about:

Energy – DYNAMICS

High or low in space – LEVELS

Pathways in space – SPACE

Actions chosen – ACTIONS

Learn each other's phrase and link them together. Each pair should now have a 16 count phrase. There should be a clear contrast for the audience in the two linked sequences, yet seamless in movement.

DEVELOPMENT (2)

NORTH = HAPPY SOUTH = SAD EAST = PROUD WEST = SCARED
Work on a travelling phrase as a transition to move around the compass points that correspond with the emotions featured in the DUET.
For example if the DUET was 8 counts SCARED followed by 8 counts HAPPY:

■ Both children perform the 8 counts of SCARED in the SCARED zone (WEST)

■ Both dancers travel from the SCARED zone (WEST) to the HAPPY zone (NORTH) continuing to base their movements on the SCARED emotion. The travelling must include I jump, I roll and I turn.

■ Once in the HAPPY zone (NORTH), both the dancers perform the 8 counts of the HAPPY phrase.

■ Both dancers then travel from the HAPPY zone to the centre of the compass remaining in the HAPPY emotion and including I jump, I roll and I turn.

KS2	Trapped – A Dance Framework and Scheme of Work for KS2 – Ludus Dance
	LESSON 1 – RECOGNISING EMOTIONS
	The travel section can be improvised at first to explore different movements, before being set. Both travelling phrases will be slightly different as the movement has been inspired by a particular emotion however, they will be similar as both contain a roll, jump and turn.
	To finish – hold a still photo that expresses an emotion that your DUET was based on.
PERFORMANCE	Divide the class into groups and show the DUETS.
APPRECIATION	Could you tell what emotions were being expressed? Was this because of the choice of movements or the way in which they were performed? What were the movements that you particularly enjoyed and why?
COOL DOWN	See Suggestions for Cool Down [not reproduced].

Sample Session Plan used by Spiral Dance 2007

Group . . . . Venue . . . .

Date of session . . . . Dance Artist(s) . . . .

Aims of session . . . .

Time	Activity (ice breakers/warm up/activity and cool down)	Music and materials	Teaching points	Evaluation notes

Overall notes/ evaluation on session . . . .

Lesson Evaluation – Take Art

Group: . . . .
Lesson: . . . .
Leader(s): . . . .
Date: . . . .

LEADER LEARNING		
What did I do well?	What did I find difficult?	What could I improve on?
What did I learn?		

PARTICIPANTS' LEARNING	
What did they do well/enjoy?	What did they find difficult?
Any comments from the group	

Any observations or feedback from staff/mentor
IMPLICATIONS FOR FUTURE TEACHING
What implications does the evaluation have for future sessions? How might I do this session differently in the future?
Any other comments/concerns/general thoughts about the session

Project Coordinator Checklist

(See Chapter 17 for further discussion on project coordination.)

- **Aims**: Who decides these? Are you working for an organisation which has set clear aims for the project or will you need to suggest aims?
- **Publicity**: Are you responsible for this? If so, how will you market the project? Do you need to make any presentations? Is there a budget for leaflets or adverts in newspapers?
- **Schedule**: How many sessions? How long per session? What time of day is best? (Check for clashes with hairdresser/chiropody visits if working in sheltered housing or care homes.)
- **Participants**: How many? What are their interests? How fit are they?
- **Venue**: Have you a choice? What type of floor/furniture/ventilation? Are there facilities for refreshments? Who will provide these? Can you get into the venue before the start time?
- **Content**: What type of dance would be most appropriate? How will you decide what to do/where to start?
- **People management**: Who will lead and support on the sessions? If you are not leading on it, how will you liaise with the lead artist? How much support does he/she need? Have you established clear lines of communication?
- **Risk assessment**: Have you done a risk assessment on venue and activities? Have you discussed existing controls and precautions with all staff involved?
- **Equal opportunities/inclusion**: Are there any issues relating to access/diversity/inclusion? Will you accept all comers? How will you decide on staff? Is written information clear and easy to understand? Have you thought about how to communicate with people who do not read?
- **Duty of care**: What do you need to do to take care of the people on the project?
- **Insurance**: Does the project have adequate insurance cover?
- **Consent form**: Will you be taking photographs/video? Who will organise the consent forms? Where will they be stored?
- **Administration**: Have you allowed time for this?

- **Resources/music/materials**: Do you need to buy/borrow any resources? Do you need a licence?
- **Celebration/final session**: Is this definitely the end, or might the funders come up with more money for another project? How will this be handled? Can you strike the right balance and end the project on a positive note? Check that your celebration does not clash with any key festivals for people of different faiths.
- **Liaison with partners**: How will you report on the project? Do you need to have meetings with host organisation/warden/arts officers/funders? Have you allowed time for this and costed it into the budget?
- **Monitoring**: What records will you be keeping? How will information be collected? Who needs to receive monitoring information?
- **Evaluation**: What will you be evaluating and what methods will you be using? Will you be using an external evaluator? Have you costed this in your budget?
- **Documentation**: Will you be providing a summary document? Will you be documenting the project in other ways? (Photographs, video, chronicler report, project diary?) Do you need to book a photographer?
- **Mentoring/support for you**: Do you need any specific help/advice? Have you created opportunities to discuss the practice with other practitioners? Do you think this is important? Have you costed it into the budget?

Ludus Dance Risk Estimation

ACTIVITY: Workshops

WHO IS AT RISK? Staff & pupils

DEPARTMENT: Touring

Probability	
Almost certain	6
Frequent occurrence	5
Fairly frequent occurrence	4
Occasional occurrence	3
Possible but unlikely	2
Highly improbable	1

Severity	
Fatality	6
Major injury	5
Prolonged absence	4
3 day injury	3
Minor injury	2
Negligible	1

Score	
01–09	Tolerable risk
10–19	Improve in 2/3 months
20–36	Urgent action required

TOTAL SCORE = P × S

BEFORE

AFTER

EVENT	P	S	Total	REMEDY	P	S	Total
Students arriving late sustain injuries by not being present for warm-up	2	4	8	Follow guidelines for workshop attendees, ensure late arrivals warm-up before joining in session	2	2	4
Floors in poor condition. Loose blocks (floor), dirty floor causing people to slip or hurt themselves on any sharp objects	3	5	15	Ensure the floor is safe to work on before beginning the session	2	4	8
Surplus equipment in the hall, e.g. ladders, chairs, gym equipment	3	5	15	Make sure to remove any equipment which is in the way. Set clear limits where the students are allowed to work. No climbing on the apparatus etc.	2	4	8
Hall too small for the number of participants	3	5	14	Follow Ludus guidelines with respect to class size	2	4	8
Danger of electrocution due to faulty electrical equipment, loose sockets, frayed cables	3	5	16	Survey electrical equipment before using	2	4/5	9
Injuries caused by inappropriate dress, shoes or accessories (jewellery and watches)	3	5	17	Important to educate the students about appropriate dress code for dance classes	2	3	6
Space being used as a thoroughfare for other students	3	2	6	Stop class when it is time for other students to enter	1	3	3
Space too hot or too cold leading to dehydration or injury	4	2	8	Inform staff member or caretaker and see if heating up or down. Tell student to dress appropriately, cancel class in extreme cases	1	3	3

Signature: . . . . **Title**: Dancer/Teacher **Date**: . . . . **Review**: 1 year from date

Freedom in Dance Risk Assessment – Mature Movers

Creative dance session in sheltered housing lounge

Participants are all aged between 72 and 94 years – many are frail

Creative movement exercises designed to promote mobility and reduce falls

Existing controls:

- Most activities take place with participants seated.
- Workshop leaders have received training from Freedom in Dance
- Participants read guidelines for exercise and sign that they agree to advise leaders of any health condition which might affect their ability to exercise
- Participants are regularly reminded not to do any movement which feels uncomfortable
- Handbags and walking sticks are stored safely under seats or out of the way so people won't trip

(*See table on next page*)

Activities	Hazards	Risk rating			Precautions to be taken	Additional information for leaders
		Low	Med	High		
Rolling large ball	Leaning too far Getting out of chair to retrieve ball	✓			Leaders be ready to retrieve ball if participants can't reach	Location of warden call button to determined prior to session beginning
Foot exercises (toe taps heel lifts, leg raises)	Too many repetitions could result in fatigue or angina	✓			Remind participants to take a rest when they need one	Observe participants carefully for signs of fatigue and be prepared to reduce actual activity time by introducing pauses for listening to music/discussion
Shoulder and upper arm exercises	Too many repetitions could result in fatigue or angina	✓			Activity to be stopped if any participant appears fatigued	
Tapping balloon	If standing participants might attempt to kick balloon and overbalance	✓	✓		If any participants are standing ensure co-leaders are next to them	
Blowing feathers	Leaning too far Getting out of chair to retrieve feather	✓			Be ready to retrieve feather if participants can't reach	
Circle dance	Losing balance/falling			✓	Special attention to be paid as participants get up and return to seats	

Assessor: . . . .

Date: . . . .

Risk Assessment of Events

Part of the Health and Safety Policy of Dance and Theatre Cornwall

Introduction

Each event is different, so our approach to risk assessment should be carefully considered in relation to the nature of the event.

In general, the safety plan could be comprised of two separate but closely linked elements:

- The overall 'Event safety plan'. The overall event safety plan is the responsibility of the Project Manager. The Project Manager will compile the plan in accordance with the guidance below taking account of risk assessments completed by group leaders.
- Risk assessments. Risk assessments are usually completed by group leaders and relate to that individual's group activity, they should be carried out and formally recorded using or adapting the *pro forma* below.

Guidance on Event Safety Plans

The following safety plan model has been drawn up to assist in preparing a plan which satisfies nationally published guidance. It should be used as a check list so that plan details under each heading can be expanded or excluded as necessary.

Event Summary

A general overview of the event, perhaps a paragraph or two of what the event is about. Include the dates.

Location and Forward Planning of the Site

State the location and directions if the site is remote. Site plans and sketches could be included showing the following: entrances, exits, fire equipment, event organizers location, toilet arrangements, any specific hazards, traffic routes, first aid stations, water points, lost children points, refreshments etc.

Organising Team Arrangements
A drawing of the command structure, indicating the roles of each. This section should include contact numbers.

Planning and Contact with Relevant Authorities
List those contacted, include dates and names of who was consulted. Consider the Police, Fire Brigade, Ambulance service, Coastguard, Lifeboat, Lifeguards, first aid bodies, Local Authority Planning and Licensing bodies.

Communication During the Event
Detail how radios and telephones will be deployed. Include individuals in control and how they might be contacted.

Training/Briefing of Events Team
Include basic instructions on evacuation plans, radio communication, emergencies, the content of the safety plan, use of alcohol and drugs, break times, positions, duties and roles, identification and personal safety equipment.

Managing Crowds Safely and Security
Consider crowd sizes and contingency plans. Traffic movement and management, parking, disabled facilities, police activity, marshalling arrangements, gate passes, overnight security, entry and exit points, arrangements around performance areas, crowd sways or surges, perimeter fencing, young children, access for the disabled, seating arrangements, stairways and ramps, slopes and viewing points, and any barriers around known hazards.

Risk Assessment
It is a requirement that these are carried out for all known hazards during the event. Also consider journeys to and from the event for vulnerable groups or individuals.

Infrastructure/Facilities/Signage

Include catering, marquees, gas and electrical equipment, barriers, stages or performance areas, PA systems, lights, toilets, welfare positions (shelters/offices/showers), waste collection and disposal, litter, compressed bottle gas, pressure vessels, temporary structures, parking for event team and authorities. Think how you intend to ensure these are installed and maintained safely.

Fire

Identify principal risks of fire or explosion, fire fighting equipment, means of escape, means of warning in case of fire and emergency procedures and their control.

Firework Displays/Pyrotechnics

Include details of who is responsible for displays and what experience or qualification they have to carry out the event safely. Also details of the display area, any nearby hazards such as overhead cables etc. and also responsibility for clearing up afterwards.

Attractions

Each attraction will have its own hazards which should be identified and record using risk assessment forms.

Emergency/Accident Management and Reporting

Detail procedures for emergency action, first aid, ambulance, medical support, the communication arrangements and who should be informed in the event.

Personal Protective Equipment/Clothing

Detail who will be supplied with what.

Environmental Considerations

Tide times, weather conditions, nearby combustible materials, any water hazards, biological hazards (e.g. cesspools or chemical risks from crop spraying).

Insurance

Any insurance that is necessary

Event Schedule – City of Lights 2006

Part of the event plan produced by Dance and Theatre Cornwall Ltd

Date	Time	Activity
20 Nov	10.00	Lanterns being transported from Boatshed to TA Centre garages – truck from Truro City Council (Russell); Falmouth lantern(s) transported to TA Centre Buckets & hi-vis jackets collected from Truro City Council Prep signage; collect radios; prep bucket labels
21 Nov	09.00–18.00	Final tweaks on large lanterns only if absolutely necessary Schools muster point signs up at TA Centre, carry poles assembled N.B. there are Children's rehearsals for the HfC panto happening at the TA Centre 09.00–17.00
	17.30	Road closures active Crowd barriers set up Lander Gallery reception set up (Amanda Lorens)
	18.00	Briefing for stewards – radios/hi-vis jackets/buckets/badges Artists arrive at TA Centre Bands & dancers arrive at loading bay
	18.30	Schools arrive at TA Centre (as per schools briefing notes) – High-vis jackets/carry poles to group leaders Street collectors arrive at TA Centre – give out buckets
	19.00	Procession starts from TA Centre Roads re-opened where possible following procession – Police
	19.40	Procession arrives at Lemon Quay School groups disperse into Tabernacle Street – parents pick up; carry poles & hi-vis jackets gathered up (buckets to gather them in); doughnuts given out to school groups in bags Finale performance (20 mins)
	20.00	Performance finishes High-vis jackets, collection buckets, radios back to Works van Reception at Lander Gallery starts Doughnuts & hot drinks available at HfC Assembly Room (NB Chairs etc. in Assembly Room not to be moved around)

Date	Time	Activity
	20.30	Clear up – lanterns to be transported (City Council truck – waiting area for truck in Lemon Street) back to boatshed; small lanterns taken home or into litter bins; Crowd barriers de-rig (as soon as roads are clear)
22 Nov		Return radios; thank you letters; collect signage from TA Centre Count street collection

This is a big event with a lot of people so EVERYONE needs to be ALERT and READY.

Ensure that you are ready and on the ball; make sure you travel light; make sure you know what you are responsible for and who you need to stay in contact with.

Good Practice Guidelines – Take Art

The following examples of good practice are recommended to provide a positive culture and a caring climate within Take Art's Services

Planning and Administration

Recruitment – All staff working for Take Art with children, young people and vulnerable adults should have an enhanced CRB no longer than three years old, two references, observations if appropriate, and opportunity for training and feedback.

There are instances where artists cannot go through all the stages of our recommended recruitment process. This often occurs when artists have come from overseas. When this occurs, partner organisations will be informed when the project is being planned or the workshop is being booked.

- When necessary, risk assessments should be obtained or at least acknowledged from partner venues.
- Consider and discuss any agreements or written permission that might need to be obtained from parents, carers , teachers or staff (e.g. photographic permission, contact details).
- Aim to discuss workshop content with all project partners, and user groups such as teachers, playgroups, day care centre, youth workers, parents etc.
- Before commencing any workshops artists ideally should be familiarised with the practicalities of the partner venue and the staff supporting the workshop, with individual roles and responsibilities clearly defined.
- Record in detail any accident, injury, bruise/scratch or unusual incident, and any treatment, in an appropriate register.
- Only registered and approved drivers with an appropriate driving licence, insurance and MOT documentation may provide transportation for young people.
- Any educational or access requirements should be discussed and accommodated in a planning session.

Interpersonal Conduct

- At the beginning of every session make sure that each child knows a named person to go to should they have any concerns.
- Treat all children, young people and vulnerable adults equally, and with respect and dignity.
- Always put the welfare of each participant first.
- Never swear, use rough language, or make any comments with sexual over-tones/implications; never allow children to use inappropriate language unchallenged
- Build balanced relationships based on trust which empower children to share in the decision-making process.
- Give enthusiastic and constructive feedback rather then negative criticism.
- Make the arts fun, enjoyable and promote equality.
- Recognise that children or young people with disabilities may be even more vulnerable to abuse than other children or young people.
- Really listen and take into account what children say.
- Develop awareness of the developmental needs/capacity of young people.
- Avoid excessive competitive activities.
- When working a small group of young people, ensure that each young person receives 'equal' amounts of attention.

Physical Conduct

- Work in an open environment where at least one other adult is present, avoiding private or unobservable situations. In fact, avoid being in a situation where you would be alone with a child.
- If you do have to take children to the toilet always take more than one child.
- Avoid doing things of a personal nature that young children can do for themselves, e.g. tying shoes, buttoning coats etc.
- Tell young people, before any workshops that involve physical contact, exactly what the intention is, and ensure that they agree and do not show discomfort.
- Unless it is part of the workshop, always maintain a safe and appropriate physical and psychological distance from young people.
- Refrain from welcoming/farewell embraces
- Seek any necessary agreements of teachers, parents and participants at the beginning of a workshop.
- Consumption of alcohol, taking drugs or smoking is forbidden or only per-mitted within the law.
- Medicine must never be administered to a child. If medicine is necessary during the day ask the parent to return to give it.
- All accidents must be recorded in the 'Workshop Accident Book'.

Guidelines for Venue Staff – Generation Arts

The following set of guidelines have been compiled to assist venue staff whose clients are participating in the Generation Arts programme. They have been produced in response to requests by Generation Arts Support Workers, Artists and venue staff. We hope the following guidelines will make your experience of being involved in the Generation Arts programme as equally rewarding as your clients'.

The Workshop Environment

In order to create an environment in which participants can feel free and safe to explore their creative selves we must strive to meet the following conditions:

- A member of staff from the venue should be aware of the activity, greet the Artist or community participants in a friendly manner and know which space the activity is taking place.
- The Artists should be permitted to start their activities on time.
- The venue staff should actively encourage their clients to participate and promote the Generation Arts programme.
- The space should remain free of interruptions for the duration of the session.
- The space should be prepared for the activity and noise levels should be at a minimum outside the activity space.
- Each individual should feel valued for their contribution to the group however great or small.
- The focus should at all times be on what is happening in the session.
- All mobile phones should be switched off throughout the session.

Assisting the Clients

We would like to adopt a participant-led approach, meaning that as far as possible the participant should feel that they can adapt any movements/activities to suit their own needs.

- Please allow the necessary time for your client to initiate their response.
- Try as much as possible to support your client physically rather than try to control their movements.
- Please try to be as attentive as possible and play an active part in the session, supporting the participants and tutors where required.
- Make it fun!

We hope these guidelines are helpful to you. If there is anything at all that you are not sure about or if you have any suggestions, ideas or observations then please feel free to discuss them with myself.

Many thanks for you help.

Signed by Jim Dixon   Signed by Lorraine Walker
Chairman of Generation Arts   *Manager of Colinshield Court*

Freedom in Dance Guidelines for Dance Exercise with Mature Movers

The Mature Movers programme includes dance activities designed to improve balance, strength and flexibility. It may also increase circulation and lessen or prevent the effects of heart disease.

If you have not taken part in exercise for a while you are advised to speak to your doctor, who will check for any condition which may make certain forms of exercise unwise. Please read the following guidelines and advise your dance leader of any health condition or medication which may affect your ability to exercise.

1. Don't exercise if you are tired, unwell or have just eaten.
2. Wear loose clothing and soft-soled shoes.
3. At no time should an exercise or activity cause pain. If it does, stop immediately and advise the dance leader.
4. It is not unusual to feel a bit stiff and tired after the first few sessions. If this continues, speak to your doctor.

Please complete the following and give it to your dance leader

Name . . . . Tel No . . . .
Address . . . .

Please tell us if you have experienced any of the following: (Please tick either Yes or No for each condition)

	Yes	No
■ Osteoporosis		
■ Coronary thrombosis		
■ Stroke		
■ Cancer		
■ Falls		
■ Recent viral infection		
■ High/low blood pressure		

- Asthma/other chest condition
- Other (please give details)

. . . .

. . . .

I have read the guidelines for dance exercise and agree to advise the dance leader of any changes in my health condition which may affect my ability to exercise.

Signed   . . . .   Date . . . . . .
PRINT NAME   . . . .
Witness signature   . . . .   Date . . . .
PRINT NAME   . . . .   © Diane Amans 2007

Equal Opportunities Policy Statement – Spiral Dance

In accordance with the statutory requirements of the Race Relations Act 1976 and the Sex Discrimination Act 1975, Spiral Dance will not discriminate against or treat an individual differently on the grounds of colour, ethnic origin or sex. Likewise, Spiral Dance will not tolerate discrimination on the grounds of age, marital status, sexual orientation, disability, religion or nationality.

Spiral Dance will develop procedures to meet its legal and moral obligations. And, where possible, employees will be given training to avoid discrimination in all processes and procedures.

Full-time, part-time employees and free-lance workers of Spiral Dance will be offered an equal opportunity to progress in Spiral Dance. Policies, procedures and practices will be constantly reviewed to ensure individuals are recruited, trained, developed and promoted on the basis of job requirements and the individual merits and abilities for the job. They may be offered, where appropriate, special training to meet their full potential.

Spiral Dance recognises the need for fair recruitment and selection of full and part-time staff and has formulated a policy statement outlining procedures and guidelines for fair recruitment and selection of all full and part time staff.

Spiral Dance also recognises the need for a Code of Professional Practice for all Freelance and Sessional Workers and has formulated such a policy in line with the requirements set out herein.

Spiral Dance also accepts the need to overcome discrimination in service delivery. This will be achieved by ensuring all employees are fully aware of their responsibilities towards the promotion of equal opportunities. Employees will be properly equipped to take account of the different and special needs of particular groups when providing services on behalf of Spiral Dance.

The Management Committee has overall responsibility for the success of this policy.

Freedom in Dance Consent Form

Freedom in Dance Consent Form   Summer 2006
Freedom in Dance 25 Hawk Green Rd Marple Stockport SK 6 7HU

Photographs from the Salford project may be used in Freedom in Dance publicity material* and to illustrate articles in journals and newspapers during the period from August 2006 – December 2009.*

Please complete the following consent form

I agree to Freedom in Dance keeping these images and my contact details and understand that Freedom in Dance will contact me to seek my permission for any other use of the images.

NAME (please print) . . . .
Signature of parent or guardian . . . .
Date . . . . Tel No . . . .
Address
    . . . .
    . . . .
    . . . .
    . . . .

The above details will be kept on file at the Freedom in Dance office and will not be circulated to other organisations without your permission.

- If you wish to stipulate any conditions relating to use of your image please do so below

*The period of consent will vary depending on the project. Sometimes a shorter period is more appropriate.

Community Activity Registration Form

CUMBRIA SPORT COMMUNITY SPORTS COACH SCHEME

Community Activity Registration Form

Thank you for taking time to complete this form. Please note that the coach/organisers must have this form completed before your child can take part in the activity.

Child's Name: . . . .

Date of Birth: . . . .   Age: Please tick one box

0 to 13	14 to 24	24+

Home Address: . . . .
. . . .
Tel No: . . . .   Postcode: . . . .
Ward: . . . .   Gender: M/F

Participant Tracking/Equity Information

The information required below is to help us track participants through their sporting life. This will help us provide evidence to funders that the programmes we undertake are of benefit to individuals and the communities they belong to.

School: . . . .   Year: . . . .

Does your child belong to a community club?   Yes/No

If Yes, which one: . . . .

Please identify your child's ethnicity

Please tick one of the five main categories listed. The information on the right-hand side of the table will help you decide which category best fits

White	British/Irish
White Other	European/American/Australian etc.
Mixed	White & Black/Caribbean/Asian/African/Other
Asian/Asian British	Indian/Pakistani/Bangladesh/other Asian
Black/Black British	Caribbean/African/other Black
Chinese/other Ethnic Group	Chinese/Any other Ethnic Group not listed

Do you consider your child to have a disability? (Please circle) YES/NO

If YES, what is the nature of the impairment? (Please tick)

Physical Impairment		Learning Difficulties	
Hearing Impairment		Visual Impairment	
Other, please specify			

DATA PROTECTION ACT 1998

The information provided on this form is confidential and it will be used only in appropriate circumstances relating to the Scheme, Cumbria Sport, and its partners.

Please be assured that the welfare and care of the child/young person are our utmost concerns.

Emergency Contacts and Medical Information

The information below is required in the unfortunate case of an emergency. This will assist us to take the relevant action and if required issue the relevant information to health professionals in the best interests of your child.

Parent or Guardian's Name:. . . . . Tel: . . . . .

Parent or Guardian's Name:. . . . . Tel: . . . . .

Emergency Contact Name: . . . . Tel: . . . . .

Child's Doctor: . . . . Tel: . . . . .

Surgery Address: . . . .

. . . .

Has your child had a tetanus injection?   YES/NO
Is your child allergic to penicillin?   YES/NO
Has your child had a meningitis vaccine?   YES/NO

Details of any allergies, health conditions etc.: . . . .

. . . .

. . . .

Any further relevant information:. . . . .

PARENTAL/GUARDIAN CONSENT FORM

Medical Consent

I consent to any treatment necessary in the event of an emergency. I authorise staff to sign on my behalf any written form of consent required by the hospital authority provided that the delay required to obtain my signature might be considered in the opinion of the doctor or medical staff likely to endanger my child's health or safety.

Signed: . . . . Date: . . . .

Publicity Consent

I consent to photographs being taken of my child during the scheme sessions that may be used in the local papers and/or other publicity material.

Signed: . . . . Date: . . . .

Community Sports Coach Scheme
I consent to my child taking part in the scheme sessions. I understand that in the event of any child putting either themselves or other children at risk, or preventing other children from benefiting from the activities on offer, the staff have the right to exclude them from the programme.

Signed: . . . .   Date: . . . .

Please inform the coach of any change in circumstances relating to this registration form. Thank you.

SIGNATURE OF PARENT/GUARDIAN/CARER: . . . .

NAME PRINTED: . . . . **DATE.** . . . .

The Foundation for Community Dance

The Foundation for Community Dance is the UK development agency for community and participatory dance. Its mission is to make dance matter, and to work for the development of dance for all.

The organisation is based in the city of Leicester in the East Midlands of England, but operates nationally and internationally. It has been a membership organisation since its formation in 1986, and has one of the largest networks of dance professionals and supporters in the UK – representing some 4,500 people including dance artists and teachers, dance-makers, companies, organisations, agencies and venues; universities and training establishments; and funding bodies, local authorities and government departments.

The Foundation is a registered charity and receives regular funding from Arts Council England, and project funding from a variety of other agencies. It has a core team of staff, and regularly works in partnership with other dance and artform organisations, and with partners outside of the arts on areas of shared concern, such as health and disability.

Our Vision
A world where dance matters to everyone.

Our Mission
To make participation in dance vital to society, people's lives and their communities.

Our Ambitions
- Access to, participation in, and progression through dance for all
- Recognition of the importance and role of dance in people's lives

- Greater understanding between diverse communities through participation in dance
- Quality assurance for practitioners and their employers, participants and their communities
- A dance profession, and audiences for dance, that are supported by services and information resources about participation in dance.

Our Work

Information, Advice and Guidance for dance artists, organisations, students and communities including: an extensive web site and web-based information service, e-newsletters, a telephone advice service, an online directory of Foundation Members, and insurance and Criminal Records Bureau disclosure services.

Professional Development for Community Dance: We support dance artists in their community dance work through professional development and networking events; we offer dialogue and debate about current practice in *Animated* – the quarterly community dance magazine; and Making a Move is our long-term initiative for the development of a UK-wide professional framework for community dance.

Strategic development: We undertake strategic programmes to support the development of community dance for new audiences and under represented communities, in areas such as diversity, health and disability.

Advocacy, Profile and Research: We work extensively to raise the profile of, and campaign for, community dance to reveal its impact, and support the development of more opportunities for people to dance. This involves representation at conferences, networks and meetings, and entering into dialogue and partnerships with other arts organisations, the public and voluntary sector and government departments, both in the UK and internationally.

Foundation for Community Dance
LCB Depot, 31 Rutland Street, Leicester LE1 1RE
Tel: 0116 253 3453
Email: info@communitydance.org.uk
Web: www.communitydance.org.uk

Contact Details

The following contact details are for organisations mentioned in the book, plus a selection of others which may be of interest. This list is not exhaustive and will inevitably exclude many excellent companies and groups. Also, these details will become outdated so you will need to contact dance agencies in your area or browse the web for up-to-date information.

The Foundation for Community Dance is a very useful starting point, as they will be able to guide you in the right direction.

National Dance Agencies

DanceXchange
Birmingham Hippodrome
Thorpe Street
Birmingham B5 4TB
0121 689 3170
info@dancexchange.org.uk
http://www.dancexchange.org.uk/

Dance Northwest
PO Box 19
Winsford
CheshireCW7 2AQ
01606 863845
admin@dancenorthwest.org.uk
http://www.dancenorthwest.org.uk/

Artist Development
The Place
17 Dukes Road
LondonWC1H 9PY
020 7383 3524

artistdevelopment@theplace.org.uk
http://www.theplace.org.uk/

Dance City
Peel Lane, Off Waterloo Street
Newcastle-upon-Tyne
NE1 4DW
0191 261 0505
info@dancecity.co.uk
http://www.dancecity.co.uk/

Dance 4
PreSet
3–9 Hockley
Nottingham
NG1 1FH
0115 941 0773
info@dance4.co.uk
http://www.dance4.co.uk/

Dance South West
PO Box 5457
Bournemouth BH1 1WU
01202 554131
http://www.dancesouthwest.org.uk/

Dance East
Northgate Arts Centre
Sidegate Lane West
Ipswich IP4 3DF
01473 639230
info@danceeast.demon.co.uk
http://www.danceeast.co.uk/

South East Dance
5 Palace Place
Castle Square
Brighton BN1 1EF
01273 202032
info@southeastdance.org.uk
http://www.southeastdance.org.uk/

Swindon Dance
Town Hall Studios, Regent Circus
Swindon SN1 1QF
01793 463210
http://www.swindondance.org.uk/

Yorkshire Dance
3 St Peters Buildings
St Peters Square
Leeds LS9 8AH
0113 2439867
admin@yorkshiredance.org.uk
http://www.yorkshiredance.org.uk/

Youth Dance England
Royal Academy of Dance Building
36 Battersea Square
London SW11 3RA
020 7924 7167
admin@yde.org.uk
http://www.yde.org.uk/

Regional Dance Organisations

Aberdeen
City Moves
c/o Aberdeen Art Gallery
Schoolhill
Aberdeen AB10 1FQ
01224 523 705

Berkshire
Berkshire Regional Dance Council
South Hill Park Arts Centre, Ringmead,
Birchhill,
Berkshire RG12 7PA
01344 351 803
http://www.berkshiredance.org.uk/

Buckinghamshire
Bucksdance
First Floor, Rear office, Rycote Place
30–38 Cambridge Street, Aylesbury
Bucks HP20 1RS
01296 395 994

Cambridgeshire
Cambsdance
6 The Old Maltings,
135 Ditton Walk
Cambridge CB5 8PY
01223 245 254 Fax:01223 248 777
info@cambsdance.org.uk
http://www.cambsdance.org.uk/

Cheshire
Cheshire Dance
Winsford Library
High Street, Winsford
Cheshire CW7 2AS
01606 861 770
info@cheshiredance.org
http://www.cheshiredance.org/

Cornwall
The works – Dance & Theatre in Cornwall
Crusader House
Newnham Quay, Truro
Cornwall TR1 2DP
01872 222 622
cornwall@dancesouthwest.org.uk
http://www.dancesouthwest.org.uk/somerset/

Devon
Dance in Devon
Exeter Phoenix, Bradninch Place
Gandy Street,
Exeter EX4 3LS
01392 667 050
devon@dancesouthwest.org.uk
http://www.dancesouthwest.org.uk/devon/

Derby
Derby Dance Centre
Dance House, Chapel Street
Derby DE1 3GU
01332 370 911

Dorset
Dorset Dance Forum
27 West Borough
Wimbourne BH21 1LT
01202 884 340
dorset@dancesouthwest.org.uk
http://www.dancesouthwest.org.uk/dorset/

Dudley
Dudley Community Dance
Netherton Arts Centre
Northfield Road, Netherton
Dudley DY2 9EP

Dundee
The Space
Dundee College
Kingsway Campus
Old Glamis Road
Dundee DD3 8LE
01382 834 934

East London
East London Dance
Stratford Circus
Theatre Square
London E15 1BX
020 8279 1050

Edinburgh
Dance Base National Centre for Dance
14–16 Grassmarket
Edinburgh EN1 2JU
0131 225 5525; Fax 0131 225 5234
dance@dancebase.co.uk
http://www.dancebase.co.uk/

Essex
Essexdance
Chancellor Hall
Market Road
Chelmsford
Essex CM1 1XA
01245 346 036

Freedom in Dance
c/o lincolnshire dance
The Stables
Wellingore Hall
Wellingore LN5 0HX
01522 811 811
freedom@lincolnshiredance.com

Glasgow
The Dance House
74 Victoria Crescent Road
Glasgow G12 9NJ
0141 334 0716

Gloucester
Gloucestershire Dance
Colwell Centre for Arts in Education
Derby Road
Gloucester GL1 4AD
01452 550 431
admin@gloucestershiredance.org.uk
http://www.dancesouthwest.org.uk/gloucestershire/

Greenwich
Greenwich Dance Agency
Greenwich Borough Hall
Royal Hill
London SE10 8RE
020 8293 9741

Hampshire
Hampshire Dance
The Point
Leigh Road

Eastleigh
Hants SO50 9DE
0238 065 2713

Hertfordshire
Hertsdance
Innovation Centre
University of Hertfordshire
Hatfield, Herts AL10 9AB
01707 281 076

Ireland
Institute for Choreography and Dance
Firkin Crane
Shandon
Cork
Ireland
+353 21 450 7487

Isle of Wight
Island Dance Initiative
The Guildhall
High Street
Newport
Isle of Wight PO30 1TY
01983 823 813

Lincolnshire
lincolnshire dance
The Stables
Wellingore Hall
Wellingore LN5 0HX
01522 811 811
info@lincolnshiredance.com

Manchester
Dance Initiative
Zion Arts Centre
Stretford Road
Hulme
Manchester M15 5ZA
0161 232 7179

Merseyside
Merseyside Dance Initiative
24 Hope Street
Liverpool L1 9BQ
0151 708 8810
http://www.merseysidedance.co.uk/
info@merseysidedance.co.uk

Norfolk
Norfolk Dance
The Garage, Chapel Field North
Norwich NR2 1NY
01603 283 399
info@norfolkdance.co.uk

Northern Ireland
Dance Northern Ireland
15 church Street
Belfast BT1 1PG
028 9024 9930 Fax 028 9024 9930
http://www.danceni.com/
vicki@danceni.com or lisa@danceni.com

Oxford
Oxford City Council
St Aldates Chambers
109–113 St Aldates
Oxford
01865 252 802

Somerset
Take Art! Dance Somerset
The Mill, Flaxdrayton Farm
South Petherton
Somerset TA13 5LR
01460 249 450
somerset@dancesouthwest.org.uk
http://www.dancesouthwest.org.uk/somerset/

Surrey and Guildford
Surrey Dance Project
County Arts Unit

Westfield Primary School, Bonsey Lane
Woking GU22 9PR
01483 776 128

Wales
Welsh Independent Dance
Chapter
Market Road, Canton
Cardiff CF5 1QE
02920 387 314

Useful web links

Arts Council England
http://www.artscouncil.org.uk/

Arts Council of Northern Ireland
http://www.artscouncil-ni.org/

Arts Council of Wales – Cyngor Celfyddydau Cymru
http://www.ccc-acw.org.uk/

Association of Dance of the African Diaspora
http://www.adad.org.uk/

Association of National Dance Agencies
http://www.anda.org.uk/

CandoCo
http://www.candoco.co.uk/

Community Dance Wales – Dawns Gymuned Cymru
http://www.communitydancewales.com/

Council for Dance Education and Training
http://www.cdet.org.uk/

Dance Books
http://www.dancebooks.org/

Dancers' Career Development (DCD)
http://www.thedcd.org.uk/

Dance UK
http://www.danceuk.org/

Dancing Times
http://www.dancing-times.co.uk/

Foundation for Community Dance
http://www.communitydance.org.uk/

Healthier Dancer Programme
http://www.danceuk.org/

Independent Dance
http://www.independentdance.co.uk/

Kutcheri Buzz.com
http://www.kutcheribuzz.com/

Alan Martin Inclusive Dance Workshops
http://www.mouseonthemove.co.uk/

National Dance Teachers Association
http://www.ndta.org.uk/

National Resource Centre for Dance
http://www.surrey.ac.uk/NRCD/

Protein Dance
http://www.proteindance.co.uk/

Qualifications and Curriculum Authority
http://www.qca.org.uk/

Scottish Arts Council
http://www.sac.org.uk/

Scottish Youth Dance
http://www.ydance.org/

South Asian Dance
http://www.southasiandance.co.uk/

Work in Dance
http://www.workindance.com/

Youth Dance England
http://www.yde.org.uk/

Suppliers of Resources

Ludus Dance Teaching Resources
Ludus Dance Touring Company
http://www.ludusdance.org/
01524 389901

Nottingham Rehab Supplies
Findel House
Excelsior Road
Ashby de la Zouch
Leicestershire LE65 1NG
0870 6000 197
info@nrs-uk.co.uk

Rompa
Goyt Side Road
Chesterfield
Derbyshire S40 2PH
0845 230117

Everyday Dancing
Jabadao Mail Order Catalogue
The Yard
Viaduct Street
Stanningley
Leeds LS28 6AU
0113 236 3311
info@jabadao.org

The Festival Shop
Multifaith, Multicultural and Citizenship Resources
http://www.festivalshop.co.uk/

Soundbeam
Soundbeam Project
Unit 3 Highbury Villas
St Michael's Hill
Bristol
BS2 8BY
0117 974 4142
tim@soundbeam.co.uk

Music for Dance
PO Box 18257
London EC1V 3XB
020 8317 4439
cb@musicfordance.net
http://www.musicfordance.net/

Information on Safeguarding and Duty of Care

Arts Council England
14 Great Peter Street
London SW1P 3NQ
020 7333 0100
http://www.artscouncil.org.uk/
Provides a directory of safeguarding advisers

NSPCC National Training Centre
3 Gilmour Close
Beaumont Leys
Leicester LE4 1EZ
0116 234 7227
consultancy@nspcc.org.uk
http://www.nspcc.org.uk/
Provides information about training courses and distance learning packages on child protection awareness

Pathway of the Biscuit
1 Appleton Close
Eldwick BD16 3LY
01274 568 094
Provides training in safeguarding and duty of care

Other Resources

Dance UK
2nd Floor, Urdang
Finsbury Town Hall
Rosebery Avenue
London EC1R 4QT
020 7713 0730

Foundation for Community Dance
LCB Depot
31 Rutland Street
Leicester LE1 1RE
0116 253 3453
info@communitydance.org.uk

Generation Arts
West Lothian Council
Craigsfarm Campus
Maree Walk
Craigshill
Livingston
EH54 5BP

Green Candle Dance Company
Unit 20.6
Aberdeen Studios
Aberdeen Centre
22 Highbury Grove
London N5 2EA
020 7359 8776
info@greencandledance.com

Spiral Dance
Falinge Park Buildings
Falinge Park
Falinge Road
Rochdale
OL12 6LB
01706 644433

Noelle Williamson
donnoelle@onetel.com

Glossary

Arts Council England

Arts Council England is the national development agency for the arts in England. It distributes public money from the Government and the National Lottery.

Arts Council of Northern Ireland

Arts Council of Northern Ireland is the lead development agency for the arts in Northern Ireland.

Arts Council of Wales

Arts Council of Wales is responsible for funding and developing the arts in Wales.

CPD

Continuing professional development or ongoing professional learning.

CRB Disclosure Check

A service run by the Home Office Criminal Records Bureau. It helps organisations make more thorough checks on people who are going to have contact with children, young people and vulnerable adults.

Creative Partnerships

The government's flagship creativity programme for schools and young people.

Dance and health

Dance companies and organisations work in partnership with other agencies to promote active lifestyles and tackle health issues through dance.

Dance animateur

A less used term for community dance artist/practitioner. Was more commonly used in the early days of community dance provision.

Data Protection

The Data Protection Act 1998 regulates how personal information is used and protects individuals from misuse of personal information.

DCMS

Department for Culture, Media and Sport, responsible for government policy on the arts and creative industries.

Developmental Movement Play

DMP is a framework for supporting the kind of movement that supports children's physical *and* neurological development. It focuses on:

- the *free-flow, spontaneous movement play* that children so readily engage in, in and out of everything they do
- some *specific movement activities* within this free-flow movement play that play a particular part in the development of the body, brain and nervous system

DfES

Department for Education and Skills: a government department with the aims of 'creating opportunity, releasing potential and achieving excellence'. In June 2007, DfES was replaced by the Department for Children, Schools and Families (DCSF).

Duty of Care

The duty which rests on an organisation or individual to make sure that all reasonable steps are taken to ensure the safety of any person involved in any activity for which that organisation or individual is responsible.

Foundation for Community Dance

UK development agency for community and participatory dance

Key Stages (KS1, KS2, KS3, KS4)

The National Curriculum in England operates at four key stages. Key Stages 1 and 2 relate to primary education (7–11years) and Key Stages 3 and 4 relate to secondary education (11–16 year olds).

Music copyright

All recorded music is covered by copyright – see Resources section for further information.

National Development Agency

Government-sponsored public body.

Ofsted

Office for Standards in Education – a non-ministerial government agency which inspects and regulates education and childcare provision.

Person centred

Practice which emphasises the value of the individual.

POVA

Protection of vulnerable adults.

PPL

Phonographic Performance Limited deals with licence applications for the public use of sound recordings in dance classes.

Process oriented

Refers to practice where the emphasis is on *experiencing* the dance. It is associated with a person-centred approach to facilitation.

Public liability insurance

This is insurance cover in case a member of the public makes a claim against you for injury or death to a third party or damage to the property of a third party.

Quality assurance (QA)

This incorporates quality management and quality control. QA is aimed at achieving consistent quality standards and is measured using agreed, quantifiable quality criteria.

Reflective practitioner

Someone who uses their knowledge and experience, together with a theoretical framework, in order to evaluate their practice and adopt a creative approach to problem solving.

Reflexive practitioner

Someone who engages in an ongoing process of internal reflection. Reflexive practitioners combine the elements of reflective practice, outlined above, with the ability to notice their own feelings and thoughts whilst facilitating dance experiences for other people. They combine sensitivity to the needs of the participants, awareness of their own needs and the ability to respond in the moment.

Risk assessment

The systematic examination of all aspects of practice to identify any hazards which have the potential to cause harm.

Safeguarding

The practice of keeping children, young people and vulnerable adults safe from abuse and neglect

Scottish Arts Council

Scottish Arts Council is the lead body for the funding, development and advocacy of the arts in Scotland.

Service provider

An organisation providing a service such as health, social care, housing.

References

Adair, J. (1998) *Effective Leadership*. Pan Macmillan, London.

Albright, A. C. and Gere, D. (2003) *A Dance Improvisation Reader*. Wesleyan University Press, Middletown, CT.

Amans, D. (1997). A Study of Process-Oriented Community Dance. *Unpublished MA Dissertation*. University of Surrey, Guildford.

Amans, D. (2006) *Survey of Community Dance Practitioners and Dance Agency Directors* (Unpublished research).

Ames, M. (2006) The shadow of a language. *Animated*, Summer, 16–20.

Anderson, B. (1991) *Imagined Communities: Reflections on the Origin and Spread of Nationalism*. Verso, London (first published 1983).

Archer, J. (2007) Dance City: embracing diversity. *Animated*, Spring, 34.

Arts Council England (2004) *Self Evaluation* information sheet. Arts Council England, London.

Arts Council England (2006) *Dance and Health: the Benefits for People of All Ages*. Arts Council England, London.

Arts Council England (2006). *Dance Included: Towards Good Practice in Dance and Social Inclusion*. Arts Council England, London.

Arts Council of Wales (1996) *Taking Part*. Arts Council of Wales, Cardiff.

Arts Council of Wales (2007) Draft Art Forms Strategy. Unpublished. Arts Council of Wales, Cardiff.

Audit Commission (1998) *A Fruitful Partnership:Effective Partnership Working*. Audit Commission, London.

Barba, E. and Savarese, N. (1991) *A Dictionary of Theatre Anthropology, the Secret Art of the Performer*. Routledge, London.

Benjamin, A. (2002) *Making an Entrance*. Routledge, London.

Brinson, P. (1991) *Dance as Education: Towards a National Dance Culture*. The Falmer Press, Basingstoke.

Burns, S. (2007) *Mapping Dance. Entrepreneurship and Professional Dance Practice in Dance Higher Education*. Palatine, Lancaster.

Cavarero, A. (1997) Birth, love and politics. *Radical Philosophy*, **86**, 19–23.

Clinton, L. and Glen, A. (1993). Community arts. In *Community and Public Policy* (ed. H. Butler), Chapter 6, pp. 92–105. Pluto Press, London.

Collingwood, R. G. (1938) *The Principles of Art*. Clarendon Press, Oxford.

Department for Education and Science (2002) *In Learning through PE and Sport: a guide to the Physical Education, School Sport and Club Link Strategy*. Department for Education and Science, London.

Department for Education and Science (2005) *Dance Links: a Guide to Delivering High Quality Dance for Children and Young People*. Department for Education and Science, London.

Department of Health (2001) *National Service Framework for Older People*. Department of Health, London.

Foundation for Community Dance (1996) *Thinking Aloud: In Search of a Framework for Community Dance*. Foundation for Community Dance, Leicester.

Foundation for Community Dance (2001) *Dancing Nation*. Handbook accompanying film commissioned by Foundation for Community Dance, Leicester.

Foundation for Community Dance (2006) Web site, http://www.communitydance.org.uk/, February.

Featherstone, M. (1995) *Undoing Culture: Globalization, Postmodernism and Identity*. Sage, London.

Finnan, K. (2003) Holding the balance. *Animated*, Summer.

Greenwood, C. (2007) Come and join the dance: young people, dance and diversity, *Animated*, Spring 2007, 23

Greenland, P. (ed.) (2000) *What Dancers Do That Other Health Workers Don't*. JABADAO, Leeds.

Greenland, P. (2005) We can do hard things. *Animated*, Spring, 30.

Halprin, A. (1979) *Movement Ritual*. Tamalpa Institute/Dancers Workshop, Kentfield, CA.

Halprin, A. (1995) *Moving Toward Life*. Wesleyan University Press, Hanover and London.

Halprin, A. (2000) *Dance as a Healing Art*. Life Rhythm, Mendocino, CA.

Halprin, L. (1969) *The RSVP Cycles, Creative Processes in the Human Environment*. George Braziller, New York.

Ings, R. (1994) No time to dance. *Animated*, Winter, 2–3.

JABADAO (1995) National Development Agency for Specialist Movement Work, Autumn (brochure), p. 1.

Jameson, F. (1991) *Postmodernism, or The Logic of Late Capitalism*. Verso, London.

Jasper, L. (1995) Tensions in the definition of community dance. *Border Tensions: Dance and Discourse. Proceedings from the Fifth Study of Dance Conference*, p. 189. University of Surrey, Guildford.

Jasper, L. (1997) *Moving Definitions of Community Dance*. Research Paper, Department of Dance Studies, University of Surrey

Johnson, D. and Johnson, F. (1991) *Joining Together: Group Theory and Group Skills*, p. 69. Prentice Hall International, London.

Kelly, O. (1984) *Community Art and the State: Storming the Citadels*, p. 5. Commedia, London.

Kirschenbaum, H. and Henderson, V. L. (eds.) (1990) *The Carl Rogers Reader*. Constable, London.

Lee, R. (2004). The possibilities are endless. *Animated*, Spring, 12–13.

Macfarlane, C. (2007) An evolving dance dialogue. *Animated*, Spring, 18.

Marks, V. (1998) Community dance? Connecting the evolution of theory and practice. In *Community Dance: Current Issues in the Field, Seminar Papers*, pp. 3–19. University of Surrey, Guildford.

Maslow, A. H. (1970). *Motivation and Personality*. Harper & Row, London.

Matarasso, F. (1994) *Regular Marvels*. Community Dance and Mime Foundation.

Matarasso, F.(1996) *Defining Values:Evaluating Arts Programmes*, p. 3. Comedia, Gloucester.

Matarasso, F. (1998) Use or ornament? The social impact of participation in the arts. Paper to *Creative Communities* conference, London.

Matarasso, F. (2005). Slow dancer: moving in the material world. *Animated*, Autumn, 20–4.

McConnell, F. (2006) A generation game. *Animated*, Summer, 13–15.

McCretton, N. (2006). Playing along with the audience. *Animated*, Winter, 12–14.

Nancy, J. (1993) *The Birth to Presence* (transl. Brian Holmer). Stanford University Press, Stanford.

National Assembly for Wales (2005). *Dance in Wales: A Review*. National Assembly for Wales, Cardiff.

Olsen, A. (2002) *Body and Earth, an Experiential Guide*. University Press of New England, Hanover & London.

Pallaro, P. (ed.) (1999) *Authentic Movement: Essays by Mary Starks Whitehouse, Janet Adler and Joan Chodorow*. Jessica Kingsley, London.

Peppiatt, A. and Venner, K. (1993). *Community Dance: a Progress Report*. ACGB, London.

Peppiatt, A. (1997) *Community Dance – Education Plus?* Research Paper, Department of Dance Studies, University of Surrey.

Powys Dance (1999). *Background Information for Tutors*. Unpublished, Powys Dance.

Poynor, H. and Simmonds, J. (eds.) (1997) *Dancers and Communities*. Ausdance, Sydney.

Risbridger, P. (2005). Peer pleasure. *Animated*, Summer, 15–17.

Ross, J. (2006) *Anna Halprin: Experience as Dance*. University of California Press, Berkeley, CA.

Rubidge, S. (1984) Community dance – a growth industry. *Dance Theatre Journal*, **2**(4).

Scholey, L. (1998) New definitions. *Animated*, Summer, 30–1.

Siddall, J. (1997) *Community Dance – Education Plus?* Research Paper, Department of Dance Studies, University of Surrey.

Spafford, J. (2005) Why dance...? *Animated*, Spring, 12.

Sylvestrini, L. (2006) Alfresco – intergenerational performance. *Animated*, Winter, 20.

Tannenbaum, R. and Schmidt, W. H. (1973) How to choose a leadership pattern. *Harvard Business Review*, May–June, p. 163.

Taylor, C. (1992) *The Ethics of Authenticity*. Harvard University Press, Cambridge MA.

Thomson, C. (1988) Community dance: what community... what dance? In: *Fourth International Conference of Dance and the Child International: An International Perspective*, Vol. iii – Dance, Culture and Community. London.

Thomson, C. (1994) Dance and the concept of community. *Focus on Community Dance, Dance and the Child International Journal*, **3**, 20.

Thomson, C. (2006) We are a dancing nation. *Animated*, Spring, 5–8.

Tomkins, A. (2006) To keep or not to keep the word community in community dance. *Animated*, Summer, 31.

Tönnies, F. (1887) *Community and Society* (transl. and ed. C. P. Loomis). Harper & Row, New York (1963 edition).

Trueman, R. (1998) Was I alright? An examination of the effect of performance on self-esteem in community dance. In: *Community Dance: Current Issues in the Field, Seminar Papers*, pp. 65–73. University of Surrey, Guildford.

White, M. (2005). Well being or well meaning? *Animated*, Spring, 10–11.

Willis, P. (1996) *Common Culture*. Open University Press, Milton Keynes.

Wilson, H. (2000) Community Dance in Performance. *Unpublished MA Dissertation*, University of Surrey, Guildford.

Wolff, J. (1993) *The Social Production of Art*, 2nd edn. MacMillan, London.

Woolf, F. (1999) *Partnerships in Learning*. Arts Council England, London.

Worth, L. and Poynor, H. (2005) *Anna Halprin*. Routledge, London.

Index